Leadership for Inclusive Schools

Praise for *Leadership for Inclusive Schools: Cases from Principals for Supporting Students with Special Educational Needs*

"Making schools inclusive demands the transformation of a wide range of long entrenched school and classroom practices. In *Leadership for Inclusive Schools*, Sider and Maich provide insights on the critical elements of effective and value-driven leadership needed to achieve that goal. The case study format draws the reader into the practical and difficult issues faced by principals in schools every day. With this book, Sider and Maich have delivered a resource that will be invaluable for the professional learning of both current and prospective school leaders."

—**Gordon L. Porter, CM, ONB, director,
Inclusive Education Canada**

"Over more than thirty years of research in inclusive practices I have found a critical element to determine success. For any organization to transform practices to become inclusive, leadership is key. This book, focused on leadership, is a welcome addition to the field. The format is engaging; presenting cases to facilitate analysis and learning is perfect for teaching. I am excited to see the innovative ways teachers and students interact with this text."

—**Vianne Timmons, president and vice chancellor, Memorial University of Newfoundland and Labrador**

Leadership for Inclusive Schools

Cases from Principals for Supporting Students with Special Educational Needs

Steve R. Sider
Kimberly Maich

ROWMAN & LITTLEFIELD
Lanham • Boulder • New York • London

Published by Rowman & Littlefield
An imprint of The Rowman & Littlefield Publishing Group, Inc.
4501 Forbes Boulevard, Suite 200, Lanham, Maryland 20706
www.rowman.com

86-90 Paul Street, London EC2A 4NE, United Kingdom

Copyright © 2022 by Steven Ray Sider and Kimberly Anne Maich

All rights reserved. No part of this book may be reproduced in any form or by any electronic or mechanical means, including information storage and retrieval systems, without written permission from the publisher, except by a reviewer who may quote passages in a review.

British Library Cataloguing in Publication Information Available

Library of Congress Cataloging-in-Publication Data

Names: Sider, Steve, editor. | Maich, Kimberly, 1969- editor.
Title: Leadership for inclusive schools : cases from principals for supporting students with special educational needs / Edited by Steven Ray Sider, Kimberly Anne Maich.
Description: Lanham : Rowman & Littlefield Publishing Group, [2022] | Includes bibliographical references. | Summary: "This book provides case studies and resources to help school principals develop skills and knowledge in leading inclusive schools for students with special education needs"—Provided by publisher.
Identifiers: LCCN 2021042409 (print) | LCCN 2021042410 (ebook) |
 ISBN 9781475852752 (cloth) | ISBN 9781475852769 (paperback) |
 ISBN 9781475852776 (epub)
Subjects: LCSH: Educational leadership—Case studies. | Inclusive Education—Case studies. | Special education—Study and teaching—Case studies. | Students with disabilities—Education—Case studies.
Classification: LCC LB2806 .L3823 2022 (print) | LCC LB2806 (ebook) |
 DDC 371.9/046—dc23
LC record available at https://lccn.loc.gov/2021042409
LC ebook record available at https://lccn.loc.gov/2021042410

Steve: I want to dedicate this book to "Scott" a student in a school where I was a principal who helped teach me an important lesson on inclusive education early in my career.

Kimberly: I would like to dedicate this book to the parents, students, and educators who continually push the boundaries and walls around inclusive education that we erect, and provide advocacy and support for change, even in the face of personal and professional fatigue.

Contents

Acknowledgments		ix
1	Introduction	1
2	Competencies for Inclusive School Leadership	15
TRANSITIONS		**29**
3	The Case of Charles	31
4	Supporting Albert	41
5	The Big Move	51
THE EARLY YEARS		**59**
6	"You Have to Trust We're Doing Our Job"	61
7	The Case of Jakob	71
8	"I Can't Believe I Was the One Who Excluded Him"	81
ELEMENTARY SCHOOL SPECIFIC CASES		**89**
9	The Grade Five Field Trip	91
10	Overstepping Boundaries	105
11	An Accident and an Injury	117
SECONDARY SCHOOL SPECIFIC CASES		**125**
12	The Incident in Mr. Mooney's Science Class	127

13	Overheard in the Staff Room	139
14	Truly Inclusive?	147

COMMUNITY SUPPORTS   155

15	Involving Community Programs: The Case of Aki	157
16	The Case of Sahar Said	167
17	"She Won't Go"	177

SCHOOL BOARD SUPPORTS   185

18	Supporting T.J. and Mr. Garcia	187
19	A Case of School Board Funding	197
20	Wandering Off: A Case of a Safe Arrival Program School Teams	205

SCHOOL TEAMS   213

21	Caught between a Rock and a Hard Place	215
22	A Dysfunctional School Team?	225
23	"No One Is Listening to Me"	235

COMPLEX CASES   243

24	"I Was on Autopilot"	245
25	The Case of Bethany	255
26	The Newspaper Article	265

SUPPORTING NEW TEACHERS   273

27	Figuring It Out on Your Own	275
28	The Case of Alexis	283
29	Over Invested?	291

References	299
About the Contributors	321
About the Authors	323

Acknowledgments

Steve: I would like to thank the hundreds of principals from across Canada, the United States, Egypt, Ghana, and Haiti who have helped me better understand the hopes, and the realities, of inclusive education. The research that led to this book was supported by the Social Sciences and Humanities Research Council (SSHRC) of Canada. My family always supports me through the process of research and book-writing, and I want to acknowledge their support. Thank you Karen, CJ, Karley, Emily, and Nate. Finally, the writing of this book was made possible through some amazing research assistants including Hillary Winger, Keifer Ciarroni, Dan Anderson, Sarah Perkins, Danika Morrison, Rachel Dobbs, Abby Breckles, and Aman Dhaliwal.

Kimberly: I would like to thank all of our research participants and those who allow us to observe, understand, and share in efforts toward inclusive school leadership at home and far beyond home, as well as my coauthor Dr. Steve Sider for leading this project, our SSHRC funding, and our research assistants. My family is foundational to any work that I do. Thanks to John, Robert, Grace & Mark, Hannah & Steven, and Quincey for being that foundation.

Chapter 1

Introduction

If we were to examine the resources available on how to support students with special education needs[1] in inclusive schools, we would quickly discover a wealth of books, websites, videos, blogs, and articles that provide a significant amount of information. Some of these are geared to parents, while many are directed at teachers and other educators. What would be curiously lacking, though, is an equally broad spectrum of resources which are available for school leaders. School principals[2] are expected to support students with special education needs and foster inclusive schools, but often without evidence-based resources which can support them in doing so with efficiency, ease, and success for all involved. This book of case stories is an answer to this gap.

But is such a resource really necessary?

Starting with our own experience as teachers, special education resource consultants, school administrators, and now university faculty members instructing courses in special education and disability, we believe the answer is "yes." In our own formal training, there was little attention given to how school leaders foster inclusive schools where teachers and other educators welcome and support all students. Yes, we were instructed in the processes involved with Individual Education Plans (IEPs), multidisciplinary teams, school-based teams, psych-educational assessments, and time-tabling, but we were not formally trained in how to build a cohesive school culture that engaged all children, even those with complex needs. We were not encouraged to explore the evidence that supports inclusive schools. We did not receive materials that provided information about the global movement to inclusive education. Much of what we learned was from our previous educational and familial experiences. There is nothing necessarily wrong with that except that these experiences might not be adequate to support the diversity of needs in schools.

Now, as educational researchers in the second halves of our careers, we encounter principals in our work across diverse contexts such as Canada, the United States, the United Kingdom, Thailand, Ghana, Australia, Haiti, Egypt, Switzerland, and beyond who have very similar experiences to us. They have had technical training that focuses on rules and procedures but not on skills, knowledge, or attitudes that can more effectively foster inclusive schools. They are often looking for evidence-based resources to help them support all students in their schools. We have written this book of case stories as a way to engage principals—and those who aspire to be—in a way that uses the real experiences of other principals, paired with evidence-based competencies, to support their growth as inclusive leaders.

Every day, school principals working in public and private education systems face situations and make decisions involving students with special education needs. What guides these interactions? As we have indicated from our own experience, they are based on school leaders' past tacit experiences with—and perceptions of—how to best support students (Cameron, 2016). However, these decisions are not necessarily based on evidence from research or even formal policy itself. That is not to say that principals or other school leaders deliberately *choose* to act in a way that is contrary to evidence; principals would not intentionally do this. However, relying on personal experiences to guide practice can be problematic if these previous experiences are limited in nature or include inappropriate or insufficient decisions. Principals need to know that they are giving direction to schools in evidence-informed ways.

Principals may also make decisions based on directives provided by their local school district but sometimes without adequate support to implement these policies. Again, this book serves as a companion to the type of in-service professional development principals are provided with so that the directives and guidance they are given are contextualized with evidence-based practices. This book supplements the lived experience of the school principal and the guidance being given by the school district to support effective decision-making. Thus, it provides an opportunity to connect educational policy, research-based effective practices, and the implementation of these policies and practices in the work that school leaders do in supporting students with special education needs in their school environments (Jahnukainen, 2015).

Finally, there seems to be a general understanding that inclusive schools are what our society needs. Research indicates that inclusive education benefits all learners (Szumski et al., 2017). This is supported by international guidelines and codes such as the Universal Declaration of Human Rights and the Convention on the Rights of the Child. International agreements such as the Sustainable Development Goals aim for school systems around the world to have equitable and inclusive education. Legislation and policy documents are either in place or in progress and support these international agreements.

How do school systems achieve the goals of international agreements such as the Sustainable Development Goals? By ensuring that teachers have the necessary guidance and resources available to enable them in their classrooms (Porter & Towell, 2017; Winzer, 2017). School systems also support teachers in striving for inclusive schools by providing staff support and training to help them realize the potential of inclusive classrooms. Staff such as educational assistants, speech therapists, psychologists, and special education resource teachers work with teachers, children, and parents/guardians to support a child's learning. School boards and districts will also provide specialized professional learning workshops and courses to further support teachers in fostering inclusive classrooms.

Yet, what is often lacking in the professional learning and supports provided for teachers is an acknowledgment that principals themselves are powerful determinants of whether these interventions and supports are intentionally and deeply supporting inclusive classrooms where all children are valued. There is compelling research that the ways in which school principals provide leadership in schools, for example, by engaging with all students and their caregivers in healthy and supportive says, is a key determining factor in how effectively and authentically teachers engage students in inclusive classrooms (Howell, 2016).

It is clear that more needs to be done to support the work that principals do in fostering inclusive schools. Researchers have identified a significant and persistent gap in research on inclusivity in K-12 education. There is a significant amount of literature examining the experiences of teachers and students in inclusive classrooms; further, there is substantial scholarly literature which identifies the critical role of school principals in effecting positive student achievements. Yet there are limited resources to support principals as they foster inclusive school environments for students with special education needs (Edmunds & Macmillan, 2010). This book comes at a crucial moment for schools, as educators face unprecedented challenges in their educational practice, including increasing rates of reported stress, verbal and physical aggression, and inclusion of diverse student needs (Sider et al., 2021). The COVID-19 pandemic has further exacerbated the challenges that principals face but has also provided an important opportunity to consider how to best support all students in their neighborhood schools (Sider, 2020).

In the remainder of this introductory chapter, the key elements of inclusive education are examined, a rationale for considering inclusive school leadership is provided, and the format for the remainder of the book is introduced.

WHAT IS INCLUSIVE EDUCATION?

Inclusion is a multifaceted concept focused on including all members of society with their many facets of diversity—including areas such as ability, culture, and family—in everyday experiences in multiple contexts (Simplican et al., 2015). The concept of inclusion reflects a movement away from viewing difference as a deficit toward understanding and honoring differences as a strength (Zaretsky et al., 2008).

More specific to this book is the concept of *inclusive education*. Inclusive education is a broadly understood term that refers to the "meaningful participation and achievement of all students who were increasingly vulnerable to the effects of marginalization in existing educational arrangements" (Zaretsky et al., 2008, p. 170). There are a wide variety of conceptions of inclusive education stemming from a number of subdisciplines of education, including multicultural education, gender-based education, special education, and anti-racist education (De Luca, 2013). Thus, the conceptualization of inclusive education considers a wide range of diverse student needs, including gender, sexual orientation, religion, language, and ability. Inclusive education is a reflection of a belief that all students, including those with special education needs such as specific learning disorders and autism spectrum disorder are capable of learning, and that every student can make a valued contribution to a classroom and school (Specht et al., 2016). The focus of this book is specifically on students with special education needs and how principals can support school environments which are supportive and inclusive of their diverse needs.

There is solid evidence that inclusive education is beneficial for all students. Inclusion is consistently seen as effective for the social and academic outcomes of all students (Kalambouka et al., 2007). A review of the literature on the academic outcomes of students with special education needs in inclusive versus segregated settings found that, generally, studies supported the inclusive environment as being more positive (or no different) than segregated settings (Canadian Council on Learning, 2009). Further, inclusion does not just benefit the child with a special education needs but is effective for the social and academic outcomes of all students (Kalambouka et al., 2007; Szumski, 2017). It appears that school settings which promote inclusion are more successful at promoting learning for all, the goal of education, and that "what is good for special education is good for all education" (Cobb, 2015, p. 231).

Inclusive education is a concept that has gained growing prominence around the world over the past three decades. Five key international agreements have provided the framework for inclusive education in countries such as the United States and Canada:

1. **United Nations Universal Declaration of Human Rights (UDHR).** Proclaimed after World War II in 1948, this agreement set out fundamental human rights which would be universally protected. Article 26 of the UDHR explicitly states that "everyone has the right to education," and multiple other parts of the UDHR refer to the equal treatment of all whether with special needs or not. For more information, please see http://www.un.org/en/universal-declaration-human-rights/
2. **United Nations Convention on the Rights of the Child** specifically addressed the rights of children globally. Adopted in 1989, the Convention states in Article 23 that all children, including those with special needs, "should enjoy a full and decent life, in conditions which ensure dignity, promote self-reliance and facilitate the child's active participation in the community." For more information, please see http://www.ohchr.org/EN/ProfessionalInterest/Pages/CRC.aspx
3. The **UNESCO Salamanca Statement** was agreed to in 1994 in Salamanca Spain by representatives of ninety-two governments and twenty-five international organizations. The statement called on governments and organizations to consider inclusion in neighborhood schools as the norm for all children, regardless of physical, intellectual, social, emotional, linguistic or other abilities. For the full text of the Salamanca Statement, please see https://unesdoc.unesco.org/ark:/48223/pf0000098427
4. A fourth international agreement, the **Convention on the Rights of Persons with Disabilities**, adopted in 2006, specifically used the term "inclusive education" in Article 24. The article states that governments "shall ensure an inclusive education system at all levels." For more information, please see https://www.un.org/development/desa/disabilities/convention-on-the-rights-of-persons-with-disabilities.html
5. The most recent relevant international agreement, the **Sustainable Development Goals**, was agreed to in 2015. These seventeen goals included one with a focus on education (SDG4) which aims to "ensure inclusive and equitable quality education and promote lifelong learning opportunities for all." For more information, see http://www.undp.org/content/undp/en/home/sustainable-development-goals.html

Countries around the world have attempted to take these international conventions and agreements and put them into practice in their contexts. For example, in Canada, the Council of Ministers of Education in a 2008 report indicated that inclusive education is "quality education that aims at the full participation of all learners" (p. 2). Since Canada is a federal system with educational responsibilities being part of provincial mandates, the implementation of inclusive education is under the purview of individual provincial

governments. For example, Ontario has an *Equity and Inclusive Education Strategy* which includes a vision statement that states:
We envision an inclusive education system in Ontario in which

- all students, parents, and other members of the school community are welcomed and respected; and
- every student is supported and inspired to succeed in a culture of high expectations for learning.

To achieve an equitable and inclusive school climate, school boards and schools will work to ensure that all members of the school community feel safe, comfortable, and accepted. We want all staff and students to value diversity and to demonstrate respect for others and a commitment to establishing a just, caring society (Ontario's Equity and Inclusive Education Strategy Quick Facts, nd).

Though beyond the scope of this book, it is important to note, briefly, that there is wide difference of implementation of what inclusive education looks like, feels like, and sounds like for students with special education needs. There are many organizations that are doing excellent work in supporting inclusive education.

Here are some websites for well-known associations and organizations supporting a variety of students with special education needs in the United States and Canada:

American Speech-Language-Hearing Association: https://www.asha.org/
Ontario Teachers' Federation: www.teachspeced.ca
Learning Disabilities Association of America: https://ldaamerica.org/
American Autism Association: https://www.myautism.org/
Attention Deficit Disorder Association: https://add.org/
American Foundation for the Blind: https://www.afb.org/
Holland Bloorview Centre: http://www.hollandbloorview.ca/
Canadian Mental Health Association: www.cmha.ca

One of the goals of many of these organizations is to support inclusive education for children with special education needs so that they have their needs met in neighborhood schools in classes with similar-aged peers. Some jurisdictions have implemented full inclusion models from kindergarten to grade 12, while others support partial inclusion models where students with special education needs may be in specialized classes or specialized schools. The implementation and monitoring of inclusive education is not yet complete—nor perfected—as its goals and objectives continue to be ongoing, core issues in related research and practice:

Teachers are often constrained by legislation, terminology, and board practices that do not fully embrace the shift towards a reconceptualization of schooling that supports inclusive learning environments for all children. Until legislation changes, we must work within a system that has enough room for adaptations, yet few explicit requirements for accountability regarding inclusion. (Killoran et al., 2013, p. 242)

Thus, there is work to be done to achieve inclusive education, none more so than to support school principals in fostering inclusive schools. This book answers such a call and provides resources in the form of case stories to support the professional learning of principals in schools which aim to support the inclusion of students with special education needs.

WHY A FOCUS ON SCHOOL LEADERSHIP FOR INCLUSION?

Research done by Cobb (2015) and Sider et al. (2021) illustrates a persistent gap in the scholarly literature indicating a lack of research and resources to support school principals and inclusion. In this section, we examine why it is important to consider "leadership principles for principals" to support inclusive schools. This focus on leadership competencies for inclusive school principals will be further examined and extended in the following chapter.

School leadership should be transformative, systematically promoting academic achievement, family and community empowerment, democratic engagement, and global citizenship (Shields, 2010). These values—always essential—are even more important in the context of inclusive schools. A significant body of literature indicates that effective principals are critical in supporting effective schools (Fullan, 2011). The effectiveness of principals is widely considered to influence student achievement and success in the classroom (Leithwood et al., 2010), although the direct effect of school leadership on student achievement is minimal or difficult to determine (Shin & Slater, 2010). Principals, however, have significant indirect leadership effects on student achievement through their influence on teachers' self-efficacy, commitment, and beliefs (Ross & Gray, 2006).

School leadership is generally characterized as the process of recruiting and managing the talents and energies of educators, students, parents, and other community stakeholders toward achieving shared educational goals. Such a view is what Leithwood et al. (2006) refer to as the "four broad categories of practices identified in research summaries: setting directions, developing people, redesigning the organization, and managing the instructional (teaching and learning) programme" (pp. 18–19). These four categories set the tone for school culture and define to a large extent schools' conditions through which the general health of the learning environment can flourish.

If it is understood that principals are key contributors to the healthy climate of schools and can impact student achievement through their interactions and support of teachers, what is known about the ways in which principals do in fact support inclusive schools? Cobb (2015) completed a meta-analysis of nineteen North American articles—mainly research studies from 2001 to 2011—related to special education leadership with school principals ranging from elementary to secondary areas of responsibility. It is clear that there are jurisdictional differences with the approaches that principals take within special education leadership, but also many key commonalities and lessons to be learned. Cobb noted that principals are essential human resources in both interpreting and implementing policy: their behaviors affect the behaviors of classroom teachers themselves, the front line of service delivery in schools. Further, principals set the tone and expectations in a range of foundational processes, including inclusion and special education, and their leadership role in the field is a top issue of great importance. Cobb identified various domains and roles that principals maintain in supporting special education inclusion in schools (see table 1.1). Table 1.1 summarizes what is a deep and rich finding: principals navigate and support school-based inclusion in multiple domains involving various relationships, bodies of knowledge, and practical skills, but they also rotate among several key roles (and therefore perspectives) in each of these domains. It is clearly a set of complex knowledge, skills, and values that principals bring to this particular role, which is only one of (again) many roles that principals play in their schools—and beyond.

Clearly, the leadership that principals provide in fostering inclusive schools for students with special education needs is both "multifaceted and complicated" (Cobb, 2015, p. 229). In chapter 2, we specifically examine leadership competencies—skills, knowledge, and attitudes—of principals to support inclusive schools.

Table 1.1 Domains and Roles of Principals in School-based Special Education Inclusion

Domains	Roles
Inclusive program delivery	Visionary, advocate, innovator, interpreter, organizer
Staff collaboration	Visionary, partner, coach, conflict resolver, organizer
Parental engagement	Partner, interpreter, organizer

Source: Cobb (2015) as presented in Sider et al. (2017).

Research we have completed provides significant opportunity to consider the roles, experiences, and competencies of inclusive school principals (see Sider et al., 2017, 2021; Sider, 2020). Commencing in 2016, the authors and an associated research team have embarked on multiple national Canadian research studies (funded by the Social Sciences and Humanities Research Council of Canada) that have examined the experiences of school principals with supporting inclusive schools for students with special education needs. In excess of 300 principals and other school leaders from across Canada have been involved in these studies which have included principals from a wide variety of school contexts including elementary and secondary schools, Public and Catholic school systems, and English-speaking and French-speaking. We have identified day-to-day activities that principals engage in to support students with special education needs. These include:

- Ongoing communication and support with students, teachers, parents/guardians.
- Participating on and giving direction to special education personnel and teams.
- Resource allocation including human personnel and assistive technologies.
- Advocacy of students and their needs with staff, school board personnel, and community agencies.
- Responding to day-to-day needs and incidents, as well as ongoing follow-up and tracking of progress.
- Reviewing documents such as IEPs (or equivalent).
- Developing and implementing safety plans (Sider et al., 2017).

Clearly, principals are incredibly busy in supporting very diverse and complex students and situations.

We have also examined the types of training that principals have experienced in supporting their ability to work with students with special education needs, their families, and the teachers who support them. Our research has demonstrated that there is a disparate variety of professional learning that principals experience in relationship to inclusion (Sider et al., 2017). Some of this professional development is informal such as reading books and dialoguing with colleagues; some is completed in formal, structured ways, for example, as in-service workshops on topics such as working with students with autism spectrum disorder or workshops on risk assessment. In our studies, principals have identified graduate courses they completed on differentiation and inclusion or professional courses that were done in conjunction with educational organizations. Leadership conferences that focus on special education as well as specialized courses in related areas such as reading and mathematics have also been identified as instrumental in the professional journey to support inclusive schools. Our research has identified that many of the professional learning experiences of principals focus on technical aspects of special education such as legislative and policy frameworks. There appears to be a lack of training that involves specific strategies and supports for principals in how to foster inclusive school environments. In other words, principals are often learning the "how" of "doing" special education but not the "how" of building inclusive school *cultures*.

Our research has also identified the importance of significant events that principals have experienced which profoundly influence their views on inclusion (Sider et al., 2021). In the final section of this chapter, we examine what we have identified as *critical incidents* in the formation of principals' values, beliefs, and practices in supporting students with special education needs in inclusive schools.

CRITICAL INCIDENTS AS A PROFESSIONAL FRAMEWORK FOR CASE STORIES

A number of studies have examined critical incidents in schools (Dollarhide et al., 2007; Hanhimäki & Tirri, 2009; Yamamoto et al., 2014). Critical incidents are significant emotional events that affect one's practice and perspective (Yamamoto et al., 2014). They can be either negative or positive and have significant effects on current and future work (Scott, 2004). Plus, critical incidents lead to ethical reflection on practice (Hanhimäki & Tirri, 2009). They provide a suitable framework within which leadership dilemmas and issues can be explored (Dollarhide et al., 2007).

The work of Yamamoto et al. (2014) noted that when school leaders explore critical incidents, "in order to make sense of the event, the leader also discovered the meaning of the event" (p. 177). Yamamoto et al. examined how critical incidents could shake leaders' confidence and shape their understanding of their beliefs as leaders. As a result, critical incidents play a significant role in influencing principals' development of day-to-day leadership practices. In this book, the importance of critical incidents as a conceptual framework is highlighted, as these incidents are crucial in the shaping of principals' views on inclusive school contexts. These critical incidents also were used to develop the case stories that are shared in this book. Thus, they are authentic cases based on the experiences of principals across the research contexts with which we have engaged.

As part of the studies we have completed, we have asked principals to describe critical incidents that have informed their understanding of, and support for, inclusive schools. This book serves as an opportunity to mobilize these examples, without including identifying information, in the form of case stories to support the development of inclusive skills and dispositions of school principals and those who aspire to be. We use the term *case story* instead of *case study* to denote that the cases are presented as narrative text that describes authentic experiences but which do not provide all of the details as would normally be present in a detailed case study. The stories are meant to stimulate discussion and learning and not to present a complete descriptive text of a particular context or situation.

FORMAT OF THE BOOK

In the following chapter, research-based principles for fostering inclusive school leadership competencies are presented. Following chapter 2, the remainder of this book is structured along nine sections—with three case stories in each—to integrate these leadership competencies with case examples. In total, twenty-seven cases are presented in this book. Each case includes a descriptive section, a commentary from one or two experts, associated leadership competencies, and resources and extension activities for further consideration and analysis. These nine sections include:

- Section 1: The Early Years
- Section 2: The Elementary Years
- Section 3: The Secondary Years
- Section 4: Transitions
- Section 5: Community Supports
- Section 6: School Board Supports
- Section 7: School Teams
- Section 8: Complex Cases
- Section 9: Cases for Supporting New Teachers

In addition to identifying leadership competencies in each case story, the presented cases also incorporate essential, integrated themes. These themes are synthesized into the case stories to illustrate the importance of understanding key aspects of leadership related to inclusion. The themes provide readers and course instructors with aspects that may be helpful to a particular context or course. For example, if a course instructor that is using this book as a resource wants to focus on cases which address the concept of collaboration, they could choose the relevant cases. These crosscutting themes are presented in figure 1.1 and include:

- Communication
- Parents, caregivers, and families

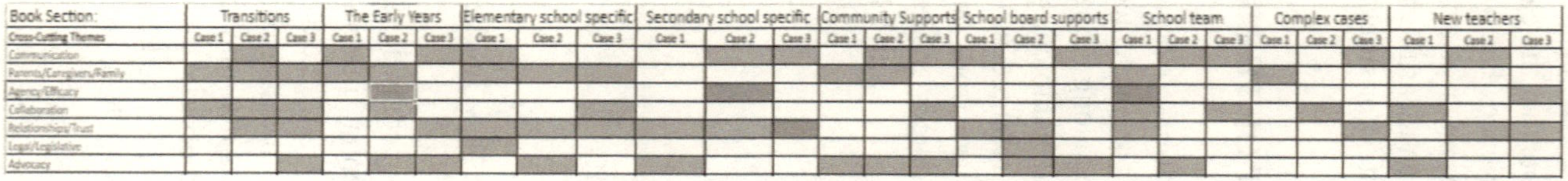

Figure 1.1 Crosscutting Themes. *Source:* Created by author.

- Agency and efficacy
- Collaboration
- Relationships and trust
- Legislative implications
- Advocacy

As you read this resource for professional learning, it is important to remember that the cases are not focused on specific exceptionalities, diagnoses, deficits, or disorders, or specific strengths, joys, positive outcomes, and new learning. Instead, the cases are meant to stimulate discussion and foster the development of leadership competencies *through* the case stories. As well, although legislative frameworks are referenced, these contexts and policies are illustrative of broader legislation which can be found in many jurisdictions and in many countries. We recognize that each jurisdiction has nuanced and differentiated policy frameworks; however, there are many commonalities across districts. Thus, the book has universal application and serves as a catalyst for professional learning in Canada, the United States, Australia, the United Kingdom, and beyond.

The cases in this resource have been written as a way to help facilitate learning and dialogue related to inclusion. The cases are all based on actual events that principals shared with our research team as part of our national studies. We are deeply grateful for research assistants—Hillary Winger, Keifer Ciarroni, Dan Anderson, Sarah Perkins, Danika Morrison, Rachel Dobbs, Abby Breckles, and Aman Dhaliwal—who helped in creating the narratives for the case stories and in supporting the research projects that helped document the experiences that shaped the stories. It is hoped that this resource will serve to facilitate deepening professional inquiry and reflection into the many dimensions associated with creating inclusive learning contexts for all.

NOTES

1. We use the term *special education needs* recognizing that this is a contested term and that other terms such as *disability, handicapped,* and *exceptionality* are alternative terms each with nuanced understandings. We define special education needs later in this chapter but use it to describe students who require special education supports and services.

2. The term *principal*, moving forward, is being used in a generic sense to refer to principals, vice principals, or other school leaders who have authority to make school-wide decisions. All terms will be used moving forward, but for the sake of efficiency, *principal* is typically used to indicate any or either of the above-mentioned roles.

Chapter 2

Competencies for Inclusive School Leadership

This book provides an opportunity to consider case stories that are based on events that have been shared with us through our research. We use these case stories as illustrative narratives to consider leadership competencies that support inclusive education. As discussed in the introductory chapter, there is a significant gap in the research between that which speaks to school inclusion and that which focuses on effective school leadership. Of course, they are not completely separate bodies of research; one certainly informs the other. However, there has been limited literature that specifically considers the types of competences that principals need to support inclusive schools for students with special education needs (Bateman et al., 2017). In this chapter, we first explore what we mean by leadership competencies and then examine leadership competencies that are specific to inclusive schools. As a result, this chapter responds to the question: What competences do principals require to lead inclusive schools? As you work through the case stories in this book, this chapter will be helpful in considering how leadership competencies can shape inclusive schools. The resources, questions to consider, and expert commentaries that are associated with each case story will help shape the development of these competencies. The case stories themselves will help highlight these competences so that principals and other emerging leaders can be aware of their importance in fostering inclusive schools for students with special education needs.

We begin by first considering what is meant by the term *competency* and then examine the scholarly literature with consideration for school leadership competencies and that which speaks specifically to leadership competencies that nurture inclusive schools.

WHAT ARE COMPETENCIES?

Competencies are knowledge, skills, and attitudes (Asia Society, 2018). A definition provided by Lambert and Bouchamma (2019) aligns with this concept: "competency (knowing how to act) must be considered as an action requiring the mobilization of a knowledge ensemble (theoretical knowledge), as well as of knowing how (abilities) and knowing how to be (attitudes, qualities, emotions)" (p. 54). When we think about leadership competencies for inclusive schools, we need to consider the knowledge, skills, and attitudes that principals need to foster inclusive education. It is important to note that scholars and professional organizations may refer to these leadership knowledge, skills, and attitudes by other terms such as dispositions, practices, capacities, and indicators. Of course, there are nuances to terms and definitions but it is important to understand that, despite subtle differences, the essential aspects of these terms are much the same.

Jurisdictions around the world have made efforts to operationalize these competencies into standards and frameworks. For example, in Ontario, Canada, the Ontario Leadership Framework (OLF) provides a description of successful leadership practices (Ontario Leadership Framework, 2013) drawing extensively on the work of Ken Leithwood. The "five core leadership capacities" identified in the OLF include: setting goals, aligning resources with priorities, promoting collaborative learning cultures, using data, and engaging in courageous conversations. The OLF also identifies the functions of school leadership as including: setting directions, building relationships and developing people, developing the organization to support desired practices, improving the instructional program, and securing accountability.

Principals' performance appraisal in Ontario is based on specific aspects of these functions. As well, school improvement efforts are often connected to these functions.

In the United States, a well-known competency framework is the Professional Standards for Educational Leaders (NPBEA, 2015). The NPBEA has identified the following standards for professional practice:

1. Mission, Vision, and Core Values
2. Ethics and Professional Norms
3. Equity and Cultural Responsiveness
4. Curriculum, Instruction and Assessment
5. Community of Care and Support for Students
6. Professional Capacity of School Personnel
7. Professional Community for Teachers and Staff
8. Meaningful Engagement of Families and Community

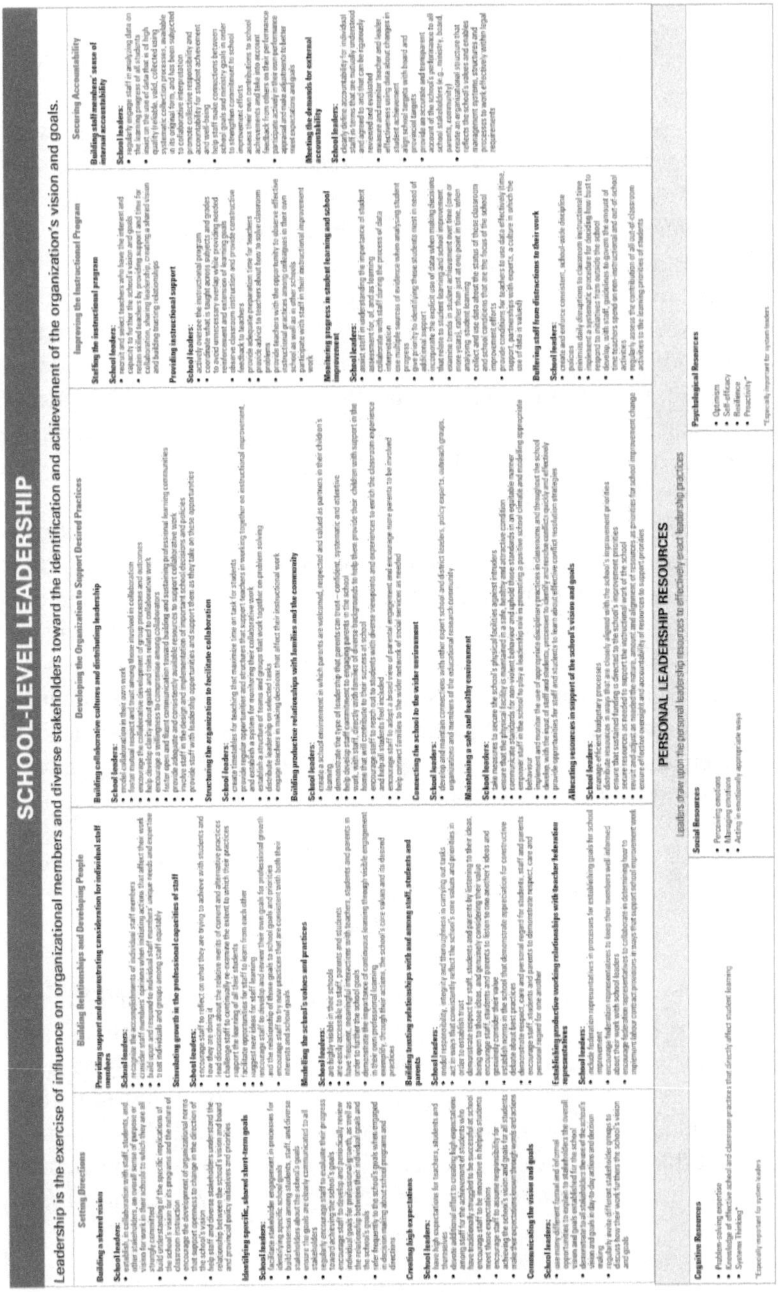

Figure 2.1 Ontario Leadership Framework. *Source:* https://www.education-leadership-ontario.ca/application/files/8814/9452/4183/Ontario_Leadership_Framework_OLF.pdf.

9. Operations and Management
10. School Improvement

The NPBEA states that these aspects (domains) of leadership should not be siloed aspects of leadership. Instead, they inform each other and often overlap. Further, these standards guide both individual principal and system-wide efforts. As such, they represent a theory of change for effective leadership (NPBEA, 2015, p. 6). They serve as an indicator of what schools, school districts, and the general public value. As the NPBEA document states, "They're designed to ensure that educational leaders are ready to meet effectively the challenges and opportunities of the job today and in the future as education, schools and society continue to transform" (2015, p. 1). Thus, we can see that the determination of competencies and competency frameworks provide an important role in forward-thinking and monitoring. That is, they help principals set direction for themselves and their schools and also help with ensuring that what needs to be accomplished is in fact being done.

These models from Canada and the United States illustrate the ways in which principals' leadership competencies may be framed. Other educational jurisdictions around the world offer other models for how leadership is conceptualized and assessed. What is important to this discussion is a recognition that leadership competencies are framed in often similar ways, but what is often lacking in these leadership frameworks is an explicit explanation of the types of leadership competencies that foster inclusive schools for students with special education needs. In the next section, we illustrate general leadership competencies before turning to a specific examination of competencies that are aligned with inclusive schools.

LEADERSHIP COMPETENCIES: COMPARATIVE PERSPECTIVES

A 2019 article by Laval University professors Monique Lambert and Yamina Bouchamma explored four competency standards for school principals from Quebec, Alberta, Australia, and the United States. In their analysis, they defined competencies as behaviors expected for principals. As noted earlier, competency standards are guidelines that address these expected behaviors in order to meet the expectations of the jurisdiction. Lambert and Bouchamma (2019) found similar standards in the different contexts which included:

- Improvement and innovation
- Decisions and responsibilities

- Mission and vision
- Community, parents, partnerships
- Laws and policies
- Material and financial resources
- Collaboration, shared leadership, empowerment
- Professional development for self and others
- Human resource management and interpersonal relationships
- Knowledge of pedagogy and programs
- Learning practices and strategies
- Supervision and teacher support
- Needs of the student
- Organizational climate
- Adaptation to change and feedback
- Communication
- Use of data results and research

They also identified competencies that appeared in some competency standards but not in others. These included:

- Technology
- Cultural diversity
- Balance between personal and professional life

These types of comparative perspectives are helpful in identifying patterns of competencies in different contexts. It is also interesting to note from this research by Lambert and Bouchamma that these jurisdictions do not specifically identify leadership competencies related to inclusion and special education, although certainly leadership practices involving communication, laws and policies, and professional development activities will intersect with supporting students with special education needs.

The purpose of this chapter is not to provide an exhaustive overview of leadership competencies but to identify competencies which are particularly important for shaping inclusive school environments for students with special education needs. It is also important to recognize that competencies and standards are dynamic. The NPBEA states that "professional standards are not static. They are regularly reviewed and adjusted to accurately reflect evolving understandings of, expectations for, and contexts that shape the profession's work" (2015, p. 2). For those interested in knowing more about competencies and standards, particularly for school leaders, the work of Pont (2013) and Leithwood et al. (2006) are very helpful. In the next section, we consider what the scholarly literature says about competencies that are specifically needed for leading inclusive schools.

INCLUSIVE SCHOOL LEADERSHIP COMPETENCIES

So what do we know about leadership competencies specific to supporting students with special education needs in inclusive schools? For those who are interested in the research on inclusive school leadership competencies, Bateman et al. (2017) provides a succinct summary of the literature that addresses competencies for school principals related to special education and how (or if) accreditation entities in the United States have incorporated these. Bateman et al. identified thirty aspects of special education that principals wished they knew about in their leadership preparation. The list uses language and legal aspects specific to the United States (e.g., Individuals with Disabilities Act) but there are many aspects that have relevance to other jurisdictions. Although the list is focused on knowledge related to special education and thus not a full representation of competencies as we define them, it does provide a very helpful framework.

The thirty aspects of special education that Bateman et al. (2017) identify are:

1. Describe the six major parts of the IDEA and their purposes.
2. Describe the child find requirement, and what is meant by an affirmative duty.
3. Describe a nondiscriminatory evaluation and its components.
4. Describe an independent educational evaluation and what should be done when one is either requested or received.
5. Describe the age requirements of students served by the IDEA.
6. Describe a multidisciplinary team and its members.
7. Describe school district responsibilities with respect to free and appropriate public education.
8. Describe the purpose of the IEP and how it relates to communication, management, accountability, compliance and monitoring, and evaluation.
9. Describe the persons required to attend an IEP meeting.
10. Describe the purpose of measurable annual goals.
11. Describe progress monitoring and its importance in the IEP process.
12. Describe the steps a school district should take to ensure parental involvement in the IEP process.
13. Describe the purpose of Section 504.
14. Describe differences between the IDEA and Section 504.

15. Describe "major life activities" as defined by Section 504.
16. Describe a manifestation determination and its purpose.
17. Describe a behavior intervention plan and what should be included.
18. Describe the purpose of a functional behavioral assessment and when it should be conducted.
19. Describe rules and factors considered in determining whether a series of suspensions would constitute a pattern of exclusions.
20. Describe related services, including when they should be provided, and limitations on their service.
21. Describe the factors an IEP team should consider in determining placement.
22. Describe and explain the continuum of alternative placements.
23. Describe how the general curriculum should be part of placement decisions.
24. Describe supplementary aids or services that may be used to help a student to be educated in the least restrictive environment.
25. Describe the purpose and expectations of the transition requirements (part C to B and from secondary to postsecondary) for a student with an IEP.
26. Describe the information IDEA requires be supplied to parents of students with disabilities regarding student records.
27. Describe how a student can be no longer eligible for special education and related services.
28. Describe the IDEA's general procedural requirements.
29. Describe the stay-put provision.
30. Describe how school districts can ensure that they do not discriminate against students with disabilities.

From this framework, what appears to be the primary differentiating factor between general leadership competencies and those that focus on inclusion for students with special education needs is the emphasis inclusive leadership models place on particular skills, such as: awareness of Individual Education Plan processes, parent-relationships, personnel development, and a flexible approach for students with special education needs. Here it is also important to note what Lambert and Bouchamma (2019) call *contextual competencies* that change over time. Contextual competencies are those that are specific to a time and place. For example, the COVID-19 pandemic required that certain competencies, such as nimbleness in leadership, were accentuated (Sider, 2020). Another example, related to individual practices, are the competencies that a principal might need when taking on the leadership of a school that is going through a significant transition in the local community, such as the sociocultural factors that occur when new cultural or linguistic groups move into a community.

Another helpful meta-analysis (a study of studies) was completed by Patrice Thompson (2017). Thompson's work focused on the competencies of special education administrators, those who specifically give leadership to special education programs and services, but still has relevance to the leadership competencies that principals require to support inclusive education. Thompson identifies eight categories of competencies: collaboration, program development and organization, program and individual research and evaluation, leadership and policy, professional development and ethical practice, shared vision and decision-making, retention of personnel, and data analyses for planned decision-making. For more information on the literature base that these competencies were drawn from, see table 2.1

Other scholars, when considering broad aspects of inclusion (such as language, race, gender, religion, socioeconomics, and sexual orientation) have

Table 2.1 Thompson's (2017) Meta-Analysis of Competencies Referenced as Being Essential to the Leadership of Special Education Programs

Special Education Leadership Competencies	References
Collaboration among personnel, families, and community members	Council for Exceptional Children (CEC), 2009; Furney et al., 2005; Lashley & Boscardin, 2003; Stevenson-Jacobson et al., 2006; Wellner, 2012; Wigle & Wilcox, 1999
Program development and organization	CEC, 2009; Johnson, 1998; Lashley, 2007; Lashley & Boscardin, 2003; Wigle & Wilcox, 1999
Leadership and policy	Bozonelos, 2008; CEC, 2009; Furney et al., 2005; Goor & Schwenn, 1997; Johnson, 1998; Lashley, 2007; Lashley & Boscardin, 2003; Passman, 2008; Protz, 2005; Stevenson-Jacobson et al., 2006; Wigle & Wilcox, 1999
Professionalism and ethical practice	Bozonelos, 2008; CEC, 2009; Lashley, 2007; Lashley & Boscardin, 2003; Wigle & Wilcox, 1999
Vision, planning, and decision-making that is shared	Furney et al., 2005; Lashley & Boscardin, 2003; Wigle & Wilcox, 1999
Retention of special education teachers	Bozonelos, 2008; Lashley & Boscardin, 2003; Stevenson-Jacobson et al., 2006; Wigle & Wilcox, 1999
Data analysis for planned decision-making	CEC, 2009; Furney et al., 2005; Wigle & Wilcox, 1999
Individual and program research-based practices and evaluation	CEC, 2009; Lashley & Boscardin, 2003; Stevenson-Jacobson et al., 2006; Wigle & Wilcox, 1999

identified other key aspects such as supporting education in as inclusive environment as possible, nurturing collaborative teaching strategies, ensuring parental rights and engagement, compliance with legal requirements, and recruitment, selection, orientation and supervision of staff (Stevenson-Jacobson et al., 2006). Passman (2008) address the importance of principal beliefs and values that align with inclusion. Cusson (2010) adds the importance of leading professional development for the school staff and providing advocacy for students with special education needs and their families. Further, it is important to consider how principals' model inclusive practices and communicate a vision that all students can learn (Schultz, 2011). Other factors, such as previous experience with special education, have been identified as positively contributing to leaders' inclusive educational practices (Cohen, 2015; Ross & Cozzens, 2016). It is interesting to note that Angelle and Bilton (2009) discovered that principals reported a significantly higher sense of efficacy simply by completing one special education course as part of their principal training programs. This speaks to the importance of resources such as this book which can be used in principals' professional learning programs to foster inclusive school leadership competencies.

Finally, this chapter would not be complete without considering dimensions of social justice in school leadership for inclusive schools. Principals who advocate for and support students with special education needs are demonstrating a commitment to ensuring that all students have a strong sense of belonging in their neighborhood school. Principals who work to this end consider the whole child and not just an aspect of their identity such as ability. In other words, principals who have a commitment to social justice will recognize the barriers that exist for students and work to dismantle them. They also recognize that children are complex beings with intersecting aspects of identity. As DeMathews et al. (2021) state, "Much of the leadership literature focuses on how well-prepared principals create inclusive schools without consideration of race and other forms of student identity" (p. 10). Thus, leadership competencies for inclusive school principals need to address and foster a social justice commitment to recognizing the whole child and engages in work to dismantle the barriers the child and their families might confront. Competencies that include skills in communication, knowledge of processes, and an attitude that values inclusion are required to ensure that all students are welcomed in their neighborhood school.

Based on our review of the scholarly literature and experience as long-term educators, we have identified the following leadership competencies which are particularly important for principals to foster in relationship to supporting students with special education needs in inclusive schools. These competencies are supported by scholarship in the field as illustrated in table 2.2 below.

Table 2.2 Sider & Maich Competencies for Inclusive School Leaders

	Competency	Explanation	Evidence and Further Reading
Skills	Communication	Communicate consistently and comprehensively with teachers, system leaders, other educators, students, parents/guardians, and other stakeholders.	Bateman et al., 2017; Lambert & Bouchamma, 2019; Schultz, 2011; Sider et al., 2021
	Differentiated instruction	Provide instructional leadership for teachers in differentiated pedagogical practices.	Lambert & Bouchamma, 2019; Schultz, 2011; Thompson, 2017
	Professional learning	Identify problems of practice and implement professional learning opportunities for oneself, for teachers, and for the staff as a whole to target areas of need.	Cusson, 2010; Thompson, 2017
	Advocacy and program development	Lobby to system leaders and community organizations for programs, services, and supports that will enhance student success.	Cusson, 2010; Lambert & Bouchamma, 2019; Stevenson-Jacobson et al., 2006; Thompson, 2017
	Collaboration	Engage educators in collaborative communities of practice to strategically develop and implement programs contributing to student success.	Duncan, 2010; Lambert & Bouchamma, 2019; Stevenson-Jacobson et al., 2006; Thompson, 2017
	Problem-solving	Ability to frame, re-frame, and examine challenges leading to effective implementation of solutions.	Bergstrom, 2012; Thompson, 2017
	Human resources	Hire, train, support, and retain staff committed to the inclusion of students with special education needs.	Bateman et al., 2017; Stevenson-Jacobson et al., 2006
Knowledge	Policies and procedures	Awareness of and ability to navigate school jurisdiction identification, placement, review, staffing, and funding issues.	Bateman et al., 2017; Thompson, 2017
	Legal requirements	Knowledge related to provincial or state regulations for inclusion and special education.	Bateman et al., 2017; Stevenson-Jacobson et al., 2006
	Lived experience of students with special education needs	Awareness of the experiences of students with special education needs and insight into the potential barriers they experience and the opportunities to overcome these barriers.	Cohen, 2015; Ross & Cozzens, 2016; Sider et al., 2017

	Competency	Description	References
	Differentiated leadership	Knowledge of flexible class and school-wide approaches to students' strengths and needs and models the way.	Schultz, 2011; Sider, 2020; Sider et al., 2021; Thompson, 2017
	Contextual knowledge	Awareness of the specific contextual factors for students and their families, individuals within the school, community (e.g., champions of inclusion, toxic naysayers) as well as knowledge of the overall school climate and of the neighboring community.	Cohen, 2015; DeMathews et al., 2021; Lambert & Bouchamma, 2019; Ross & Cozzens, 2016; Schultz, 2011
Attitudes	Values inclusion	Actively communicates and models a belief that all students should be included in their neighborhood schools.	DeMathews et al., 2021; Passman 2008; Sider et al., 2017; Sider, 2020; Stevenson-Jacobson et al., 2006
	Agency	Actively engages students, their family members, teachers, and others in the educational environment to work from an asset-based perspective, focusing on strengths and opportunities as opposed to only focusing on the challenges and needs.	DeMathews et al., 2021; MacCormack et al., 2021; Passman, 2008; Sider et al., 2017
	Fosters relationships	Recognizes that relationships are fundamentally important to the successes of all students and actively works to foster professional relationships that model acceptance and inclusion.	Bateman et al., 2017; Sider et al., 2021; Stevenson-Jacobson et al., 2006
	Embodies professional standards	Holds up ethical standards such as trust, respect, integrity, and care in their work to support all students.	Sider, 2020; Thompson, 2017

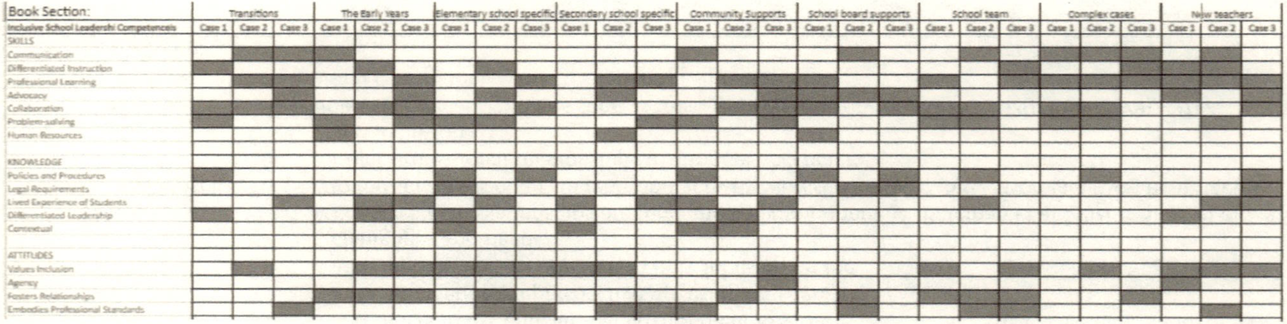

Figure 2.2 Leadership Competencies Connected to Cases. *Source:* Created by author.

What is clear from our research is that more studies need to be completed to better understand leadership competencies for inclusion. As well, those responsible for principals' pre-service and in-service professional learning need to explicitly provide training in inclusive practices. From our examination of inclusive school leadership practices and the related literature, what we do know is that certain knowledge, skills, and attitudes will help foster inclusive school leadership competencies. This chapter has helped outline these competencies.

The cases that follow in this book are designed to help foster leadership competencies so that principals can effectively support all students in their schools. Although many of the cases address the multiple, intersecting competencies that we have addressed in this chapter, we have specifically addressed the following leadership competencies in these cases (see figure 2.2).

We make explicit connections to these competencies in each of the case stories to follow. The resources, questions to consider, and expert commentaries provide further insights into these leadership competencies.

TRANSITIONS

Chapter 3

The Case of Charles

CASE 1: TRANSITIONS

Crosscutting Themes: Collaboration, Parents/Caregivers/Family.
Leadership Competencies: Collaboration, Differentiated Leadership, Problem-solving, Differentiated Instruction, Policies and Procedures.

I have been a school administrator for about five years now. I recently moved from being a vice principal at a small, rural high school to being a vice principal in an urban high school with over 1,700 students and two other vice principals. The school has a large percentage of students with special education needs. It was certainly a huge change, but I was prepared for it as I have specialized in special education most of my career. The school has a very collaborative approach to special education; there is a school-based team made up of a vice principal (me), resource teacher, paraprofessionals, and the head of the Special Education Department.

Collaboration is certainly key when supporting students who have special and unique needs. My philosophy is that we should never work in isolation to support these students; it requires collaborating with staff, parents, the school board, and our students. Trying to solve problems on our own can be very difficult and lonely, which leads to more stress. This is why I believe it is really very important to work as a team within the school.

One particular student at the school, Charles, presents us with a unique case. Charles was diagnosed with autism. He participates in a regular cooking class each morning and spends the rest of the school day in a class with other students with special education needs. He is normally a quiet and well-behaved student who is well liked by his peers and staff. However, Charles has begun acting in ways that are unusual. He has begun swearing at other students and staff—and even spitting on them—as he walks from his cooking class to his other classroom at the other end of the school. Before I arrived at the school, the team had tried a few different strategies with little success and was starting to lose hope for effective ways to address, and change, the behaviors. The current strategy that was in place when Charles acted out was sending him to a vice principal's office—*mine.*

I began witnessing Charles' strange behavior on a daily basis. Each time it occurred Charles was sent to me, and I would reiterate the fact that this behavior was not OK. I also had to deal with the victims of Charles' spitting. I worked on building a stronger relationship with him and tried my best to better understand why he was behaving the way he was. He was always very quiet and reserved when he entered my office, so it was very difficult to build a strong relationship with him.

The school-based team eventually identified that transitioning between classes was very stressful for Charles and caused him to act out in the halls. The noise and chaos of students changing classes in the hallways was overwhelming for him.

When Charles entered the hallways, he became agitated, angry, and stressed. I worked with our cooking teacher to release Charles from class five minutes before the bell rang so he could avoid the chaotic halls. Immediately we noticed a huge difference in his behavior. The spitting had stopped in the

Figure 3.1 Student Waiting Outside of a Principal's Office. *Source*: https://www.istockphoto.com. Credit: DGLimages.

Figure 3.2 **Crowded School Hallway.** *Source*: https://www.istockphoto.com. Credit: kali9.

hallways. He also seemed much less stressed and on edge throughout the day.

Before long, however, spitting incidents began happening in the cafeteria over lunch. We figured it was for similar reasons: the cafeteria was loud, energetic, and overwhelming for Charles. Similarly, transitioning from the cafeteria back to class and vice versa was causing a lot of his anxiety. Once again, we adapted his daily routine so that he could eat in a quieter place and avoid the busy transition of lunchtime. But his inappropriate behavior continued.

One morning when Charles was in my office following a spitting situation, he provided some clues about his behavior. He told me that he was mad at the school for "kicking him out in the fall." He said, "I don't know what I'm going to do in the fall. I want to stay here at the school. But I'm getting kicked out because I'll be 21."

This is when I first realized that Charles is twenty years old, turning twenty-one in the fall. In our province, students are allowed to remain in secondary school until they are twenty-one, which meant that Charles only had a couple more months left at the school. I wasn't aware of his age and wondered if a plan had been put in place to help him transition out of high school.

I got in touch with the special education teacher primarily responsible for the Individual Education Plan for Charles. I learned that the transition plan that was in place had not been updated for three years. We decided to get in touch with Charles' parents to identify possible places for Charles to attend in the fall. They seemed reluctant at first to come to the school meetings, but once they saw how hard we were trying to ensure Charles' success, they quickly became quite supportive. Both of Charles' parents expressed that they were nervous about their son leaving high school and weren't sure what he was going to do in the fall. I focused on building trust with them. We're all currently looking for an appropriate day program for Charles to attend in the fall.

Charles' situation has shown me the different transitions that students experience: transitions within the school day and in life. These transitions are difficult for all students, especially those with special education needs. I think it is important for us, as school leaders, to collaborate with the right stakeholders and identify possible strategies to help students who need extra support. We can truly change their school experience, as well as their life after leaving our school building. My advice for any new principal or vice principal is to make sure they create an environment that supports effective communication, inclusion, and collaboration. We must avoid trying to do everything on our own to better support students as they make transitions—whether big or small.

Questions To Consider:

1. What strategies have you found effective in assisting students who have a hard time with transitions within a school day?
2. Why is it important to collaborate with the whole school team as well as the student and their parents in order to address a situation? How do principals help to make sure that this happens in schools?
3. The school-based team decided that Charles should eat in a quiet area over the lunch break and not in the busy cafeteria. Do you think this was a good idea to exclude him from eating with his peers in the cafeteria? What could the team have done differently to allow Charles to eat with others?
4. The principal used some language when talking about Charles that maybe viewed as problematic. In what ways is language important when discussing a student who has special education needs? Is the use of the word *victim* in this context problematic? Why or why not?

Expert Commentary:

When I read the case about Charles, several issues were highlighted for me. First and foremost was the idea of transition. As the vice principal noted, they can be big or small and can be overwhelming for all students. The second issue that came to me through the discussion of the strategies tried was the assumptions that we tend to make based on behaviors exhibited by students. Finally, the issue of self-determination seems to be an overarching point of discussion. The work of Michael Wehmeyer and colleagues has for decades focused on self-determination in the education of students with disabilities. Self-determination is the ability, motivation, and volition for people to set goals for themselves and to take and sustain the action to achieve those goals (MacCormack et al., 2021). As students age, we give them more and more choices and provide guidance about their futures with their input. Too often we take choices away from students with disabilities, especially as they age. I was struck by the statements of the vice principal and wondered about the choices that had been afforded to Charles. In trying to determine the cause of his behavior many strategies were implemented and failed. The vice principal also stated that they were working hard with the parents to find places for Charles for next year. I wondered where Charles was in all these conversations. I wondered if removing him from class early and having him eat lunch in quiet places had been his idea or forced upon him by people who were trying to determine the reason for his behavior. We need to do a better job in schools of preparing students to be adults. We need to involve students in the discussion of their future. If not, we end up with situations such as the one that Charles is in when he stated "I don't know what I'm going to do in the fall. I want to stay here at the school. But I'm getting kicked out because I'll be 21." Students with disabilities want the same things as students without disabilities. We must not assume otherwise.

To prepare students with disabilities for adulthood, we can do a few things within our secondary school settings to prepare them. Keeping their world small in a special class only with other students with disabilities and a few teachers is not the way forward. Charles likely wants to stay in school because he knows nothing else. We need to create opportunities for experiences beyond the classroom. Career development and career experience are as important for students with disabilities as they are for those without. Providing opportunities for students to know the activities that they can participate in after school finishes and providing experiences in those activities are important. Cooperative learning is useful; job coaches may help. If we continue to focus only on what goes on for students with disabilities within the walls of the school, we will continue to have students who age out of school and transition to the couch in their parent's house. We can do better and we must do better.

REFERENCES:

MacCormack, J., Sider, S., Maich, K., & Specht, J. (2021). Self-determination and inclusion: The role of Canadian principals in catalysing inclusive-positive practices. *International Journal of Education Policy and Leadership, 17*(2). https://journals.sfu.ca/ijepl/index.php/ijepl/issue/view/213

Name: Jacqueline Specht
Position: Professor and Director of the Canadian Research Centre on Inclusive Education
Institutional Affiliation: Western University

Resources

Books

Hughes, J., & Lackenby, N. (2015). *Achieving successful transitions for young people with disabilities: a practical guide.* Jessica Kingsley Publishers.
This book is an expansive transition guide for multiple scenarios. Jill Hughes and Natalie Lackenby have committed to defining key information such as policy and legislations, duty of local authorities and health, housing and education agencies, as well as the impact of education, health and care plans. This book provides resources on services for young people age 16–25 on transitions from moving from children to adult services, school to college, and gaining work experience. This book is aimed as a guide for practitioners and students as a step-by-step process to managing transitions. With evidenced-based models this book also cites resources and suggestions for any and all stakeholders involved in supporting student transition (i.e., social workers, occupational therapists etc).

Maich, K., & Hall, C. (2016). *Autism spectrum disorder in the Ontario context.* Canadian Scholars.
This book is written by professors Kimberly Maich and Carmen Hall who are clinicians and educators in the field of autism. It is unique in its focus on an Ontario, Canada context, as well as its focus across the lifespan from early childhood to adulthood. It is divided into three sections: introduction, interventions, and a look across the lifespan. The book has ten chapters covering the history of autism to ways to support today's parents and families.

Rigler, M., Rutherford, A., & Quinn, E. (2015). *Independence, social, and study strategies for young adults with autism spectrum disorder.* Jessica Kingsley Publishers.
This book explores the BASICS college curriculum which was constructed as a hands-on learning approach for students with autism to teach essential life and study skills. The book is broken down as a life skills guide and expands on the transition to college, organization in academics, communication in academics, organization in life, communication in personal life, stress management, personal responsibilities in academics, campus social life, and relationships. This book is an expansive look at large social and academic transitions for individuals with autism it also includes next steps, a back to basics chart, as well as a guided discussion.

Storey, K., & Hunter, D. (2014). *The road ahead: Transition to adult life for persons with disabilities.* IOS Press.

This book describes assistive technology and its role in successful transition from school to adult life for people with disabilities. The book provides strategies for people working with school transition age students as well as those who continue to work with adults with disabilities. The strategies are all explored and explained in detail with resources and actionable steps to create experiences for individuals to learn independence, career development, independent and supported living as well as community functioning skills. These are supported by informing the reader of person-centered transition planning, employment assessment, and collaboration between agencies for a seamless transition.

Academic Articles

Hume, K., Sreckovic, M., Snyder, K., & Carnahan, C. (2014). Smooth transitions: Helping students with Autism Spectrum Disorder navigate the school day. *Teaching Exceptional Children*, 47(1), 35–45. doi:10.1177/0040059914542794

This research article specifically looks at strategies for smooth transitions and helping students with autism navigate the school day. First, there is an explanation of the frequency of transitions and what characteristics may be associated with autism and transitions. Transition supports are techniques used to support students with autism in changes or disruptions of activities. The article identifies steps such as identifying the problem, selecting appropriate supports, implementing supports, and collecting data to problem solve for successful transitions. Each section is detailed in suggested supports and resources.

Kokina, A., Kern, L., Bambara, L., Cole, C., & Wood, B. (2012). Social Story TM interventions: An examination of effectiveness in addressing transition difficulties of students with Autism Spectrum Disorders [*ProQuest Dissertations Publishing*].

This dissertation-based piece examines the effectiveness of social stories when addressing transition difficulties. The authors' accurately explains the practice of social story interventions, identified theory related to transition difficulties and why students with autism may experience these difficulties through assessment. Supports such as auditory and visual cues, visual activity schedules, video priming/modeling, classroom structuring, behavioral interventions, and comparisons of methods are all explained and explored in this paper.

Szidon, K., Ruppar, A., & Smith, L. (2015). Five steps for developing effective transition plans for high school students with Autism spectrum disorder. *Teaching Exceptional Children*, 47(3), 147–152. doi: 10.1177/0040059914559780

Kathernine Szidon, Andrea Rupparm, and Leann Smith explore aspects of special education in a high school and its special education team's request for professional development. The school has recognized barriers to student learning such as the challenge of transition planning and IEPs for students with autism due to the large variance between social, academic, language, and behavioral skills. This article lists steps as a guide for writing transition plans by identifying goals, linking post-secondary goals with IEP goals, troubleshoot and adjust transition and IEP goals, and evaluating progress. Each section details specific considerations and strategies that can support student success.

Professional Articles

Autism Advocate. (2009). *School transitions in the elementary grades*. Autism Advocate, https://www.autism-society.org/wp-content/uploads/2014/04/school-transitions-in-the-elementary-grades.pdf

This is an adapted resource by the Indiana Resource Center for Autism which focuses on school transitions in the Elementary Grades with practical suggestions for families. This document focuses on transitions being common in all lives, and how, for individuals with autism, these transitions require specific considerations and planning from school staff and families. The document walks through types of transitions from pre-school to more formal education, how to find out who will provide support for your child's school, what supports are offered, and how to contact the person/organization. This document provides tips and information for parents as well as answers to frequently asked questions surrounding transitions.

Ontario Ministry of Education. (2019). *Supporting students with autism spectrum disorder*. Edu.gov.ca. http://www.edu.gov.on.ca/eng/general/elemsec/speced/autism.html

This document was created to outline the current Ontario Ministry of Education initiatives which are in place to support students with autism. These initiatives include policy updates, ABA therapy, a breakdown of funding and continued support. This resource is helpful for parents and teachers looking for ways to find resources in school. This resource helps to enhance understanding and smooth communication between schools and parents.

Roberts, J. (2016). *Let's behave as a team.(cooperation of schools and parents in addressing students' behavioral problems) (Parents' View)*. Times Educational Supplement, 5218.

This piece discusses communication strategies to manage student behaviors. This article includes the importance of identifying the root of the problem, and then creating authentic and personal communication to discover what options are best to support that student, from consequences, and possible disciplinary efforts. The article also explains the importance of a foundation of trust between school and parents to rectify any miscommunication or negative emotions associated with discussion on student behavior.

Websites

Autism, Life skills, Social Skills. (n.d). *Necessary life skills for teens with Autism*. Learning For a Purpose. https://learningforapurpose.com/2018/01/11/necessary-life-skills-for-teens-with-autism/

This website dives into the perspective a person with autism may want to convey, first starting with statements to explain why certain behaviors are exhibited and what contributes to these behaviors or feelings of unease. The website has a variety of links to resources such as checklists, social stories, other helpful websites, and parent guides. These resources are ordered under the headings which include a description and a few considerations for individuals with autism, of skills, self-advocacy, personal safety, how to care for one's self, everyday life skills, executive functioning skills, job skills, and how to manage one's emotions. All of these headings are detailed descriptions on the impact each of these have on students and strategies to help students learn, cope and manage.

Davis, M. (2013, May 16). *Transition resources for parents, teachers, and administrators.* Edutopia. https://www.edutopia.org/blog/transition-resources-teachers-matt-davis

This website contains resources for parents, teachers and administrators that can help students make the transition into elementary, middle, and high school, as well as further in life. The website is broken down by division (elementary, middle, high school, and beyond) these sections include a multitude of links with annotations to guide those seeking resources to the most appropriate link for their interests. These links range from conversation starters, to strategies and goal setting for students.

Ellerbrock, C. (2012). *Help students transition to high school smoothly.* AMLE. https://www.amle.org/BrowsebyTopic/WhatsNew/WNDet/TabId/270/ArtMID/888/ArticleID/117/Help-Students-Transition-to-High-School-Smoothly.aspx

This article written by Cheryl Ellerbrock, an assistant professor at the University of South Florida, focuses on her research on the developmental needs of young adolescent learners. This website discusses the move from middle to high school and the emotions associated for learners. From procedural, social, and academic changes Ellerbrock speaks to the details of how to support students through this transition. She breaks down an explanation as well as tasks for the student to complete/experiment with to ease these transitions. This website is a great resource for both parents and schools' to understand a deeper level of what these transitions need to look like for students with special education needs.

Logsdon, A. (2020, May 17). *Using person-first language when describing people with disabilities.* Very Well Family. https://www.verywellfamily.com/focus-on-the-person-first-is-good-etiquette-2161897

The website explores the importance of stakeholders in a child's life using person-first language. Teachers, parents, principals, and friends need to prioritize the individual and not the issue or disability the student has. The website explores considerations and perspectives, and alternatives to person-first terminology as people are not their disability, but may consider it an important part of their identity so it is important not to remove it from one's vocabulary.

Solomon, M. (2018, August 7). *How to help young adults with autism transition to adulthood.* Spectrum News. https://www.spectrumnews.org/opinion/viewpoint/help-young-adults-autism-transition-adulthood/

This website offers an opinion piece by Marjorie Solomon, a professor at the University of California. She speaks of her experience working with individuals with autism and their specific concern with navigating the adult world such as college, career path, succeeding in the workplace, living independently as well as forming social and romantic relationships.

Chapter 4

Supporting Albert

CASE 2: TRANSITIONS

Crosscutting Themes: Parents/Caregivers/Family, Relationships/Trust, Communication, Collaboration.
Leadership Competencies: Communication, Collaboration, Values Inclusion, Professional Learning.

Samuel Bakar's Perspective

I am a grade four teacher at Cedarview Elementary School. My class this year is unique because most of the students identify as male. The boys in the class have a lot of energy and can quickly increase the energy of the whole class. Most days it is a struggle to get through a whole lesson without being interrupted numerous times. I also have three students who are all on the autism spectrum and have a particularly difficult time settling down. Frankly, it has been a difficult year for me.

One of my students, Albert Cummings, presents some unique challenges. I taught him when he was in grade three as well and, although some of his behaviors were problematic then, they were not a frequent distraction. This year is a completely different story. Albert is particularly out of sorts in the mornings when he first steps into the classroom from playing outside. It tends to take him the first thirty minutes of class—*at least*—to even get his planner message finished. By this point, Albert's frustrations have elevated because his peers have already started on something else. Once he feels he is behind the rest of the class, Albert becomes so agitated that he can't do anything. All he can concentrate on is the fact that he won't be able to finish on time. He also gets agitated when I can't come to his desk to help him immediately.

His agitation spreads to the rest of the class. Albert also speaks very loudly as I teach and interrupts when others are speaking. He blurts out whatever is on his mind—sometimes he blurts out inappropriate words or makes rude comments about other students.

Last week I reached out to Albert's parents to learn more about how Albert behaves at home. I ended up speaking with Albert's mom, Leanne Cummings, for nearly an hour. She said that she has noticed that mornings are especially difficult for her son. He often has trouble waking up and getting ready for school. He often yells—and even swears—at her in the mornings and complains that he doesn't want to go to school. She is concerned because he has a hard time regulating his emotions and calming himself down. Leanne suspects that her son may have some sort of disorder. She has booked an appointment with Albert's family doctor but is worried that the doctor may want to put Albert on medication and she doesn't want to do that. As we ended the phone call, I told Leanne that I understand her concerns and am here to support Albert.

I also spoke to the school principal, Kim Young, about Albert and my frustrations. I am feeling tired and, frankly, not all that sympathetic toward my student. He is always in my personal space, yelling, and trying to get more attention from me. He gets very close and expresses himself very loudly. The more I try to talk to him and try to calm him down, the more intense his reaction is. He gets to a point where he is so stressed and anxious that he can't even hear what I am saying to him and he just continues to yell over top of me. It's really frustrating. I shared with Kim that I usually send Albert into the hall for a "break time" if he's really disrupting the class. I could sense that Kim isn't particularly happy with my strategy; she said that he may decide to run off if he's unsupervised in the hall. I figure that there are plenty of teachers and other staff walking in the halls so he should be just fine out there. Kim told me to send Albert to her office if he is acting out, but she didn't offer any other support than that. I know Kim is busy and all, but she can't provide more help to me than *that*?

I am now feeling quite concerned because I feel like I'm *always* sending Albert out into the hall to calm down. This means that Albert is missing a lot of class time.

He also seems to find the transitions to and from the breaks quite difficult. The breaks, in some ways, cause Albert to become more frustrated because when he returns to the classroom, he feels like he is behind the other students in his work.

I recently had a meeting with Kim and the special education resource teacher, Marta, and discussed ways that we could improve Albert's daily routines. Marta suggested that we try soft entries with Albert in the hope that it will improve his mornings and set a positive tone for his day. She explained

Figure 4.1 Student Sitting Alone. *Source*: https://www.istockphoto.com. Credit: Ridofranz.

that soft entries usually involve a paraprofessional taking a student to another room, like a special education resource room, and doing a few calming activities with them before entering the busy classroom with the other students. The paraprofessional will teach the student some strategies to help them better manage their own behavior. The student is given the opportunity to have a calm, relaxed morning routine, away from the busyness of the classroom. Once the student is feeling relaxed and in control, they are able to reenter the classroom. I think this is a great idea and might be really helpful for Albert. And it might help my own mental health.

Kim Young's Perspective

It was early in the fall when Samuel Bakar, the grade four teacher, came to me with his concerns about Albert Cummings. He shared with me that he was at a breaking point and is feeling exhausted by Albert's problematic behavior, especially in the mornings. I knew that a plan needed to be put in place to help Albert, particularly with his transitions and regulating his emotions.

I told Samuel that I understood the way he was feeling. I also told him that I am here to support him and that we will come up with a solution together. I emphasized that he isn't alone in this process. There is nothing worse than feeling like you are on your own island when dealing with situations like this one. I sensed, however, that Samuel didn't really appreciate my words. I think he wanted me to do more to help him, but I don't know what he is expecting of me at this early stage.

Samuel explained to me that he often sends Albert on breaks when his temper escalates. While this strategy gives *Samuel* a break from Albert, it concerns me that Albert is in the hall so much and is missing important instruction time. My hope was that we could help him control his emotions better so that he could have a better opportunity to learn.

Last week I spent a morning in Samuel's classroom to observe Albert. I could see how the transition into the classroom was particularly stressful for him. I have been meaning to ask a paraprofessional to do soft entries with Albert to help him ease into the classroom in the mornings. Marta, the special education resource teacher, made this suggestion and I think it's a good one.

I have also tried to build a relationship with Albert. One day I asked him about why he doesn't like to come into the classroom in the mornings. "Because I don't like Mr. Bakar. He just sends me out of the classroom," Albert told me, looking down at the ground and not making eye contact with me. "I don't like leaving all the time. It makes me sad." I told Albert that I will do my best to come up with another solution. I agreed, in my head, that the breaks were most likely not that helpful. I had told Samuel to send Albert to my office if he is acting up, but he hasn't sent Albert to me yet. I need to have another conversation with Samuel about Albert. We need to help Albert be the best he can be. The problem is that Samuel is frustrated by Albert's behavior and doesn't seem very willing to help him. I need to figure out how to effectively support Samuel as he supports Albert. But how?

Questions To Consider:

1. Do you think that the principal, Kim Young, handled the situation with Samuel Bakar, the teacher, well? How else can she support him as he supports Albert?
2. Transitions are a particularly challenging aspect of the day for students with special education needs. What other solutions could help address Albert's problematic behavior and difficulty with transitions?
3. How would you ensure that Albert would be able to remain in the classroom for the majority of the day, without being a major distraction for the rest of the class?
4. As a principal, what steps would you take to communicate with Albert's parents?

Expert Commentary:

A school principal must know how to effectively lead their staff so that the whole school team can meet each and every student's needs. One indicator of effective leadership is how well a leader can actively listen—and not just simply hear—their subordinates' request for assistance (Mishra, 2020). Active listening by school principals first translates into prioritizing effective internal communication with staff, as much as they prioritize external communication with parents, superiors or community members.

The case study of "Supporting Albert" is an excellent example of how a school principal's intentions to support a teacher and student, both in need of

Figure 4.2 **Principal Communicating with a Teacher.** *Source:* https://www.istockphoto.com. Credit: SolStock.

assistance, do not necessarily translate into efficient internal communication between them, nor into the co-implementation of timely transition strategies for Albert, an at-risk student.

School principals, like Ms. Young, are busy problem solving, and preventing other problems from occurring while also still trying to motivate their staff to learn and grow. Yet, they need to remember the necessity of using complementary leadership skills alongside staff members in order to meet each and every student's needs. As school principal, Ms. Young's leadership skill set should include effective communication strategies that ensure that staff members can achieve success in the classroom so they may, in turn, ensure student success and well-being. Clearly, that is not the case regarding Mr. Bakar or Albert. In other words, it is not enough for Ms. Young to observe Albert in the classroom once, nor is it acceptable to have forgotten to do follow-up with paraprofessionals about the implementation of soft entry transitions for him. It is also not realistic nor conducive to inclusion for her to offer Mr. Bakar the possibility of sending Albert to her office at any time. Simply put, these are not solutions that ensure a safe and secure environment for Albert while also maintaining a stimulating and inclusive one for him.

Complimentary school leadership strategies require strong, consistent, and regularly scheduled communication with the teacher and the student needing support, as well as an action plan based on specific goals, between the school principal, various staff members, Albert and his family. Together, everyone could complete a student transition profile as a first step to identifying the primary and secondary issues impeding Albert's success and well-being (see Moore, n.d.). The common goal being to effectively achieve Albert's inclusion in his classroom, through his goals, and objectives, and—in turn—his well-being and success. For example, in this case study, Albert has more than made it clear that he feels unwelcome in Mr. Bakar's classroom, and Mr. Bakar is aware that he is sending Albert out into the hallway more often. Therefore, Albert's team needs to further investigate the important breakdown in this previously good student-teacher relationship.

Finally, complementary school leadership skills between the principal and their staff require that each professional develop self-leadership skills. This less-known form of leadership is about "recognising, developing and leveraging the levels of individual self-leadership so these individuals can lead their organisations more authentically and towards desired outcomes" (Kotze, 2016, p. 97). In this case study, Ms. Young needs to: (1) recognize and acknowledge her current limitations in terms of not having been able to contribute effectively to meeting either Mr. Bakar's or Albert's needs; (2) ask Mr. Bakar what he specifically needs/wishes from her in terms of support for Albert and himself, and then to develop the strategies with him to meet those needs/wishes instead of her simply proposing them herself, or making empty promises; and (3) involve other staff members, such as the special education resource teacher, by leveraging her expertise in discussions with Mr. Bakar about Albert for his success and well-being.

References:

Kotze, T. (2016). Self leadership as an antecedent to leadership: an empirical study among public sector employees. *African Journal of Public Affairs*, 9(2). https://repository.up.ac.za/handle/2263/58194

Mishra, S. (2020). Listening as a leadership tool: A survey of subordinates' perception towards listening skills of effective leaders. *Journal of Xidian University*. https://doi.org/10.37896/jxu14.6/170

Moore, S. (n.d.). *Student transition profile*. https://blogsomemoore.files.wordpress.com/2015/02/student-transition-profile.pdf

Name: Mélissa Villella
Position: Assistant Professor in School Administration
Institutional Affiliation: Université du Québec en Abitibi-Témiscamingue

Resources

Books

Arneson, S. (2017). *Communicate and motivate: The school leader's guide to effective communication*. Routledge.
This book by author Shelly Arneson helps to facilitate effective principal-teacher communication. The book has a student-centered approach to communication within a school and includes strategies for different forms of communication.

Videos

Knox County Schools TV. (2018, June 6). *Calming corners*. [Video]. YouTube. https://www.youtube.com/watch?v=U2HdaOyh09Q
This short video by the Knox County School Board is all about creating a calm down space or corner within the classroom. The goal of a calm down corner is to stop interruptions for behavior as it allows students to learn and use self-regulation techniques. Students can go themselves or teachers can direct them there, and a short timer is normally set to tell the student to return to the class activity.

Academic Articles

Cook, C. R., Coco, S., Zhang, Y., Fiat, A. E., Duong, M. T., Renshaw, T. L., Long, A. C., & Frank, S. (2018). Cultivating positive teacher-student relationships: Preliminary evaluation of the establish-maintain-restore (EMR) method. *School Psychology Review, 47*(3), 226–243. doi: 10.17105/SPR-2017-0025.V47-3

The study that is the focus of this article examines how to improve teacher-student relationships. The study evaluated the establish-maintain-restore (EMR) method of professional development which included follow-up support.

Professional Articles

Finley, T. (2017, March 13). *Mastering classroom transitions.* Edutopia. https://www.edutopia.org/article/mastering-transitions-todd-finley

The article includes five steps to a successful transition as well as how to troubleshoot when they aren't going as planned. Other informative pieces explaining why transitions may not be going well are included in the article.

Ontario Ministry of Education. (2013). *Engaging parents in their children's learning.* Edu.gov.ca http://www.edu.gov.on.ca/eng/policyfunding/leadership/pdfs/issue20.pdf

The online resource for school leaders "Principals want to know" presents a two page, five section, recommendation document to help get parents invested in their child's education. The goal with this document is to improve parent communication through five simple steps. .

Rosenberg, D., & Miles, K, H. (2018). *Growing great teachers: How school system leaders can use existing resources to better develop, support, and retain new teachers and improve student outcomes.* ERStrategies. https://files.eric.ed.gov/fulltext/ED593368.pdf

This document presented by the team at ERS looks to help school leaders develop the educators in their schools. The document includes five recommendations to implement in your school to better support teachers. This resource is helpful for both new and struggling teachers.

Websites

Dabbs, L. (2012, March 26). *A school principal must be a support to teachers.* Kids discover. https://www.kidsdiscover.com/teacherresources/school-principal-support-teachers/

This article by Lisa Dabbs is all about supporting classroom teachers. The article includes Dabbs own story and opinion on supporting classroom teachers and links to resources to create a professional learning community. While acknowledging that a principal's job is complex, it also important to remember that there is always room for improvement.

Education World. (2015, March 30). *Stress relief for teachers and students.* https://www.educationworld.com/a_curr/strategy/strategy063.shtml

Stress is prevalent in a lot of educators' and students' lives, so this article presented by Education World includes an array of stress reliever tips. The article has links to other articles and other online resources like videos to help teachers, principals and students find relief from stress. The resources for the students are great online tools to use with one student or the entire class.

Ontario Teachers Federation. (n.d.). *Transition skills.* Teach Spec Ed. https://www.teachspeced.ca/transition-plans?q=node/728

This website shares different teaching strategies. The strategies can be implemented at different levels, during instruction, within the physical classroom or at the time of assessment. Using multiple strategies can help students better adjust to transitions within the classroom.

Robson, D. (2018, April 16). *How to help kids who struggle with daily transitions.* CBC. https://www.cbc.ca/parents/learning/view/how-to-help-kids-who-struggle-with-transitions

This article is a helpful resource to learn about daily transitions in a child's life. The article includes five tips that can be used both at home and at school to help a student transition from one task to another. This article is helpful for classroom teachers and also for parents at home struggling with the same issue.

Chapter 5

The Big Move

CASE 3: TRANSITIONS

Crosscutting Themes: Collaboration, Relationship/Trust, Parents/Caregivers/Family, Advocacy.

Leadership Competencies: Collaboration, Communication, Lived Experience of Students, Advocacy, Professional Learning, Embodies Professional Standards

Derek McDonald is a thirteen-year-old student at Windemere Lane Elementary School. He is in grade eight and getting ready to make the big move to high school. His stepfather, Peter Steinfold, is concerned about Derek's upcoming transition. Derek is diagnosed with attention deficit hyperactivity disorder and struggles with social anxiety. A few of Derek's teachers have wondered if he may be on the autism spectrum, but he hasn't been diagnosed. He has a difficult time socializing with his classmates and tends to get stressed when he is faced with change.

Derek really struggled in grade seven last year. He had trouble concentrating on his work and often had emotional outbursts when transitioning into different classrooms. Once he threw some school supplies around the classroom and slammed his fist down on his desk, which was unsettling for other students and for his teacher. These outbursts occurred almost daily that year, but his teacher and the special education resource teacher put a plan in place to help Derek in his transitions this year. The plan has helped him significantly.

Derek's stepfather, Peter, has been thrilled with the progress that Derek has made from grade seven to grade eight. But, with high school in the near future, Peter is concerned that Derek is going to struggle with the transition.

He decided to have a conversation with the school principal, Iris Singh, and special education resource teacher, Stan Brownlee. The three met in April to talk about supporting Derek in his transition to Mackenzie High.

"I'm worried about Derek," Peter admitted during the meeting. "High school is so much different than elementary school. I'd really like to set a plan in place to ensure that Derek is successful in his transition. I don't want him to backtrack. He's done so well this year."

"I understand your concerns," Ms. Singh said.

We certainly understand how important it is to help support students during these transitions, especially for a student like Derek who struggles with changes. In fact, transition planning is a part of the legal requirements in the province. So school boards have strategies and plans set in place to help students transition successfully to high school.

Iris explained that, in her experience, many students experience isolation, a decline in academic performance, and a decrease in confidence when transitioning to high school. While these experiences are natural and cannot be totally avoided, she promised that the school would help prepare Derek.

"I think one of our first steps of action should be to connect with the head of special education and the principal at Mackenzie High," Iris suggested.

Figure 5.1 Parent Meeting. *Source*: https://www.istockphoto.com. Credit: monkeybusinessimages.

"I agree," said Stan.

I also think it would be helpful if Derek visits Mackenzie a few times before the fall. The school offers a Head Start program in August for students with special education needs. It might be helpful if he participates in that. That way he can get his timetable, classroom numbers, and teachers' names ahead of time. He'll also get a tour of the school—classrooms, washrooms, the cafeteria, all that.

Iris also suggested that Derek join a peer-to-peer mentorship program at Mackenzie. He would be matched up with another student who could help him navigate the school for the first couple weeks. That way he would have someone to talk to right away and would hopefully feel less isolated.

Peter felt relieved. He didn't know that these types of programs existed at Mackenzie. He thought the programs would help Derek feel more at ease on his first day of high school since he would already know where everything is and would be comfortable navigating a new building.

Months passed, and the team at Windemere Lane did all that they could to prepare Derek for his transition to high school. Stan had frequent conversations with Peter over the telephone to check in and see how Derek was doing at home. Peter said that he mainly seemed like his normal self but was much more anxious than usual, which, he thought, was to be expected. The school continued to provide Derek with coping strategies for his anxiety.

Figure 5.2 Student Helping a Younger Student. *Source*: https://www.istockphoto.com. Credit: lisegagne.

Stan even worked on some mindfulness techniques with Derek hoping that it would provide Derek with a technique to use to ease his anxious mind. Derek was also able to participate in the Head Start program where he met Bruce Smith, the head of the special education department, and was matched up with a grade twelve student, Evan, to help him in the first few weeks of high school.

September

The first day of classes quickly arrived and Derek was off to his first day at Mackenzie High. Peter decided to bring him to the school early so that he could go in and help him adjust. Before long, the hallways were filled with hundreds of students. Derek immediately felt overwhelmed and anxious. He didn't know where his peer mentor, Evan, was, who had promised to help him find his homeroom. Evan was supposed to meet him in the school foyer but never showed up. Derek decided to find his homeroom himself and, when he did, he found a seat at the back of the classroom. He was too nervous to look at any of the other students, let alone talk to them. He felt restless and fidgety, so he decided to open up his new agenda and start drawing. After a couple of minutes passed, he heard the teacher talking in the background but decided to continue to draw to help ease his nerves.

Suddenly Derek heard, "You! In the red shirt! Your name is . . . let me see . . . *Derek*! Derek, are you listening to me? You need to stop drawing and listen to my instructions so that you know what to do."

Derek looked up at the teacher and saw all the other students turned and staring at him. His heart began to race and he felt his face go red. He felt like he was losing control of his emotions. He began sobbing.

The teacher recognized that Derek was having a panic attack. He called Bruce, the special education resource teacher, who took Derek out of the classroom.

As Bruce walked Derek to a quiet office space, he said, "I'm going to call your dad and see if he can pick you up. I think you should head home for the day and come back tomorrow. Start fresh."

Derek nodded silently.

When Peter received a phone call from the school and was asked to come pick up Derek, he immediately panicked. *I don't understand why this happened*, he thought as he rushed out of work and drove madly to the high school. *I thought I did everything to avoid this. I met with Derek's elementary school to develop a transition plan. Derek went to the Head Start program. He has a peer mentor. How is he going to get through high school if he can't even get through the first day?*

Peter continued to drive, feeling defeated and not sure of what to do next.

Questions To Consider:

1. What steps were taken to support Derek's successful transition to high school? Would you have advised other steps to take? Given the steps that were taken, why was the first day not a success?
2. Could Iris have provided more support to Derek and Peter? If so, how? Should other people have been further involved in the transition? What is the role of the secondary school administrative team in supporting the transition?
3. What are some strategies you would set in place during a student's final years of elementary school to help them transition to high school?
4. This student has some specific learning and behavioral needs. How could those have been better supported during this transition to secondary school?

Expert Opinion:

Perhaps the lack of continuity in Derek's transition plan (and its implementation) from Windermere Lane Elementary School to Mackenzie High School is what led to him experience a panic attack and then being escorted out of the classroom that day. This case highlights several concerns within Mackenzie High School. It must be stated that, although support programs are put in place to *ease* student's transitions, Derek's program proved to be executed ineffectively. To begin, issues of communication are obvious. Bruce Smith, the head of the special education department, clearly did not prepare Derek's teachers well enough for having a student with ADHD and social anxiety. More saliently, the elementary and secondary principals appeared to assume that all teachers have a preliminary understanding of special education and yet are not held accountable to uphold an appropriate level of competency with respect to teaching and responding to students with special education needs. The DSM-5 states that experiencing social anxiety can lead to withdrawal and isolation; thus, overall quality of life is negatively affected (American Psychiatric Association, 2013). It is the responsibility of schools to have strategies in place in order to enhance all student's experiences in their learning environments. In Derek's experience, however, his teacher instead became a catalyst for the negative consequences of his social anxiety.

Moving forward, Derek's case should now act as a learning experience for both the elementary and secondary princpals. Ideally, the principals would take the lessons learned from the abovementioned shortcomings and apply them to not only Derek, but the entire student body: both current and future. Possible arrangements that the principals could make include, first, facilitating disability sensitivity training across all faculty at Mackenzie High School. Second, the principals could promote parent-teacher communication even before classes begin in September to allow for effective preparation of student support strategies. Efforts to maintain these solutions can be supported through embracing an organizational behavior management (OBM) model. Specifically, the principals could focus on the *performance management* component of OBM, where, behavior analytic principles would be applied to manage the performance of faculty (Wilder et al., 2009). An OBM model focusing on performance management could facilitate effective leadership by way of collaboratively selecting shared goals within classrooms and across students to promote inclusivity. In this way, faculty behavior would be shaped to achieve agreed-upon organizational values. The following questions could be addressed as part of this type of process.

1. What are effective self-regulatory practices that should be taught to students?
2. How can school faculty eliminate alienation of students with special education needs?
3. How can faculty address both academic needs and mental health needs compassionately? How can compassion be practiced in the classroom?

In the event that the above questions can be answered, and those answers are applied by faculty, Mackenzie High School would be engaging in inclusive, research-informed practices as per the guidance of the principals.

References

American Psychiatric Association. (2013). *Diagnostic and statistical manual of mental disorders* (5th ed.). Arlington, VA: Author.

Wilder, D. A., Austin, J., & Casella, S. (2009). Applying behavior analysis in organizations: Organizational behavior management. *Psychological Services*, 6(3), 202–211. doi: 10.1037/a00153

Name: Emma Hosey
Position: Graduate Student
Institutional Affiliation: Yorkville University

Resources

Books

Olender, R. A., Elias, J., & Mastroleo, R. D. (2010). *The school-home connection: Forging positive relationships with parents.* Corwin Press.
Authors Rosemary Olender, Jacquelyn Elias and Rosemary Mastroleo write about their professional experiences and research when they created this book about creating positive school-home relationships. They talk about common reasons for both negative and positive relationships with students' families.

Videos

ABC10. (2019, May 17). *Teens talk about the transition from middle school to high school* [Video]. YouTube. https://www.youtube.com/watch?v=rojP6Tj2OF4&feature=youtu.be

This video presented by ABC10 shows the transition to high school from the students' perspective. Having a better understanding of how students perceive the change can be very helpful in how educators support students during the transition.

Academic Articles

Benner, A. D., Boyle, A. E., Bakhtiari, F., Buchmann, M., Malti, T., & Steinhoff, A. (2017). Understanding students' transitions to high school: Demographic variation and the role of supportive relationships. *Journal of Youth and Adolescence,* 46(10), 2129–2142. Springer Science and Business Media LLC.

This article examines how the transition to high school can be affected by many different factors. This qualitative study concluded that positive connections with peers and educators positively affect the student the most. The study also found that keeping as much of the student's life as stable as possible during this time leads to a better transition.

Weymouth, B. B., & Buehler, C. (2018). Early adolescents' relationships with parents, teachers, and peers and increases in social anxiety symptoms. *Journal of Family Psychology,* 32(4), 496–506. doi: 10/1037/fam0000396

This study by Bridget Weymouth and Cheryl Buehler looked at the dynamic relationship between students, parents, teachers, and their peers. The study noted that the parent and teacher relationships with the student was the biggest predictor for the student's social anxiety. Poor relationships between students and parents can affect the student in many ways, and this study showed some of the negative outcomes.

Professional Articles

Connections for Students Phase II Regional Advisory Group. (n.d.). *Connections for students: Meeting minutes templates.* Edugains. http://www.edugains.ca/resourcesSpecEd/ASD/BoardDevelopedResources/CapacityBuilding/ConnectionsForStudents_Meeting_Minutes_Template-3.pdf

This document uses checklists and timetables to help manage a student's transition. Whether the student is transitioning from home-school or elementary-secondary, this resource is a very practical tool for principals and teachers. The document includes three other resources that could be useful for supporting students through transitions.

EduGains. (n.d.). *Educator support guide for transition planning.* Ontario Ministry of Education. http://www.edugains.ca/resourcesSpecEd/IEP&Transitions/BoardDevelopedResources/TransitionPlanning/SupportGuides/EducatorSupportGuideforTransitionPlanning.pdf

Transitions between home-school, elementary-secondary, and secondary-work can be extremely challenging and so this support guide was created for educators as a two-page infographic on transitions. The document has three goals to keep in mind when planning for a student to transition both between academic settings and between lessons, in the mornings and at the end of the day.

Grade 8 to 9 Transition Planning. Pathways & Student Success. (2021). Retrieved 3 May 2021, from https://studentsuccess.hcdsb.org/sample-page/transition-planning/.

This article presented by the Halton Catholic District School Board is useful for educators, parents, and students alike who would like to know more about transitioning to high school. The article is divided into months so that you can better know when to do what to prepare students for grade nine.

Perras, C. (2016). *Elementary to secondary: transition planning for students with LDs*. LD@School. https://www.ldatschool.ca/transitionelementarysecondary/

This article by Cindy Perras, an educational consultant, is part of a series on helping students with learning disabilities transition to high school. This article is filled with links to other resources as well as checklists so that everything is in on place when trying to support the transition to secondary for students with a learning disability.

Websites

Davis, M. (2013). *Transition resources for parents, teachers, and administrators*. Edutopia. https://www.edutopia.org/blog/transition-resources-teachers-matt-davis

This blog entry from Matt Davis, is for parents, teachers, and school leaders. The blog shares information to help students transitioning at any level, home-school, elementary-secondary, secondary-college, or the workforce. Every heading includes three to six points with extra resources to look through for more information.

Foundation for People with Learning Disabilities (2013). *Moving on ... Tips for pupils moving to secondary school*. https://www.mentalhealth.org.uk/sites/default/files/moving-on-top-tips-for-pupils.pdf

This resource presented by the Foundation for People with Learning Disabilities is a great resource for students who are making the transition to secondary school. The document includes pathway style pages that students can follow to have a more successful entry into high school. There are also checklists and other resources available within the document.

Horne, V. (2015). *Five useful ways teachers can help pupils transition to secondary school*. The Guardian. https://www.theguardian.com/teacher-network/2015/jul/01/five-useful-ways-teachers-pupils-transition-secondary-school

Vicky Horne, a school administrator, shares how teachers can support their students through one of the most challenging transitions in their adolescent lives. Horne shares five tips to share with students: make contact with secondary schools, share information, alleviate fears, teach resilience, and don't panic.

THE EARLY YEARS

Chapter 6

"You Have to Trust We're Doing Our Job"

CASE 1: THE EARLY YEARS

Crosscutting Themes: Communication, Parents/Caregivers/Family
Leadership Competencies: Human Resources, Fosters Relationships, Communication, Problem-solving, Advocacy.

Rosa Lopez is a student in the Kindergarten class at Northview Elementary, where I've been the principal for just three months.

Rosa has a great deal of difficulty sitting still and paying attention in class. She often disrupts our ten-minute circle time by wandering around the room and playing with various toys. If her teacher, Jennifer Littlefield, asks her to join the rest of the class on the carpet, Rosa will often fall to the floor and cry—very loudly and for a long time. Because of this problem, Mrs. Littlefield has resorted to ignoring Rosa—when she can—and just continuing on with her lessons. But it has become increasingly apparent that this strategy isn't working, as Rosa will often get more upset that she missed out on activities with her classmates. Her tantrums are getting longer and louder and her time on the carpet is getting shorter and shorter. On top of this, the school is in a constant flux of hiring new special education teachers. Not that Rosa is officially a student with a special education need. As a result, many teachers end up in *my* office to discuss supports for their students because we don't have a consistent special education teacher.

One afternoon when the school day had ended, Jennifer Littlefield knocked on my office door. We talked casually until she brought up the reason she had come to see me. "I'm really concerned about Rosa," she said. "I've tried to help her, but haven't had any luck. I'd really appreciate your support here."

Figure 6.1 Distracted Students. *Source*: https://www.istockphoto.com. Credit: princigalli.

After listening to Jennifer's frustrations and concerns with Rosa and then observing a few hours in the Kindergarten classroom a few days later, I thought it best to connect with Rosa's family. I wanted to communicate what had been happening in the classroom and to see if there were any similarities or differences between her behavior at home and her behavior in class.

Jennifer and I met with Rosa's family about a week later. Mr. Lopez shared that his daughter often has difficulty doing one task for extended periods of time and has trouble sitting still at home. He admitted that he didn't think much of it and assumed it was just a restless phase. However, after hearing about her struggles to pay attention and sit still in class, we all realized that there might be something more significant involved and Rosa's parents said that they wanted to take her to see a doctor. We also agreed that, for the time being, it would be beneficial to Rosa's learning to bring a paraprofessional into class to provide increased support and attention.

The meeting ended well, and I felt like the Lopez's were happy with the support that we could provide Rosa and their family. However, I began to get frequent phone calls from the Lopez's. They would ask me for updates on Rosa and how she was doing in class. At first, I didn't mind these calls. As a parent myself, I understood their concerns about their daughter. But the calls started increasing in number and began to test my patience.

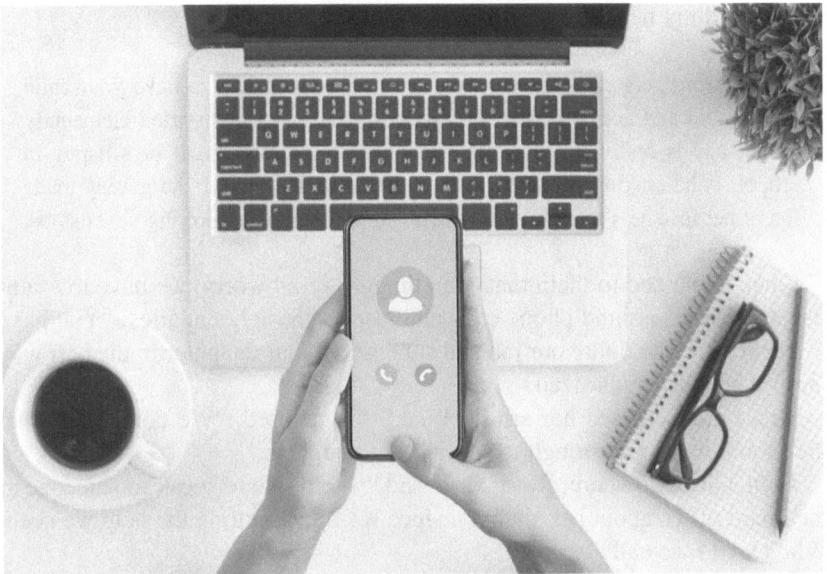

Figure 6.2 Incoming Call. *Source*: https://www.istockphoto.com. Credit: Prostock-Studio.

I started to get *really* annoyed. The Lopez's would call my office phone as early as 7:00 a.m. and as late as 6:00 p.m., demanding to talk to me. If I wasn't in the office, they would leave long messages on my voice mail, telling me to call them back immediately.

One morning I vented to my vice principal, Kassia Jones, about the situation. Kassia had been at the school for over six years and knew the Lopez's and their other child, Henry, who was in the third grade. "The Lopez's are intense! They're calling me constantly, as if I don't have anything else to do. I care about Rosa, of course, but there have to be some boundaries established, right?" I asked her.

Rather than taking the calls, she encouraged me to invite the Lopez's to the school for another in-person conversation to discuss their concerns. This way, she suggested, they would see that I was willing to put the time into supporting Rosa the best way that I could.

The next day, I reluctantly organized a meeting with the Lopez's. I included Jennifer Littlefield and the classroom's new paraprofessional in the meeting. After a number of deep breathing exercises to ground myself, I entered the meeting room. During the meeting, it was clear that Rosa's parents were most worried about how her learning challenges would affect her ability to make friends. They also expressed that it had been a difficult transition for them to have Rosa in school and away from home.

I nodded my head in agreement and said,

I know from personal experience what an adjustment it is to have your child start school and not be home every day. My little guy just started elementary school and is really shy. I worry about him constantly and if he's happy in school. Is he making friends? Do the other kids like him? Is he getting made fun of because he's a really slow reader? As a parent, the worrying never stops.

I then explained to them that even though we all worry, we have to establish boundaries around phone calls and respect those boundaries: "You have to trust that we're doing our job and supporting your daughter in the best way that we can," I emphasized.

Mrs. Lopez crossed her arms. "Well," she retorted. "We don't think that the school has done enough to support our daughter."

Then, out of nowhere, Rosa's dad said, "We'd like to speak to someone at the board office about her situation since we're not getting the help we need. Who should we call?"

Questions To Consider:

1. How have you effectively fostered trust with parents of Kindergarten students? What are some challenges that you have faced?
2. In your jurisdiction, is it likely that a paraprofessional would be implemented in a situation like this where there is no diagnosis but a child demonstrates having challenges in the classroom? What processes might be put into place for a situation such as the one in this case?
3. Do you think that the principal should have been more tolerant toward the Lopez family and their constant phone calls? Why or why not?

Expert Opinion:

> We don't accomplish anything in this world alone . . .
> and whatever happens is the result of the whole tapestry
> of one's life and all the weavings of individual threads
> from one to another that creates something.
> *Sandra Day O'Connor*

The threads that parents contribute to the tapestry of a child's growth and learning is multicolored, strong, resolute, and bountiful. As teachers, our threads are just as strong; however they vary in length, vibrancy, and impact since children have numerous teachers with different approaches to teaching and learning throughout their lifetime. Recognizing that the mainstay of the tapestry are the threads from parents, it is up to us as teachers to ensure parental engagement and voices are listened to in a mindful, respectful, and intentional way.

According to Pushor (2011), "there is an inherent hierarchy in [the] relationship" (p. 67) between teachers and parents. In many classrooms, it is evident that teachers hold the power of the relationship since "they decide when and how parents will play a part in their children's schooling" (Pushor, 2011, p. 67). It is often the school's decision how communication is shared with parents, how strategies related to students' behavior and inclusion are implemented, and when parents are called in for a meeting, and so on. This unilateral agenda usually moves "in one direction, from the school to parents and families" (Pushor, 2011, p. 67) leaving fractures of mistrust and shaky parent-teacher partnerships.

Fostering a culture of trust with parents is foundational to the success of a child (Ontario Ministry of Education, 2015). It is the role of the teacher, administration, and school staff to nourish a trusting relationship with parents that is "founded on active listening, sharing information, building partnerships, and finding common ground" (CODE, 2012, p. 3). It is through transparent, invitational, and leaning in actions by the teacher, that determines if a culture of trust with parents can be established (Sinay et al., 2016). Sometimes parents have intergenerational trauma related to trust building and the school system, so teachers must find creative ways to build reciprocity that honors and validates parent's strengths and highlights the common ground that both parents and teacher have related to the same shared high expectations, hopes, and dreams for the student.

Looking at the early years case featuring Rosa Lopez, it is evident that several of the conditions outlined above for meaningful parental engagement advocacy are askew. Since this is the first experience Rosa's parents have had with the school system, her parents more than ever want to know that Rosa's teacher has care, compassion, and commitment toward her wholistic growth. They are unfamiliar with ethical parent-teacher boundaries. They are seeking guidance on supports and strategies they can provide, and they want to know that Rosa's behaviors are being ameliorated by school staff through skill building and direct instruction.

In the early years, part of the initial parent meeting could be to establish the roles and responsibilities of each stakeholder (e.g., parents, teacher, child, administration, etc.) (Ontario Ministry of Education, 2007). Sharing information about Rosa's behavior in an objective and quantifiable manner (i.e., using ABC chart) and using open, invitational language asking parents to share their observations at home may find common ground needed to determine an action plan whereby all stakeholders have a purposeful role. Agreeing upon a communication protocol enables parents to expect updates from the teacher on an acquiescent basis, thus relieving the fear and anxiety parents may have about their daughter's progress. Lastly, documenting the meeting using an Interview Organizer template (ETFO, 2011, pp. 90–93) and sharing a copy with family helps keep the agreements transparent so that trust between stakeholders can develop.

According to Pushor (2011), "when we give our heartfelt care and commitment, time to listen and learn, and space for parent knowledge to be shared alongside our own knowledge, what we get is stronger schools, families, and communities" (p. 68). In the case of Rosa, the threads of both parents and teachers need to be woven together in a more synchronous manner. There is common ground evident alongside mutual care and commitment; however, both parents and teachers feel their past encounters have distressed their relationship and their partnership has eroded. They need to find a way to make alliances and renew the strength that their togetherness will have for Rosa's growth and tapestry.

References:

Council of Ontario Directors of Education (CODE). (2012). Building confidence in public education. *Advisory,* 21, 1–4. http://www.ontariodirectors.ca/CODE_Advisories/Downloads/CODE%20Advisory%20No%2021%20Web.pdf

Elementary Teachers Federation of Ontario (ETFO). (2011). *The heart and art of teaching and learning: Practical ideas and resources for beginning teachers,* pp. 71–94. ETFO. https://heartandart.ca/wp-content/uploads/2011/08/heartandart.pdf.

Ontario Ministry of Education. (2007). *Shared solutions.* http://www.edu.gov.on.ca/eng/general/elemsec/speced/shared.pdf

Ontario Ministry of Education. (2015). *Achieving excellence: Enhancing public confidence.* https://www.edu.gov.on.ca/eng/about/confidence.html

Pushor, D. (2011). Looking out, looking in. *Educational Leadership,* 69(1). ASCD. https://familyengagement.nipissingu.ca/wp-content/uploads/sites/26/2014/12/Looking-Out-Looking-In.pdf

Sinay, E., Presley, A., Douglin, M., & De Jesus, S. (2016). *Fostering a "culture of trust" within and outside a school system.* (Research Report No. 15/16-11). Toronto District School Board. https://www.tdsb.on.ca/Portals/research/docs/reports/FosteringACultureOfTrustWithinAndOutsideASchoolSystem.pdf

Name: Erin Keith
Position: Limited-Duties Assistant Professor
Institutional Affiliation: Western University

Resources

Videos

Edutopia (2015, April 7). *Sharing data to create stronger parent partnerships.* YouTube. https://www.youtube.com/watch?v=kL5lO8gMrR0

This video published by Edutopia in 2015 focuses on the benefits sharing student data has on parent partnerships with the school and teachers. Teachers from Humboldt Elementary School provide insight into how they communicate student progress, their pedagogy, and delivery methods to parents regularly. Maureen Holt discusses the very specific feedback she gives to parents to best fully support her students in the classroom and at home. This video would be helpful for educators hoping to develop professionally through their communication techniques and data sharing methods with colleagues and parents alike. This video focuses on elementary school environments but could be transferable to secondary schools as well.

Academic Articles

Westerberg D., Newland R., Mendez J. L. (2020). Beyond the classroom: The Protective role of student–teacher relationships on parenting stress. *Early Childhood Education Journal*, 48(5), 633–642. doi: 10.1007/s10643-020-01024-w.

The authors conclude that the protective role of close student-teacher relationships for children and parents and have implications for how teachers and their communication with families may positively impact parents and families. The authors conducted a study that examined student-teacher relationship quality to the home environment and parenting stress in preschoolers, teachers, and parents. Home and school bidirectional communication was observed in relation to student-teacher closeness and its impact on child negative or positive affect and parenting stress.

Professional Articles

Campbell T. A., Brownlee A., Renton C. A. (2016, February). *What works? Research into practice: Pedagogical documentation: Opening windows onto learning.* Ontario Ministry of Education. http://www.edu.gov.on.ca/eng/literacynumeracy/inspire/research/ww_pedagogicdoc.htm

This research monograph (#61) was written by Terry A. Campbell, Amanda Brownlee, and Carole A. Renton for the Ontario Ministry of Education. With the focus on what educators can do to communicate what they are learning about their students' learning, these authors go on to provide insight into how to relay this information to guardians, parents, and members of the wider school community. They hone in on the importance of documentation, whether that be through visuals or blogs. While this is not directly focused on parent-teacher relationships, it can help promote trust and strengthen this partnership.

Moran, K. (2020, March 12). *9 of the biggest parent communication mistakes (plus how to fix them).* We Are Teachers. https://www.weareteachers.com/parent-communication-mistakes/

As an educator, Kimberely Moran speaks to her experience in spending time trying to form relationships with parents and missteps that occurred in communicating with them along the way. Common mistakes the author mentions; using one-way communication tools, communicating too infrequently, failing to document communications, taking a passive approach to issues, and assuming a parent can read and speak English. She also includes; fighting every battle, refusing to admit personal mistakes, taking parent issues personal, and telling parents what to do as common mistakes.

Rogozinsky, D. (2018). What to do when parents don't understand boundaries. *Study.com*. https://study.com/blog/what-to-do-when-parents-don-t-understand-boundaries.html

This article provides some insight into steps teachers and educators may consider taking when they feel there is a misunderstanding with parents about boundaries. Rogozinsky discusses that, while parents may have good intentions, they may also have difficulty in communicating these effectively to their children's teachers. She shares and explains three key overlapping steps involved on the road to effective parent-teacher communication; be clear, be strong, be cooperative.

Rubin, A. (2018, April 9). *4 professional boundaries principals need to consider*. We Are Teachers. https://www.weareteachers.com/principal-professional-boundaries/

Some of the topics covered in this professional article include; school leaders connecting with colleagues on social media, principals presence in the staff or lunchroom, principals being invited to social events by teachers, and how principals deal with reprimanding a teacher. This article explains that being an official or authority member is not an easy job and it is important to set social boundaries to fulfill this job successfully.

Websites

Council of Ontario Directors of Education. (2014). *Parent tool kit: What parents can do to help their children develop healthy relationships*. Retrieved from http://www.ontariodirectors.ca/Parent_Engagement/2014_PE_Docs/40714_Code_ParentToolKit_E.pdf

In 2014, the Council of Ontario Directors of Education shared strategies parents can add to their toolkit when developing healthy relationships with their children. Though not specific to communication between teachers and educators, this toolkit touches on important topics involving six sections titled; Be a Mentor, Be Involved, Be a Role Model, Be a Learner, Be a Coach, and Be a Guide. This document includes contributions from parents and professionals who have shared their experiences and expertise in a variety of key areas in children's lives.

Fischer, M. W. (2005, November). *Handling parent complaints—The good, the bad, and the ugly*. Education World. https://www.educationworld.com/a_curr/voice/voice082.shtml

This article written by Max W. Fischer, focuses on how educators and teachers should handle parent or guardian complaints. Fischer speaks from his thirty years of experience as a teacher and describes how to handle difficult situations involving parents of students. With a detailed four-point approach he explains how to successfully engage in meaningful and proactive conversation with parents through: not procrastinating, genuinely acknowledging a parent's concern, being assertive but not abrasive, and documenting all efforts. Fischer also provides examples of scenarios he has dealt with involving displeased parents and what worked, as well as what did not, in terms of communication approaches.

Ontario Teachers' Federation. (2015). Parent engagement. *Ontario Teachers Federation.* https://www.parentengagement.ca/

This website is a portal created by the Ontario Teachers' Federation to allow teachers and educators to access multiple modules on the following topics surrounding parent engagement: establishing positive relationships, modeling effective communication, supporting students' academic success, contributing to school life, engaging in wellbeing and safety issues, addressing equity issues and concerns, and managing and resolving conflicts. Each module contains context, background, big ideas, questions, practical tips, helpful resources, references and opportunities for ongoing learning. These modules are designed to support teachers and educators in working with parents and guardians effectively.

Chapter 7

The Case of Jakob

CASE 2: THE EARLY YEARS

Crosscutting Themes: Collaboration, Parents/Caregivers/Family, Advocacy, Agency/Efficacy.
Leadership Competencies: Values Inclusion, Differentiated Leadership, Lived Experience of Students, Collaboration, Fosters Relationships, Differentiated Instruction.

It was the second week of school at Weatherbee Elementary and I was the new Kindergarten teacher. It was my first time teaching Kindergarten. Since becoming a teacher, I've only taught grade three and four—but I was up to the challenge of teaching younger students. The school was in a rough area of town and many of the students came from lower-income households. The previous schools at which I had taught were in well-to-do neighborhoods, and the majority of students were from middle income and wealthy families. I knew that this year was certainly going to be different for me.

One of my students, Jakob, was particularly challenging, and this became apparent even in the first week together. It was difficult for him to focus on anything for long and he became frustrated and annoyed when he didn't understand something or would take much longer than his peers.

He often acted out in class. He would grab toys and materials from centers and would throw markers around the room. It was also difficult for him to interact with other kids in the class. Some of the other children started to avoid him because of his difficult, and sometimes aggressive, behavior. By the end of the first week, children were already tending not to sit near him at carpet time.

Figure 7.1 Excluded Student. *Source*: https://www.istockphoto.com. Credit: DGLimages.

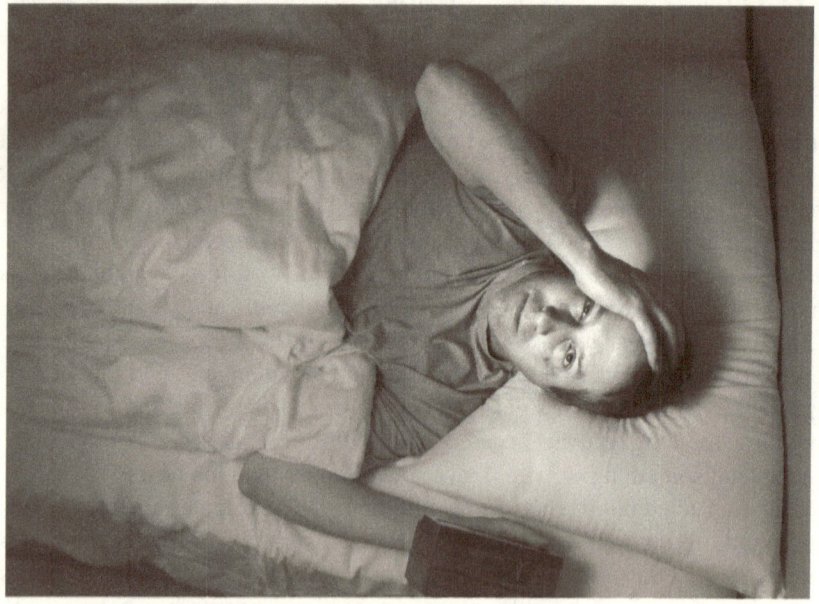

Figure 7.2 Teacher Unable to Sleep. *Source*: https://www.istockphoto.com. Credit: tab1962.

He didn't realize that he was isolating himself from the rest of the class. I knew it was early in the school year, but some of his behaviors were so unusual that it made me think some sort of medical or psychological assessment would be needed. I also noticed that he didn't always come to school with packed food. Sometimes he would sit at snack time and watch the other students eat. I knew early on that it was going to be an interesting year with Jakob.

As we progressed into the second and third week of the year, Jakob's behavior became more and more challenging to handle. One morning he yelled out a string of curse words while I was reading a book to the class on the carpet. I told him that the words he was saying were inappropriate and should not be used—but this simply encouraged him to yell the words *louder*.

He was also continuing to struggle with making friends. It didn't help that he had tried to steal a little girl's granola bar, which made her break down and cry. I had tried to call the phone number listed in the student information database, but there wasn't even an opportunity to leave a voicemail. Notes home in his backpack were not answered.

I started to lose sleep over Jakob. It consumed me—thoughts and guesses about what was going on with him.

I also wondered about his home life and why he didn't have food for snacks or lunch. I wanted to do something, but also felt ill-equipped to handle such a situation. I didn't want to cross any boundaries that would put him or me in a difficult position with the school or his family.

At the end of September, one afternoon during snack time, I asked Jakob to come see me at my big comfy chair. I wanted to get more information about his family life. I began by asking him how many brothers and sisters he had. He proudly told me that he had one brother and three sisters. I asked, "What do your parents do?"

He became really quiet and looked down at the ground. He quietly said, "Mommy isn't home a lot. I don't have a daddy." Tears started rolling down the little boy's face. I was angry at myself for being so insensitive. And I felt defeated.

At the end of the day, I decided to go talk to the special education teacher, Mrs. Bloomsbury, about Jakob's situation. I told her about Jakob's difficult behavior and the little I knew about his home life. I told her that I felt so ill-equipped to handle Jakob's situation and doubted my teaching abilities.

"I should have never taken this job," I cried.

> I'm making a mess of things already. I assumed that Jakob's behavior was just a sign of him struggling with the transition to the classroom. But I think there's more to it. And I made him cry when I asked about his parents . . . I desperately want to help him. Is it possible to get a paraprofessional in the class to help me?

Mrs. Bloomsbury assured me that I was a good teacher. She said that she would try to call Jakob's mother multiple times during the day to see if she could reach her. And, if she could, she promised to organize a meeting for us to sit down with Jakob's mother and discuss his behavior and create an action plan to help support him in his learning.

Two days later, Mrs. Bloomsbury came down to my classroom to tell me that she had finally reached Jakob's mother and she was coming in that afternoon. When we met with Jakob's mom, Helena, that afternoon I learned that Jakob's dad had been killed in a car accident just weeks before Jakob was born. Helena worked three part-time jobs to support her four kids, but clearly struggled to put food on the table. Jakob's twelve-year-old sister was responsible for taking care of her younger siblings after school, which often meant that Jakob could get away with doing and saying whatever he wanted.

After the meeting, I felt like I had a better understanding of Jakob and where he came from. I found that I responded to him with more patience. Instead of labeling him as a "problem kid" in my class, I understood that he needed more individualized support and care in the classroom. With the help of Mrs. Bloomsbury and the school principal, Mr. Bee, we brought in a paraprofessional to the classroom for a trial run to see if that made a difference for Jakob's behavior.

I was still a bit embarrassed about the way I handled things and my tearful confession in Mrs. Bloomsbury's office. However, her response of kindness and patience helped me as an educator understand that this should be my first response to my students' challenges. I now understood that behavior is never isolated by itself and that Jakob's outbursts were a way for him to receive the attention that he didn't receive at home. I thought to myself, *I've got this!*

A few weeks later, I walked into my office to see a note sitting on my desk. It said, *Ms. O'Reilly, please come see me in my office. —Mr. Bee*

"*Oh no*" I thought. I headed to Mr. Bee's office, bracing myself for the worst. Mr. Bee and I talked casually before he got to the reason why I was in his office. He said that there were many children at the school who didn't come with lunch. This had been an ongoing challenge at the school for a number of years. "I wanted to talk to you to see if you'd be interested in organizing a lunch program for the school," he said.

I certainly was interested!

After months of meeting with the other teachers, Mr. Bee, and the school board, I helped implement a lunch program that was open to all students at the school.

The program ran over the lunch break on Mondays, Wednesdays, and alternating Fridays. With the help of the school board, we partnered with a local grocery store and worked with nutrition specialists to create healthy, balanced lunches and snacks for the students. All of the teachers worked together to create a breakfast monitor schedule and would take turns serving and supervising the breakfast.

As I look back at those first weeks at Wetherbee, I can now see how important resource teachers and principals are to the success of a school. And I'm reminded that I'm part of that equation too.

Questions to Consider:

1. Do you think that Ms. O'Reilly let the situation with Jakob go on for too long before she spoke with him? Should she have spoken with a school administrator first?
2. When have you advocated for a student to make the school environment more inclusive, like Ms. O'Reilly advocated for Jakob?
3. What strategies do you use to communicate with teachers who are struggling?

Expert Opinion:

There are two main aspects that this case highlights for me: (1) Thinking about what inclusion means for individual children, and (2) How leadership in the school can create the most supportive learning opportunities through strong mentorship. For the first, I think that educators are often limited through their preservice training to think about inclusion only with regards to children who have a "label," a specific diagnosis, or some other visible/invisible disability. Through strong mentorship and a focus on reflective practice, it is important for all educators to learn that inclusive practice means supporting *all* children where they are at through understanding that each child is their own unique package. When thinking about individual children like Jakob who are exhibiting challenging behaviors, this way of thinking can help us to keep an open mind and see behaviors as a form of communication or "red flags" that something else is going on in that child's life that is limiting their ability to be present in the classroom and truly learn. When we shift from interpreting challenging behaviors as symptoms rather than problems, we are more likely to spend time digging deeper to understand where they are coming from, especially with young children who aren't capable of communicating this information or being self-aware enough to understand why they are acting that way.

This case also highlights the need to provide leadership in a way that educators don't feel like they have to struggle with a challenge alone; that struggling with a challenge is not a failure but, rather, a learning opportunity. They need to know that they can "call on the troops" by collaborating with others and requesting support early on. Approaching mentorship and leadership in this way improves the strength of the team by reducing feelings of isolation. The first step to mentoring is to establish a trusting relationship. Consider having an initial meeting to discuss your mentor's preferences for communication, how to request/receive feedback, and when/how to meet helps to level the playing field, be transparent, and start in a positive way. Keep in mind that an approach that worked for one person doesn't necessarily work for another—some people prefer direct, immediate feedback, while others may prefer to have an opportunity to decompress and then have a debrief at a later time to receive their feedback. In order to be a good mentor, it is also important to establish open communication with new teachers and those transitioning to new roles/grades. Consider how the note left on the teacher's desk was enough to instill fear and anxiety even though it was not likely meant that way at all. Staff going through challenging transitions or periods of time, especially new staff, are more likely to worry about being reprimanded. Consider how changing that brief note to *"Ms. O'Reilly, I have an exciting opportunity to discuss with you. Please come see me in my office. – Mr. Bee"* could have changed Ms. O'Reilly's experience.

Two specific areas of literature come to mind for this case. First is considering Maslow's hierarchy of needs, especially when working with children experiencing adversity and/or coming from disadvantaged backgrounds. In particular, the level of food insecurity present in each student population should be considered. Even if a school breakfast or lunch program is not feasible, consider an emergency (and non-perishable) snack cupboard that can be accessed as needed (these are easily run through donations). Second is resilience research; one useful concept here is Michael Ungar's concept of hidden resilience that acknowledges that some children use atypical strategies to cope with adversity and that these strategies are often misjudged—in Jakob's case, the externalizing behaviors that we, as educators, can misinterpret as problems may be a form of a hidden resilience strategy for him. Keeping this in mind can be helpful in shifting your thinking about the behaviors as I have already discussed.

References:

Kline, T. (n.d.). *Applying Maslow's hierarchy of needs in our classrooms.* http://www.changekidslives.org/actions-4

Masten, A. S. (2014). *Ordinary magic: Resilience in development.* Guilford Press. (see Chapter 9 Resilience in the context of schools, pp. 218–239)

Name: Tricia van Rhijn
Position: Associate Professor

Institutional Affiliation: University of Guelph

Resources

Books

Jones, P., Whitehurst, T., & Egerton, J. (2012). *Creating meaningful inquiry in inclusive classrooms: Practitioners' stories of research*. Routledge Ltd. https://doi.org/10.4324/9780203112670
This book offers guidance to readers who are teachers as well as researchers, in promoting meaningful participation within the inquiry process for all students in inclusive classrooms. Alongside illustrative examples, readers are able to explore evidence-based educational solutions for a population of students which is complex, diverse, and dynamic in nature. The value of research about meaningful inquiry is emphasized during the teaching and learning process within inclusive classrooms.

Videos

Sider, S. (2012, Dec 12). *Working as a team*. Vimeo. https://vimeo.com/55498214
In this video, Dr. Steve Sider, one of the authors of this book, discusses the importance of working as a team in a school environment in supporting students with exceptionalities. The success of students with exceptionalities is largely based on a collaborative approach of resource teachers, homeroom teachers, school principals, school board specialists, parents, caregivers, and the child. Dr. Sider explains the significance of a multidisciplinary or school-based team approach, as all the members bring new input and insight into a child's progress, abilities, and needs.
TEDx Talks. (2013, November 7). *Building relationships between parents and teachers: Megan Olivia Hall at TEDxBurnsvilleEd* [Video]. YouTube. https://www.youtube.com/watch?v=kin2OdchKMQ
Megan Olivia Hall explains the importance of teachers building relationships with parents to ensure student success. Hall speaks to her own experiences as a teacher and how maintaining strong relationships with students' parents helped her better understanding her students and therefore be better prepared to support their learning. She offers recommendations such as calling parents with good news about their child's learning rather than only calling them when something goes wrong. Hall explains that on difficult days parent connections get her moving and often helps to bridge the understanding gap between herself and her students.

Professional Articles

Conners, H. (2016, December 2). *"Inclusion" is the classroom challenge teachers are too afraid to talk about, educator says*. CBC.ca. https://www.cbc.ca/news/canada/nova-scotia/nova-scotia-teachers-classrooms-inclusion-work-to-rule-1.3879240
In this 2016 article written by Holly Conners, the challenges that educators face in creating an inclusive classroom are discussed. Incorporating varying learning

capabilities into one classroom can be seen as a challenge when ability levels range from primary to grade nine. Inclusion also entails that each student participated fully and is accommodated, regardless of ability or behaviors. Individual program plans are created to suit the needs of each student and is based on their strengths and needs. There may be challenging behaviors with classrooms that are rich in diversity, and these factors can be difficult to accommodate.

Egalite, A. J. (2016, February 17). *How family background influences student achievement*. Education Next. https://www.educationnext.org/how-family-background-influences-student-achievement/

In this article, Anna J. Egalite does a deep dive into the impact of family background on student achievement. Socioeconomic factors were found to be very influential on the school achievement of pupils in a U.S. Office of Education report. Furthermore, it was found that family background explained more about a child's achievement than school expenditure levels, class sizes, and teacher quality. Egalite discussed other key factors that were found to be influential such as parental level of education, family income, parents' criminal activity or incarceration, and family structure. The cruciality of the U.S. "promise neighbourhoods," early childhood education, and small schools of choice are highlighted in conclusion, along with the importance of educators taking steps to learn about student family background.

The Understood Team. (n.d.). *4 Benefits of inclusive classrooms*. Understood.org. https://www.understood.org/en/learning-attention-issues/treatments-approaches/educational-strategies/5-benefits-of-inclusion-classrooms

This article provides details and examples of how inclusive education is beneficial to students. Inclusive classrooms and education take into consideration student ability, background, and many more factors to ensure that all students are able to participate fully. This article highlights tailoring teaching for all learners, making differences less apparent, providing a variety of support to all students, and creating high expectations for all students. Some key takeaways from this are to teach students based on their specific learning needs, provide extra support for students even if they aren't eligible for special education, and to lean on a collaborative team-teaching model for supporting students with or without special education needs.

Websites

Ontario Teachers' Federation. (2020). *Modeling effective communication*. Ontario Teachers Federation. https://www.parentengagement.ca/modules/modeling-effective-communication/context-background/

This Ontario Teachers' Federation module focuses on modeling effective communication in the larger context of parent-teacher relationships. Tips to avoid misunderstandings and missed opportunities to communicate are explained. Opening lines of communication with parents and keeping them open through transparency are discussed through this module portal as well. Parents and guardians are only able to lend their support when they are kept informed in a timely manner about their child's progress, abilities, and needs. Furthermore, understanding about situations or issues must be present before constructive problem-solving can occur. This module offers context, background, big ideas, questions, practical tips, suggestions, opportunities for ongoing learning, and helpful resources to assist educators seeking more professional development.

Shmoop. (2020). *Understanding your students' home lives.* Shmoop. https://www.shmoop.com/teachers/beyond-teaching/personal-care/students-home-lives.html

This article emphasizes how vital it is to know your students and understand their home lives. While educators have been known to experience apathetic burnout every now and then, it is key to try to put oneself in the shoes of their students. Factors which can impact student learning and behavior that are explained in this article include: poverty, family dynamics, mental illness, disability, abuse, divorce, and their own relationships. These factors can manifest themselves in a variety of ways, as seen through the actions, reactions, triggers, and behaviors demonstrated by students and children.

Teachnology. (n.d.). *Inclusion in the classroom.* Teachnology.com http://www.teach-nology.com/teachers/special_ed/inclusion/

This article revolves around inclusion and its relationship with students who fall beneath the umbrella of special education needs issues. Teachnology explains that each child and their individual experiences will be different, and this includes the impact had on their education as well. Success and failure with inclusion are discussed to be situationally dependent, and one must take each case on a student-by-student basis.

Chapter 8

"I Can't Believe I Was the One Who Excluded Him"

CASE 3: THE EARLY YEARS

Crosscutting Themes: Advocacy, Communication, Relationships/Trust.
Leadership Competencies: Advocacy, Professional Learning, Fosters Relationships, Lived Experience of Students, Collaboration, Problem-solving, Values Inclusion.

The first time I met Abdel was when he and his parents came into my office at Oak Park Elementary for a pre-Kindergarten enrollment interview. Abdel has Down syndrome and was a happy, bright kid. He was attentive and listened carefully in the interview, observing everyone and everything happening around him. I could sense that his parents were anxious about their son starting Kindergarten. At the end of the interview, I assured Abdel's parents that Oak Park was safe for Abdel to learn and grow. I told them that we would ensure Abdel was well cared for in the school and promised that he would receive any individualized supports he needed.

When Abdel began Kindergarten in the fall, the transition was smooth. He became near and dear to his teacher, Mr. Rodriguez. They developed a special relationship and Mr. Rodriguez was a constant advocate for Abdel. When Abdel had difficulty reaching some of the equipment on the playground, Mr. Rodriguez was in my office rallying to get a more accessible play structure.

When Abdel had difficulty hearing people speak in the auditorium, Mr. Rodriguez asked me if we could get a better speaker system installed. Mr. Rodriguez, who had been teaching at Oak Park for nearly a decade, was one of the most compassionate individuals and educators I had ever met. It was no surprise to me that Mr. Rodriguez and Abdel had formed a close connection.

Figure 8.1 Accessible Playground. *Source*: https://www.istockphoto.com. Credit: fstop123.

As the school principal, I organize weekly school-based team meetings with all staff members who work with students who have special education needs. The team includes teachers, paraprofessionals, the resource teacher, our vice principal, and me. When I began my role as principal at Oak Park, my vision was to create an environment where staff felt comfortable approaching me with their classroom challenges—so I worked hard to build trust within our team. I had heard that staff had not always got along well with the previous principal, largely because of his communication style, so I wanted to change how staff viewed the role of principal. When I was hired, our staff began to do professional development workshops every other month on nurturing inclusive school environments for students as well as conflict management with parents and guardians. My background as a special education teacher compelled me to foster inclusive classes and school spaces not just for students with special education needs but for *all* students. I also tried to regularly visit all of the classrooms in my school and talk with students and teachers letting them know that I cared about them.

One day as I was making my rounds and talking to students, I noticed Abdel sitting by himself, away from the rest of the kids. I approached him and asked how he was doing.

"I'm good," he responded. "But sometimes I wish I could do stuff that the other kids do."

"What do you mean, Abdel?" I asked him gently.

"I didn't get to bake cookies today. The other kids got to bake. But I didn't get to 'cause I was reading with Mrs. Arnold." He crossed his arms and frowned up at me, tears forming in his eyes. Abdel was referring to the resource teacher, Mrs. Arnold, who helped him with reading for thirty minutes each day.

"I'm sorry you didn't get to bake, Abdel," I said, my heart aching for the boy who so badly wanted to be included in everything that the rest of class did. "I have some chocolate chip cookies in my office. Do you want to come eat one with me?"

Abdel smiled up at me, clearly excited that he was going to have cookies. We walked back to my office and enjoyed a snack together.

I returned to Mr. Rodriguez's classroom at the end of the day. I told him about my conversation with Abdel and how he felt excluded from the rest of the class. Mr. Rodriguez got very quiet and told me, "I feel so badly. I didn't mean for Abdel to be excluded from baking." Then, to my surprise, Mr. Rodriguez opened up to me about his niece who also has Down syndrome. He told me that he had been nervous that she wouldn't get the specialized supports that she needed, especially with reading, which is why he advocated for Mrs. Arnold to work with Abdel on his reading skills each day. Things started to click for me. I began to understand where Mr. Rodriguez's protection of Abdel stemmed from because Abdel probably reminded Mr. Rodriguez of his niece, and he placed his worries for her on Abdel. He cared about Abdel so much and wanted him to be included—but had unintentionally excluded him from a fun activity.

The next day, Mr. Rodriguez sat down with Abdel. He apologized for making him feel excluded from class and told him the class would bake again that day.

Later that day, Mr. Rodriguez chatted with me in the staff room. He told me, "All I see when I'm working with Abdel is my niece. All I want for them is to be included. I can't believe I was the one who excluded him."

Questions to Consider:

1. Do you think that Abdel's parents and/or the school's resource teacher should have been included in this situation? Why or why not?
2. If you were to write the next part of this story, what would it look like?
3. What is the line between advocating for students and overstepping your position?
4. What strategies could you as principal use to support teachers when they approach you because they don't feel confident in their teaching abilities?

Figure 8.2 Students Baking at School. *Source*: https://www.istockphoto.com. Credit: FatCamera.

Expert Opinion:

This case is written from the perspective of a principal, a person we often think of when we think of school leadership. This work illustrates though that leadership can come in many forms; in particular in the form of advocacy. Abdel's parents advocated for him, asking the school questions and expressing their thoughts and feelings. It is essential that parents are part of the conversation. Time and time again the research tells us that parents experience stress, disenfranchisement and frustration when engaging with schools. Parents are an essential part of successful schooling and our interactions and practices must be respectful and seen as important.

Abdel's teacher was a leader in advocacy. It is often not possible for a school administrator to know the day-to-day issues of students, but teachers have the privilege of seeing close up what happens each day for their students. Speaking up and making the educational environment successful for ALL students is a great responsibility and a leadership role. In terms of his personal relationship with a student with disabilities, while in this case it led to an exclusion, research shows having a relationship with a person with a disability is often a positive factor in inclusive practice.

For parents and teachers to have that role it is essential that school administrators create a community where speaking up and shared leadership is welcomed and nurtured. Changing the tone of conversation providing both formal and informal ways to communicate and taking personal interest all serve to enhance a successful school environment. By creating such an environment, this principal was able to create a more inclusive setting for Abdel but in doing so for other individuals as well. Perhaps Abdel was not the only student or educator who benefited from some of the changes Mr. Rodriguez suggested. Being able to hear well and having easier access to play equipment creates fewer problems and more opportunities for everyone. The teacher who may have mild hearing loss normal with aging, or the child who couldn't access the play equipment in its previous configuration, also benefit from these changes.

Inclusion is not something that you do once. With every new teacher and new principal challenges can remerge. Ensuring an inclusive mindset and maintaining practices that support this mindset take vigilance and effort. Good leaders at all levels play an important role in maintaining best practice for all.

Name: Sheila Bennett
Position: Professor
Institutional Affiliation: Brock University

Resources

Videos

Edutopia (2019, January 14). *The power of relationships in schools.* YouTube. https://www.youtube.com/watch?v=kzvm1m8zq5g

This 2019 YouTube video created by Edutopia touches on the importance of relationships in school environments. Dr. Linda Darling-Hammond explains that learning environments need to be created with strong long-term relationships for children to become attached and feel safe, as well as supported by the adults at their school. When children have the feelings of attunement and trust they are able to come to the important adults in their lives and express any negative emotions or feelings of not being included that they may be experiencing.

Academic Articles

Burriss, K. (2002). What general educators have to say about successfully including students with Down Syndrome in their classes. *Childhood Education*, 78(3).

This article focuses on successes general educators have shared of their inclusion of students with Down syndrome in their classes. Katleen Burriss, the author, received feedback from parents on which teachers were successfully working with their children, and then sent a questionnaire to this group. The study found that positive collaboration between teachers and parents allowed for higher rates of successful inclusion. The article suggests that small group instruction, hands on activities, and computer-assisted programs were the most effective learning arrangements and materials for children with Down syndrome.

Elksnin, K. L., & Elksnin, N. (1989). Collaborative consultation: Improving parent-teacher communication. *Academic Therapy.* 24(3). doi: 10.1177/105345128902400302

The article written by Linda and Nick Elksnin, although older, highlights a collaborative consultation framework for parent-teacher conferences. This notes preparation, planning, a mock letter to follow, creating an environment, specifically how the conference should go from objectives to creating a plan, and finally a checklist to ensure teachers are on the right path. This journal article highlights the importance of parent understanding and collaboration for student success. When collaboration is prioritized, cooperative problem-solving activities, which benefit the students, are achieved.

Grant, L., Burrello, L., Black, W., Hoppey, D., & Kleinhammer-Trammill, J. (2013). How does a principal use intention and strategy in the enactment of advocacy leadership? *ProQuest Dissertations Publishing.*

The study found that principals use vision, intentional strategies of expectations, modeling, decision-making processes, reflection, authentic conversations, and stories to facilitate change in schools. The study defines transactional leadership and transformational leadership. The dissertation breaks down leader-follower relations and the moral components to leadership. Finally, the paper discusses advocacy for transformative leadership to understand how principals construct meaning, deploy action and employ strategies to affect change.

Guralnick, M., Connor, R., & Johnson, L. (2011). The peer social networks of young children with Down Syndrome in classroom programs. *Journal of Applied Research in Intellectual Disabilities,* 24(4), 310–321. doi: 10.1111 1468-3148.2010.00619.

Michael Guralnick, Robert Connor, and Clark Johnson examined Down syndrome (DS) in classroom settings to discover patterns in behavior. School is an ideal environment to establish relationships with peers and friendships. The researchers looked into children with developmental (cognitive) delays and found they usually have difficulties interacting with peers in these settings. It was found that peer social networks were fostered when teachers support children's peer social networks with many strategies such as social play activities.

Professional Articles

Bennett, S. (2009). *What works? Research into practice: Including students with exceptionalities.* ETFO-OTS. http://etfo-ots.ca/wp-content/uploads/2013/08/Including-Students-with-Exceptionalities.pdf

This article focuses on what we can do as educators to develop and maintain inclusive environments for students with exceptionalities. Dr. Sheila Bennett from Brock University found that research speaks to the benefits of principals' promoting inclusive school culture, that the environment and school setting influences student perceptions on acceptance, that including those with exceptionalities does not negatively impact the academic achievement of other students, and that social benefits are observed both regular and exceptional students. Bennett advocated for all students being able to learn in regular classrooms and to focus on active and productive involvement.

Down Syndrome Association of Greater St. Louis. (n.d.). *What students with down syndrome want teachers to know: Information for para professionals.* DSAGSL .org. https://dsagsl.org/wp-content/uploads/2019/02/Paraprofessional-Powerpoint -20141.pdf

A PowerPoint deck compromising of myths about Down syndrome, common health concerns that may impact learning broken down into definitions and what this may look like in the classroom, communication and behavior guidelines, and a guide to how students with Down syndrome learn. These resources explore strategies for teachers, curriculum adaptations to suit students' needs as well as various video examples of situations or case studies. Resources for teachers and ways to get involved are listed with helpful websites.

Tavanger, H. (2017, November 8). *Creating an inclusive classroom.* Edutipiahttps:// www.edutopia.org/article/creating-inclusive-classroom

The article written by Homa Tavanger discusses the most important factor of an innovative team is psychological safety. This has also been cited as an essential 21st-century skill. In the classroom it is important to build a safe and inclusive, multicultural school settings. Tavanger's suggestions are to focus on empathy, diversify your exposure of news and to engage and listen, build your vocabulary related to social justice, explore stories and perspective, and create and display class values. This article is filled with techniques to prioritize safety and inclusion.

Websites

ASCD Guest Blogger. (2018, June 6). *Inclusive classrooms: Looking at special education today.* ASCD in Service.http://inservice.ascd.org/inclusive-classrooms -looking-at-special-education-today/

This blog is an educational resource containing tools to support the whole child. The emphasis in the blog is that inclusion stems from positive attitudes, commitment to meet student needs, school leadership, and adaptive instructional methods.

Department of Health & Human Services, State Government of Victoria, Australia. (n.d.) *Down syndrome and learning.* Better Health Cannel. https://www.betterhealth.vic.gov.au/health/HealthyLiving/down-syndrome-and-learning

The Department of Health and Human Services in Australia has compiled a set of click-button resources for parents (and/or teachers) orienting around children with special needs, specifically Down syndrome. Children with Down syndrome often experience gaps in skills and learning from children their own age, but it is important to remember that they will continue to learn and grow when given the opportunity. The page explores early intervention programs to help children reach their potential, the benefits of young children attending childcare centers, playgroups and preschool settings. The most important influence on early development is daily interaction and activities with family and children, as well as benefits from structured learning opportunities.

Canadian Down Syndrome Society. (n.d.). *Down syndrome resources for teachers & schools*. CDSS.ca. https://cdss.ca/teachers-schools/

The Canadian Down Syndrome Society has created a website to help teachers explore Down syndrome and education. The site discusses how full inclusion creates better learning environments. The site also explores resources for teachers such as an Educator package, question and answer, and curriculum guides. This website offers additional resources such as how integration and inclusion are different.

Canadian Human Rights Commission. (n.d.). *Left out: Challenges faced by persons with disabilities in Canada's schools*. Canadian Human Rights Commission – Commission Canadienne des Droits de la Personne. https://www.chrc-ccdp.gc.ca/eng/content/left-out-challenges-faced-persons-disabilities-canadas-schools

A report created by the Canadian Human Rights Commission identified barriers to education, the negative impacts of disabilities on Canadians' education, as well as statistics on the highest educational attainment for persons with disabilities when monitoring the implementation of the UN Convention on the Rights of Persons with Disabilities. Education has a powerful influence on people's economic well-being and physical health.

Down Syndrome Education. (n.d.). *Resources*. Down-Syndrome.org. https://www.down-syndrome.org/en-us/resources/

A website which includes resources and comprehensive information about development and education for individuals with Down syndrome. Included are click buttons for See and Learn (an online learning system/aid) speech, language, reading, and numbers as a resource for parents and teachers. There are also videos to support effective early intervention such as inclusion practice and speech and language activities for children with Down syndrome.

Kelley, K. (2017, August 10). *50 tips and tricks to facilitating a more inclusive classroom*. We Are Teachers. https://www.weareteachers.com/tips-tricks-inclusive-classroom/

Kirstin Kelley has created a comprehensive list of how to create a more inclusive environment by modeling and removing barriers or marginalization of students. The ideas include incorporating less commonly heard points of view in lessons, educating students on why their language matters and when harmful language is used, to redirect students. The article also discusses using inclusive fonts and ensuring field trips and classrooms are accessible. Restorative justice and consistent consequences are tools for inclusive classroom management. This article focuses on school culture and the role of the principal, and professional development days and IEPs as an asset.

ELEMENTARY SCHOOL SPECIFIC CASES

Chapter 9

The Grade Five Field Trip

CASE 1: ELEMENTARY SCHOOL SPECIFIC CASE

Crosscutting Themes: Communication, Parents/Caregivers/Family, Relationships/Trust, Legal/Legislative.
Leadership Competencies: Problem-solving, Contextual, Values Inclusion, Policies and Procedures, Legal Requirements, Differentiated Leadership.

Abena Abara is a grade five teacher at Sunview Elementary School and has been a teacher for just over two years. She absolutely loves her job. Her number one priority is her students, and she prides herself on always treating them fairly and with respect. Her class is a challenging one this year as she has thirty-one students, many of whom have special education needs. It is a busy class, but Abena has a very positive mindset and strongly believes that each child should feel included. She believes she is very good at accommodating her lessons to fit the needs of all of the students in her classroom.

Abena decides to organize a field trip for her class to an outdoor education center. The center runs a variety of educational programs with links to the grade five curriculum expectations. A key learning task involves the students going on a hike on the center's grounds to learn about the different native plants and animals in the area.

Abena received approval from the principal to take the students on the trip and had finished filling out and collecting the necessary paperwork, including consent forms from parents. This was the second field trip that she had ever planned; the previous trip she had co-led with another, more experienced teacher, so Abena is feeling a bit nervous about the trip. Nevertheless, she is excited to give her students an opportunity to learn about nature while being outdoors.

Figure 9.1 Students Getting off the Bus. *Source*: https://www.istockphoto.com. Credit: kali9.

Abena's major concern about the trip has to do with one of her students, Ron, who has significant behavioral needs. He often becomes agitated in class by other students and different sounds in the room. He often slips out of the classroom, causing Abena or other staff members to search for him in the school. Abena worries that Ron would be a danger to himself if he went on the trip. She decides it is best if he stays at the school with a paraprofessional, rather than attend the trip. She decides to give Ron's parents a call and inform them of her concerns and decision to leave Ron at the school.

A few days later, Shirley McGregor, the vice principal at Sunview, receives a phone call from Mrs. Young, Ron's stepmom. She is furious that Ron's teacher intentionally excluded Ron from a class field trip. She tells

Shirley that Ron had been looking forward to the trip, and it was unacceptable that he can't join. She is hoping that Shirley will intervene and allow Ron to go. Shirley reassures Mrs. Young that she will speak with Abena and that the situation will get sorted out. Before ending the phone call, Shirley asks if Mrs. Young or her husband are available to join the class trip. Unfortunately, both parents have to work. Shirley tells Mrs. Young not to worry. She tells Ron's stepmom that she'll be in touch soon.

After the phone call ends, Shirley heads straight to Abena's classroom. She needs to have a conversation with Abena about this. It is unacceptable that she has taken it upon herself to exclude a student from a classroom activity without consulting the administrative team *and* has contacted the parents to inform them of her decision.

After some initial small talk with Abena, Shirley says,

The reason I'm here is that I just got off the phone with Ron's stepmom. She's *really* upset. I was told that you're not letting Ron join the class on the trip. Is this true? What were you thinking? You should have had a conversation with me about the situation before going to Ron's parents.

Abena is taken back.
"Oh . . . I'm sorry she is so upset," she says. "That wasn't my intention, Shirley." Abena pauses and then continues on.

"*But* I really think it's in all of our best interest if he doesn't come on the field trip to the outdoor education center. It's a difficult place to monitor students. I worry that he'll take off in the woods. What if he gets lost and I can't find him? I have thought about this for a long time and think that the best possible solution is for him to stay at home or the school. It is the best way to keep him safe. That's my main concern—Ron's safety."

Shirley takes a breath and says,

"I know you're invested in Ron's needs and that you are trying to do what you think is best for him. I recognize that your main goal is to ensure his safety, which is my priority too. But I think that we can accomplish this *without* excluding him from the trip."

"But how?" Abena asks. "I just don't think it's worth the risk. He is better off remaining at the school. Or perhaps he could stay at home for the day. I really don't want to be liable if anything happens, Shirley."
"I'll find someone to accompany you on the trip," Shirley responds.

I know you don't have a ton of experience planning field trips and taking your students elsewhere. I remember being a new teacher and feeling extra stressed about this as well. It is still stressful even after twenty years of teaching. But I know that, with the right support, we can include Ron on the trip.

"Fine," Abena says, annoyed. She really doesn't want to deal with any problems on the trip due to Ron's behavior. *He is hard enough to deal with at school*, she thinks. She can't imagine him being in a new environment—least of all, the middle of the woods.

Abena is also feeling like Shirley is being a bit condescending, which is abnormal. *Shirley is usually great*, Abena thinks. Shirley likes to get to know all the students and always talks about the importance of building solid relationships with students, especially students with special education needs, to better understand where the child is at and gain their trust. Shirley is always so positive and approachable, so Abena can't understand why she perceives her as being so condescending in this situation.

"I think it might be helpful if we look at this situation from Ron's point of view," Shirley says.

He's a grade five kid. Everyone in his class is going on a trip. His friends are going to talk about the trip when they come home and ask him why he wasn't there. He has been told by his teacher that he can't go. How do you think that would make him feel?

Abena sighs.

"It's really important that we all do our best to include all our students, regardless of behavioural issues," Shirley says.

Elementary school is such a critical time in students' lives. We want to unlock our students' potential by giving them opportunities to flourish. They're developing skills that they'll use throughout their lives. We also must remember that we have human rights legislation that we must adhere to. We have to give all students with special education needs the opportunity to participate in regular school events, like field trips.

Shirley continues,

When I was teaching, I brought students with special education needs on trips. I'll admit that it was challenging, but it was *always* worthwhile. All students benefit from going on trips. It shows them that their learning shouldn't only happen in the classroom. So you and I will come up with a plan that will allow

Ron to come on the trip while also keeping him safe. Would you please call the Youngs today and tell them that Ron can join the trip?

Questions to Consider:

1. What do you think about the way Shirley approached Abena to talk about the field trip? Was Shirley fair in her discussion points?
2. What strategies would you implement in order to ensure Ron's safety on the trip?
3. Abena thinks of herself as an accommodating teacher who always puts her students first. How do you deal with staff members who *think* they're accommodating but don't always *act* in inclusive ways?

Expert Opinion:

This case highlights several aspects of inclusion and school leadership for me. I think it is important to recognize the perceived challenge that Abena is confronted with allowing Ron to attend the class trip is not an uncommon experience. Her concerns are real and riddled with complications. Educators (as well as administrators) are under scrutiny from the public regarding their ability to meet the needs of the students in their care, especially on field trips which many school boards now require risk assessments to be completed for the perspective destination. Parents are also required to sign a risk waiver for their child to participate in any activity that could pose a potential risk no matter how small.

Safety is the utmost concern for any educator, especially a new teacher, going offsite to a location that they cannot control. Abena's biggest concern

Figure 9.2 Students Safely Crossing the Street. *Source*: https://www.istockphoto.com. Credit: Roland Magnusson.

is the safety of Ron on the trip: "What if he runs off into the woods?" "What if he loses control and get hurt or hurts someone else?" We can't really blame her for feeling concerned and unequipped for her first solo class trip. She is a new teacher with little experience.

When the parents contact the vice principal (Shirley) expressing their dissatisfaction with the teacher's decision to not allow their son to participate in the school trip, Shirley decides to immediately confront Abena. Shirley is upset about her staff member's decision to exclude the student based on her view of inclusion and rights. Shirly has many years of experience including children with various challenges, and she strongly feels that Abena should not have made this decision without consulting with admin.

Although Shirley is upset about the decision Abena has made, her reactive response in confronting Abena creates tension between the two. From the administrator's perspective, this is an urgent matter that needs to be dealt with immediately. Shirley is clearly passionate about ensuring students are included in field trips and strives to uphold this human right. Abena, on the other hand, believes she is doing what is in the best interest of all of the students and herself and the liability of losing a child, or worse, on a field trip.

At the time when Abena received approval for the trip from the administration would have been the best opportunity to discuss her concerns about Ron. Abena may have felt that approaching Shirley would indicate that she was not competent to take her students on the outdoor trip and may have been told to plan a "safer" trip for her class. For some reason, Abena did not feel that asking for support was a possible solution for her concern.

I think it is important for Shirley to inquire about Abena's reasoning/rational for not wanting Ron to go on the trip. When she approaches Abena, likely in the middle of the school day, Abena is caught off guard, feels attacked and told she must change her mind. Shirley is not taking into account that Abena did not make this decision lightly and could probably benefit from some support. If Shirley had a discussion with Abena about her plans for the field trip, keeping in mind the variety of needs in the class, this would have allowed Abena to discuss her concerns and reservations regarding the participation of all students on the trip. It would have been reassuring for Abena to know that going on any trip with thirty-one students, let alone an outdoor education trip, would be a great deal of worry for any teacher. Together they could figure out a way to best support Abena and her students. Educators need to know that they have support from their administrators to ask questions and ask for support for instances such as field trips.

This case can be supported by some of the research that is presented in the document "If inclusion means everyone, why not me?", which indicates that 71.9% of parents said that they were asked to accompany their children with intellectual disabilities on a field trip, or they would not have been allowed to go (Reid et al., 2018). This data represents experiences from across the province of Ontario, Canada and are not tied to any one region or school board. If parents are identifying this issue, then it is not surprising that Abena thought excluding Ron from the trip was a reasonable solution. These practices of excluding students from excursions are occurring and being supported at high rates within local schools.

Also, administrators cannot make assumptions that their new teachers, or experienced teachers alike, despite how excellent they may be, are prepared to deal with the myriad of needs found in any given classroom that takes years of experience to understand. Both teachers with years of experience and new teachers need opportunities to experience successful inclusion in order to have positive perceptions about inclusion (Somma & Bennett, 2020).

According to studies with preservice and new teachers specifically, they do not feel prepared to manage the demands of diverse classrooms based on their lack of training and classroom experience (Howell et al., 2018). Specht and Metsala (2018) found that one's efficacy to manage student behavior was directly linked to the amount of teaching experience they had. In fact, early results of a cross Canadian study indicate that about 52% of new teachers indicate workshops, training, and experience as factors influencing their beliefs about including students with exceptionalities (Howell et al., 2018). Even if administrators are modeling inclusive pedagogy, they cannot assume that their staff will have the ability or the belief system to demonstrate the same.

This case prompts questions regarding support for new teachers and how adminisrators can best ensure their staff have open communication and access to necessary supports, including safety on school trips so that children are not being excluded from school opportunities they have a right to participate in. How can school administrators promote an inclusive school culture in order for their staff members to model inclusion? How can administrators support their staff to reach an inclusive pedagogy, where they feel empowered to support all learners in all aspects to school?

References:

Howell, G., Fairbrother, M., Ismailos, L., Vanderloon, M., Specht, J., Gallagher, T., & Whitley, J. (2018). *Beginning teachers study – the development of inclusive practice: Thematic analysis of responses to interview questions.* Canadian Association for Educational Psychology (CAEP), Canadian Society for the Study of Education (CSSE) Conference, May 208, Regina, Canada:

Reid, L., Bennett, S., Specht, S. White, R., Somma, M., Li, X., Lattanzio, R., Gavan, K., Kyle, G., Porter, G., & Patel, A. (2018). *If inclusion means everyone, why not me?* https://www.inclusiveeducationresearch.ca/docs/why-not-me.pdf

Somma, M., & Bennett, S. (2020). Inclusive education and pedagogical change: Experiences from the front lines. *International Journal of Educational Methodology,* 6(2), 285–295. doi: 10.12973/ijem.6.2.285

Specht, J. A., & Metsala, J. L. (2018) Predictors of teacher efficacy for inclusive practice in pre-service teachers. *Exceptionality Education International,* 28, 67–82.

Name: Monique Somma
Position: Assistant Professor
Institutional Affiliation: Brock University

Expert #2

School trips are a critical part of learning for students and a key component of educational programs throughout many levels of education. The active learning opportunities provided by school trips provide multi-experiential learning, contribute to the perception of being a part of the class, increase academic understanding, and expand students' awareness of their community (Monaco et al., 2019).

Legal and Legislative Issues

Human rights legislation dictates that as educators we have to give all students with special education needs the opportunity to participate in regular school events, like field trips. It is important that we include all our students, regardless of behavioral issues.

Part 4 of the Disability Discrimination Act 1995 (as amended), indicates that schools must not treat students with disabilities less favorably than their peers without justification and they must plan strategically to increase access to schools and the curriculum over time, including school trips.

While there's no law saying that there should be a one-to-one ratio of students with disabilities to adults, when planning for field trips, having an extra adult along for any student who might have special needs beyond the regular student population can help to ensure all students stay on-track, with the group, and don't wander off.

While a school may invite a parent to accompany a student with a disability on a field trip, federal law, in particular Section 504 of the Rehabilitation Act of 1973, prohibits schools from requiring parents of students with disabilities to attend a field trip, if a similar obligation is not imposed upon the parents of students without disabilities. A school that requires only students with behavioral issues to be accompanied by a parent on a field trip discriminates on the basis of disability.

Refusing to allow a student with a disability to attend a field trip may be a denial of a Free and Appropriate Public Education (FAPE) under the Individuals with Disabilities Education Act (IDEA), as well as Section 504 of the Rehabilitation Act. Prior to excluding a student with a disability from a field trip, the school must consider if accommodations and supports will allow the student to attend, thereby giving the student equal access to the school program.

Communication with Administrators and Parents

It is important to develop and maintaining relationships and open lines of communication with parents, administrators, and other educators. Teachers must build relationships with parents so that the parents will support the teacher in correcting the problem (Meador, 2020). Teachers need to seek out advice, as no teacher should attempt to tackle a problem alone. Teachers need to be able to ask questions and solicit advice from their principal and should be encouraged to learn from each other (Meador, 2020). It is important to maintain an open line of communication with parents of young students, and as the students get older, be sure to listen to them and encourage them to advocate for themselves. When a field trip is in the planning stage, consult with your student and any involved family members.

Strategies

Teachers should begin planning well in advance and should talk about what will happen on the trip far ahead of time. Teachers can create Social Stories to help students learn what to expect the day of the trip—including waiting, taking turns, and the need to be flexible if the plan gets disrupted. In addition, teachers can customize a written or picture schedule of the day of the field trip. The schedule should include breaks and how time will be spent during downtime. When possible, teachers should develop a plan to warn students prior to a transition or provide a time limit for activities (Center for Autism Research, 2016).

Teachers should also review how students will get to the destination. Some schools use a "buddy system" on field trips or break into small groups. All students need to know what to expect, who they sit with, whether there be assigned seats with class "buddies" or whether there will be an aide nearby. If adults other than the students' regular teachers will be involved with the trip, teachers should explain who these people are ahead of time—providing pictures, names, and responsibilities of these individuals—so that students know which adults (chaperones, staff at the field trip destination, etc.) are "in charge" (Center for Autism Research, 2016).

Sensory sensitivities need to be taken into account, and there should be a plan in place for what happens if a student has a meltdown. The student should be taught how to communicate discomfort and how (and to whom) to request a break. Teachers should review safety rules, and where necessary take safety precautions, such as having children wear an identification bracelet (Center for Autism Research, 2016).

A student safety plan is a plan developed for a student whose behavior is known to pose an ongoing risk to themselves, other students, workers or other people in general. Recommended components of a student safety plan include a description of the observable behavior concerns (e.g., escape/avoidance behavior), triggers or antecedents (e.g., noise), prevention and intervention strategies to support workers and student safety, and communication procedures for all workers. It can serve as a crisis-response plan that outlines the roles and responsibilities of the workers in dealing with specific problem behaviors.

When approached with preparation, a field trip can be a wonderful opportunity for students to practice important skills, such as flexibility, positive social interactions, and safety. Because the goal of education is ultimately to prepare students for life experiences outside of the classroom, a field trip can be a step toward generalizing skills learned at school. All students benefit from going on trips. Field trips are an excellent learning activity, and all students can be accommodated with a little planning.

References

Center for Autism Research (2016). *CAR Autism roadmap.* https://www.carautismroadmap.org/supporting-students-with-asd-on-field-trips/

The Disability Discrimination Act 1995 including part IV: Education 2001. http://www.skill.org.uk/I-sheets/ISheet08-print.htm

Meador, D. (2020). *How teachers can build a trusting relationship with their principal.* ThoughtCo, February 11, 2020. https://www.thoughtco.com/build-a-trusting-relationship-with-their-principal-3194349

Monaco, N., Giri, M., & Burns, D., & Wynarczuk, K. (2019). *Participation in school trips for students with disabilities: Identification of barriers and strategies by school trip sites.* https://www.researchgate.net/publication/330367456_Participation_in_school_trips_for_students_with_disabilities_Identification_of_barriers_and_strategies_by_school_trip_sites

Name: Gabrielle Young
Position: Associate Professor
Institutional Affiliation: Memorial University of Newfoundland

Resources

Academic Articles

Ruef, B. Michael., Higgins, Cindy., Glaeser. C. J.Barbara., & Patnode, Marianne. (1998). Positive behavioral support: Strategies for teachers. *Intervention in School and Clinic.* 34(1), 21–31.

This journal article highlights Positive Behavioural Support (PBS) as a comprehensive, research-based proactive approach to behavioral support. Readers are provided with classroom strategies to try when students experience challenging behaviors as well as relevant resources. Teachers must first assess student behavior, and then collaborate with parents to devise a plan to support that student's success in a new environment, or learning. This article re-defines the perspective of behaviors as problems to understanding what is impacting the student from setting to skill deficiency. The article solidifies the understanding that a responsive and personalized setting is empowering for student success and growth.

Specht, J. A., & Metsala, J. L. (2018) Predictors of teacher efficacy for inclusive practice in pre-service teachers. *Exceptionality Education International,* 28, 67–82.

Jacqueline Specht and Jamie Metsala have concluded that high teacher efficacy is a positive contributor to student achievement. The authors conducted a study which found that the level of experience that an educator has with individuals with exceptionalities was a contributing factor to high teacher efficacy. Another finding was that student-centered belief was integral for inclusive instructional practices. This article speaks to the importance of ongoing education, awareness, and strategies for teachers to build efficacy and comfort with engaging positively with students with special education needs.

Professional Articles

Sheila, A. R., & William, H. L. (1996). "GOTCHA!" twenty-five behavior traps guaranteed to extend your student's academic and social skills. *Intervention in School and Clinic,* 31(5), 285–289. https://journalssagepub. doi:10.1177/105345129603100505

This article dives into the importance of creatively engaging students, with or without behavior concerns. It is necessary to allow choice for these students to grow, practice, and learn important skills. One strategy is a behavior "trap" in which teachers can use natural contingencies and consequences of reinforcement to create an environment that promotes and maintains generalized behavior changes. The idea is to have a simple prompt (or lure) to influence a behavior change, then reinforce the positive behavior. In the classroom this may look like a peer-to-peer conversation, prompting teamwork and appropriate behavior, the students are able to learn what is acceptable in those scenarios, and incorporate that behavior into future tasks while the teacher re-directs when needed and positively re-enforces the concept.

Hurlington, K. (2010, February). *Bolstering resilience in students: Teachers as protective factors.* What Works? Research into Practice. http://www.edu.gov.on.ca/eng/literacynumeracy/inspire/research/WW_bolstering_students.pdf

This research brief explains the benefit of building resilience in students no matter what they "lack" from stable home environments, or other support systems. It is important to focus on a strength-based model with students as a combination of traits and external protective factors will impact student resiliency. The article emphasizes the importance of key protective factors which are integral; caring relationships, high expectations, and opportunities or meaningful contribution. Along with seven strategies for creating an environment that fosters resiliency, this article also includes tips for classroom practice.

Website

Community Living New Brunswick. (n.d.). *Other strategies for achieving social inclusion through recreation.* New Brunswick association for community living. https://nbacl.nb.ca/module-pages/other-strategies-for-achieving-social-inclusion-through-recreation/

Community Living New Brunswick shares strategies for achieving social inclusion through recreation. Though not specific to field trips, the information such as addressing barriers such as cost, possible modifications and adaptations to programming, who may need to be involved from parents to administration, and safety protocols are all relevant to the content. Specifically, in terms of adaptations and modifications this web page explores the concept of identifying other ways for people to participate in programs or activities to prioritize inclusion. These programs are important to promote socialization and opportunities to build relationships.

Mastros, S. (2014, October 31). *Field trip management for special needs students.* BusBoss. https://www.busboss.com/Blog/bid/202049/Field-Trip-Management-for-Special-Needs-Students

This article includes strategies and best practices for successful trips for all. This includes assessing and being aware of needs (physical, medical and dietary), recruiting volunteers, and assess and ensure safety at trip site for all students participating.

Meador, D. (2019, February 21). *How teachers can build a trusting relationship with their principal.* ThoughtCo. https://www.thoughtco.com/build-a-trusting-relationship-with-their-principal-3194349

Derrick Meador's web article breaks down the principal-teacher relationship into twenty-four considerations. These relationships are integral to maximize potential for opportunities to grow and improve. These suggestions include leadership traits such as dependability, organization, and professionalism to suggestions in job proficiency. The article also supports professional development and consideration for student growth with a few final "tips" to creating the environment for these positive and collaborative interactions.

Ontario Ministry of Labour, Training and Skills Development. (2019, October 21). *Student safety plan.* Ontario.ca. https://www.ontario.ca/document/workplace-violence-school-boards-guidelaw/student-safety-plan

The Student Safety Plan website outlines the recommended components of a safety plan such as the student's observable behavior, triggers or antecedents, prevention and intervention strategies, communication procedures for all workers, and emergency communication procedures. Those who should be involved range from the school board and administration to parents/guardians. Safety plans support students in behaviors which are known to be ongoing risks. These plans should be reviewed and work with the student should occur on an ongoing basis to ensure they are accurate and complete.

Bethel School District. (2013). *Field trip checklist teacher's responsibility.* http://media.bethelsd.org/home/services/operations/documents/risk_management/forms/field_trip/Teacher_Checklist_Nov_2013.pdf

A checklist is provided which encompasses logistics of a field trip such as transportation, double checking necessities such as supervision, which children need medication, etc. The checklist also provides a timeline break down of the planning, implementation and action phases to ensure communication is clear and consistent. This list encompasses participation forms, buddy arrangements, safety considerations and ensures teachers review relevant policies such as chaperones. There is also a post-trip evaluation prompt.

Ontario Human Rights Commission. (n.d.). *Appropriate accommodation.* Ontario Human Rights Commission. (http://www.ohrc.on.ca/en/guidelines-accessible-education/appropriateaccommodation)

The Ontario Human Rights Commission has broken down the components of appropriate accommodation. Beginning with basic principles and the duty to accommodate that respects and provides dignity to students while meeting individual need. The webpage then details specific forms of accommodation, placement considerations for educational environments, the accommodation process as a continuum to continue to alternate and individualize student experience as well as a breakdown of how to modify educational requirements. These components are integral for teachers to be aware and able to follow policy and procedures related to human rights.

Chapter 10

Overstepping Boundaries

CASE 2: ELEMENTARY SCHOOL SPECIFIC CASES

Crosscutting Themes: Parents/Caregivers/Family, Relationships/Trust, Advocacy.
Leadership Competencies: Embodies Professional Standards, Values Inclusion, Fosters Relationships, Problem-solving, Lived Experience of Students, Advocacy, Differentiated Instruction.

My daughter, Mia, is entering grade four this year at a new school since her father, Phil, and I had a terrible experience with the students and staff at her previous school. It's exhausting talking about it, but I'm still angry about it and feel that I need to tell my side of the story.

Over the past year, we received frequent phone calls from Mia's teacher, Gerry Strong, as well as the vice principal, Tim Lui, about Mia. It became exhausting and discouraging as a parent to be constantly told that my daughter is "behaving poorly," "not listening" and "isn't doing well at school." Mia certainly struggles with social relationships and often becomes angry when she doesn't get her way with her classmates or the teacher.

Although I recognize that she is difficult to handle at times, Phil and I have done everything we can to be cooperative with the school. But the discouraging phone calls continued. At one point, Phil called the principal, John Master, and told him that the teacher and vice principal needed to stop harassing us with phone calls. Phil actually went to elementary and high school with John, so he knows him fairly well. We both respect John and think he's a good educator, but he needed to know that we were not impressed with Tim and Gerry constantly complaining to us. In my opinion, they were being unprofessional.

Figure 10.1 Student not Listening. *Source*: https://www.istockphoto.com. Credit: Marco VDM.

It was during this period of frequent phone calls in early May that Mia had a particularly troubling incident at school. She made a number of rude comments about a boy in the class who has a special education need. She upset the boy, who broke down in tears in the middle of class. Mia then went on to berate the little boy for crying. When Gerry Strong explained the incident to me, I couldn't believe it. *Where is this coming from?* I thought. *We've had challenges with Mia before but we've never seen this kind of behavior from her.*

A few days later, John called and asked Phil and me to come to the school to be a part of a team meeting about Mia. He told me that the school had already had a team meeting to discuss possible supports for Mia and he thought it was best if we were a part of the next team meeting. I was nervous and a bit defensive at the time as I didn't know what to expect from the meeting. I felt like my daughter was being judged. I felt like Phil and I were also being judged as parents. The situation started to take a toll on our marriage. Phil was always angry at Mia for being such a problem at school and I felt like I was always defending her.

Phil and I arrived at the meeting both feeling on edge. I figured Phil wouldn't say much in the meeting so it was up to me to advocate for our daughter and protect her. When we entered the meeting, the first thing I noticed was that there were more people than I expected. I recognized Gerry and Tim. There were three people there that I didn't know. *Is my daughter so much trouble that we need all these people here to talk about her?* I thought.

Tim shook our hands and explained that John, the school principal, was unable to attend the meeting. That was frustrating since John was the one who had called us and requested that we come to the meeting. I felt like he should have mentioned to us that he couldn't be there. After all, Phil and I both took time off work to be there.

The meeting started off reasonably well. Tim introduced me to two special education resource teachers and a paraprofessional who works with students like Mia. Tim shared the school's concerns about Mia's behavior, particularly her inability to interact with other students in appropriate ways. Tim said that he and the others wanted to do everything that they could to support my little girl and help her develop her social skills. He apologized for the stress the school had caused by calling us so often and hoped that there would be a better solution for everyone after this meeting. He then looked to Gerry and asked him to share his observations on Mia's behavior in the classroom. Before Gerry even began to speak I could tell he was agitated.

"Mia is a very intelligent girl," Gerry began. "I'm not at all worried about her academic performance. She is excellent at all she does. She excels in math, writing, reading. I often will find her reading a book during recess."

> But I worry about her because she's unable to connect with other students. She often makes rude remarks to other kids and doesn't understand the consequences of her words and actions. She isn't empathetic at all. She's condescending and

Figure 10.2 Student Reading. *Source*: https://www.istockphoto.com. Credit: Hakase.

thinks she's smarter than the other kids. She interrupts them all the time and doesn't seem to understand that others need a turn to speak.

Gerry went on to explain about my daughter,

Beyond that, she obsesses over objects in the classroom. We were doing a mathematics lesson where I wanted the students to identify patterns in nature. So I had collected a bunch of different items from the forest by my house like pinecones and leaves. Mia became fixated with a specific leaf, when I asked her to put it away because we were moving on she refused. I let her hang on to it and she continued to stare at it for much of the rest of the class. She then had a hard time keeping focused on my lessons.

Gerry paused. I could tell he felt awkward.

I think Mia may have some sort of condition that hasn't yet been diagnosed. I had another student with similar behaviors a few years ago. I would highly recommend you get in to see a specialist as soon as possible. She might be able to get some support or therapy.

I was shocked by Gerry's words. How *dare* he diagnose my child and tell me that she needed therapy? I was angry and embarrassed all at once. I looked to Tim, who was avoiding eye contact with me. I replied to Gerry by saying that I didn't think he should be telling me that my kid needs therapy. I told him that I thought Mia was just going through a phase and that I didn't think he had thought about her own needs.

Gerry responded with, "I still think you need to be open minded to the idea that Mia might have a special need. She would benefit from going to a specialist and getting diagnosed."

I started to cry at that point and I excused myself from the room. I couldn't believe what he was saying to me. I felt like he was being so condescending and rude—who was he to tell me how to deal with my daughter? Phil remained in the meeting for a couple of minutes to finish up the conversation. Afterward he told me that Gerry continued to emphasize the importance of Mia seeing a specialist and that he thought this was the only solution at this point. I was frustrated and felt like I was failing as a mother.

My problems with Mia's teacher and administration were the main reasons why we decided to move Mia to another school. We didn't feel like the meeting was handled professionally at all. The teacher overstepped his place and the vice principal never attempted to fix things. I was also disappointed that the principal, who my husband knew personally, simply didn't show up to the meeting. It made me feel like my daughter wasn't all that important to him.

That was last year. Now, it's the end of August and Mia is ready to start her new school. She is such a bright girl. I am so proud of her and only want what is best for her, which is why we decided to switch schools. I hope and pray that Mia will have a better experience at this school this year. We will see.

Questions to Consider:

1. If parents/guardians phoned to ask you to stop calling them regarding "problems" their child was having at school, how would you handle that situation? What might you say to the parent and then to the teacher? What steps could the school take that didn't involve complaining to the parents/guardians?
2. How may you have better communicated with the family in order to avoid them feeling attacked, defensive, confused, and so on? What support was missing by the administration to the family?
3. How would you have created a more positive and trusting relationship with Mia's family? How might this have impacted the way that the family handled the school meeting?
4. What should the vice principal have said to the parents and the teacher after the conversation went "wrong"?
5. Do you agree or disagree with Gerry's choice to informally diagnose Mia and suggest treatement to the family?

Expert Opinion:

This case highlights a number of issues related to special education, inclusion, and school leadership. In relation to special education, it appears that Mia's teacher felt some urgency around establishing a "diagnosis" to explain Mia's behavior and the recommendation to seek further intervention appears to have been made outside of any real discussion or authentic relationship with Mia's parents. The focus on securing a diagnosis was prioritized over strategizing how to foster a more positive relationship with Mia and include her in class activities. Additionally, the school's examination of any structural, social or climate-related factors, including the educator's pedagogical approach within the classroom, appears to have been largely ignored. The most important relationship educators and administrators have outside of their relationships with students, is their relationship with students' parents. In this case, through incessant complaints to parents, the relationship forged by the educator and vice principal was adversarial. Parents must be brought in as partners as they know their child best. With parents as partners, there may still have been calls home, but the substance of those calls would be ones of solidarity, co-planning and co-strategizing on how best to support Mia. In terms of leadership, the principal in this case, who was thought to be an ally and advocate, failed Mia and her parents by setting up a highly sensitive meeting and not showing up.

If I were a mentor to the principal in this case, I would advise that they support their educators in identifying classroom and school practices that can trigger or exacerbate student behavior. Coaching educators on how to foster positive relationships with students and a sense of belonging in the classroom is also key. The example of what transpired in the team meeting indicated a compounded effort to impress Mia's parents that something was "wrong" with Mia and that they needed further intervention to "fix" it. This approach does not value Mia as a whole person nor promotes social or disability justice. My final advice to administrators would be "Be there." If you are in an advocacy role, with parents depending on you, be there. Your presence sends a message to the value of your relationship with particular students and their families, as does your absence.

Mitchell (2010, 2015) has compiled a review of international empirical evidence on special and inclusive education. In these reviews, research shows that there is assumed homogeneity within exceptionality labels or diagnoses, but this is not true. Therefore, regardless of "diagnosis" or "label," educators still must work to develop relationships with their students to better understand how they learn and accommodate accordingly (Ridgeway, 2017). The example of Mia's fascination with the leaf presented an opportunity for the educator to make use of Mia's interest and differentiate the lesson/work accordingly. However, the educator opted to view Mia's fascination with the leaf as an example of disordered learning. Disability studies in education ask educators to examine the structural and social conditions of schools for ways in which the contributions of disabled students (and their families) are devalued, marginalized and excluded (Baglieri & Lavlani, 2020). That Mia was able to participate in the oppression of a fellow classmate and disabled student may exemplify how particular behaviors are enabled by the conditions within her classroom and school.

New questions that arise: What role do relationships play in enabling educators to suggest/support parents in seeking external support/intervention for their children? What process is available to ensure parents are supported during team meetings?

References:

Adams, K. S., & Christenson, S. L. (2000). Trust and the family–school relationship examination of parent–teacher differences in elementary and secondary grades. *Journal of School Psychology,* 38(5), 477–497.

Erikson, E. (1968). *Identity youth and crisis.* W. W. Norton & Company.

MacCormack, J. W. & Matheson, I. (2017). Bear with me: Teaming up with parents of students with special needs. *Education Canada,* 57(4), 20–23.

Stitt, N.M., & Brooks, N.J. (2014). Reconceptualizing parent involvement: Parent as accomplice or parent as partner? *Schools: Studies in Education,* 11(1), 75–101.

Wilder. S. (2014). Effects of parental involvement on academic achievement: A meta synthesis. *Educational Review,* 66(3), 377–397.

Name: Jeffrey MacCormack
Position: Assistant Professor of Educational Psychology and Inclusion
Institutional Affiliation: The University of Lethbridge, Faculty of Education

Expert #2

I'm not going to guess at what Mia needs right now, even though that is typically how case studies work—looking at clues in a case study and hazarding a guess is a superb way to teach pedagogy. But, we don't know enough about Mia to make meaningful suggestions, yet. And that is the first of three reasons why Gerry should not have pushed hard for diagnosis and therapy. He doesn't have enough information. How do I know? Well, he can only learn so much from classroom observation. To develop any worthwhile program, he has to speak to the student's family members. Sheesh, that is Teaching 101! So, yeah, because this was the first meeting, I feel pretty safe saying that Gerry is letting his enthusiasm get the best of him. So, reason #1: connecting with parents can be essential when it comes to understanding students' special education needs.

The second reason is that Gerry, like all of us, is not a diagnostician. Do Mia's observed behaviors have passing similarities to the types of behavior used to identify autism spectrum disorder? Yes. Or attention deficit hyperactivity disorder? Yes! Or a dozen other emotional or behavioral disorders? Of course! But, diagnosticians are trained to take the entire child in consideration and not jump to the first evidence. They have that training; we do not. We must avoid weighing in with labels. As we saw with Mia's mother's response, when educators try to guess at a diagnosis, they are stepping beyond their professional and ethical boundaries (and potentially opening themselves up to legal trouble).

And the third reason why Gerry should have avoided pushing for a particular diagnosis is that Mia may not have a diagnosable disorder. Based on my years in elementary school, I don't see anything atypical in Mia's behavior. I mean, her behavior is unfortunate, and I hope that poor little trooper who she made cry had a chance to talk to a mental health counselor about that very negative experience he had, but, um, that's how kids talk to each other from time to time. Students in grade three are feeling big emotions and may not have the words to describe them. Mia's age is usually when we learn about emotions and how they can be affected. Elementary students must learn how they fit in with their classmates, in terms of social status and competence; that process is often messy and undignified. Elementary classes are filled with the kind of casual savagery Mia showed because those students are beginning to experiment with their own senses of morality. As noted by Erickson, the all-star thinker behind psychosocial stages of development, kids are "remarkably clannish, intolerant, and cruel in their exclusion of others who are 'different'" (1968, p. 132). Erikson wasn't talking about emotionally disordered children. He was talking about *all* children.

While it may be true that Mia's behavior is very normal for someone her age, that doesn't mean that we don't do anything about it. By pointing Mia's parents toward diagnosis and therapy, Gerry seemed to be saying that Mia's behavior comes from an underlying medical or psychological issue far beyond the scope of the school. But that is not true. Helping students develop prosocial behaviors and attitudes is fundamental to an elementary teacher's job. Has anyone had a frank conversation with Mia about how people differ? Or, how to be a positive force within a community? That might be a good place to start. Of course, we are concerned with what Mia said to the other student, but what is even more important is *why* Mia said it. As I tell my students until I am hoarse, *all behavior is communication*. So, what does Mia's behavior tell us? Mia's behavior suggests that she might have old-fashioned ideas about disability. She might also need some help understanding how to have positive interactions with classmates. And, as elementary teachers, we are very well positioned to help Mia update and enrich her social decisions.

In short, even if we wanted to try to diagnose Mia, we should avoid that temptation because we are not diagnosticians, and even if we were, we don't have enough information yet, and although Mia's behavior is admittedly unpleasant and worrisome, her behavior is age appropriate. So, what are we to do? This situation calls for communication between home and school. So, let's talk for a bit about how to build home/school relationships.

"*Go on the offensive and don't let them push you around*," is the terrible advice commonly given to new teachers as they head into their first parent/teacher meetings. In spite of the evidence that reciprocal and respectful home/school relationships are crucial to the well-being of students (Adams & Christenson, 2000; Stitt & Brooks, 2014; Wilder, 2014), early career teachers are still encouraged to treat parents like adversaries, instead of allies. We can see in the case study how toxic and combative home/school relationships can harm the student. In a perfect world, the meeting with Mia's parents would have been an opportunity to see how Mia behaves at home and to brainstorm solutions together. Unfortunately, the meeting was a disaster. But how did it go so wrong?

Parent and teacher meetings can feel combative if educators are not respectful, so it should not be a surprise that Mia's mom felt a little ambushed at the meeting. Numbers count, when it comes to meetings. Why populate the meeting with three extra people? And, how did it help that Gerry spoke with an "agitated" manner? The educational team did those things because they did not value Mia's parents as collaborators in this situation. Gerry wanted Mia's parents to accept his (shoddy) guesswork and submit to his (short-sighted) plan.

When building an educational team, educators need to "recruit" the family (MacCormack & Matheson, 2017). How do you do that? When educators speak with parents, they should use *describing language*, not *prescribing language*. When we use *describing language*, we share our observations (without judgment) and ask the parents to describe their observations. When Gerry suggested that Mia might have "some sort of condition that hasn't yet been diagnosed," his message was "we already know what the problem is." To build collaborative home/school relationships, Gerry should have instead asked "what are you seeing at home?" Those "describing questions" opens discussions, instead of closing them.

In sum, when we treat families like know-nothing complainers who are just going to get in the way of our pedagogy, well, we cut the student's advocacy team in half. We need the parents to feel like they are a part of the team because they have crucial information and their cooperation will be important for transferring skills learned in school to the community more broadly.

References

Baglieri, S. & Lalvani, P. (2020). *Undoing Ableism: Teaching about disability in K-12 classrooms*. Routledge

Mitchell, D. (2010). *Education that fits: Review of international trends in the education of students with special educational needs*. University of Canterbury.

Mitchell, D. (2015). *Education that fits: Review of international trends in the education of students with special educational needs*, 2nd edition. University of Canterbury.

Ridgeway, R. (2017). Supporting struggling learners: Teachers, learners and labels of SEN. In Caroline Walker-Gleaves & David Waugh (Eds). *Looking after literacy: A whole child approach to effective literacy interventions*, Chapter 5, pp. 67–86. Sage.

Name: Gillian Parekh
Position: Canada Research Chair in Inclusion, Disability and Inclusion
Institutional Affiliation: York University

Resources

Books

Gadsden, V. L., Ford, M. A., & Breiner, H. (2016). *Parenting matters: supporting parents of children ages 0-8*. The National Academies Press. https://www.nap.edu/read/21868/chapter/7

This book revolves around supporting parents of children in pre-schools and elementary schools. Chapter 5 centers on targeted interventions for supporting parents of children with special needs, parents facing special adversities, and parents involved with child welfare services. Through the use of evidence based and evidence informed interventions used in a variety of settings the authors were able to draw conclusions and recommendations. Strongest evidence was found for programs that teach parents how to support the learning and development of their children with special needs, promote positive parent-child interactions, and focus on reducing the children's problem behaviors. Instructional interventions as well as open and positive communication of behaviors with parents had been shown to bring about advantageous outcomes including decreased parental stress.

Manitoba Education. (2004). *Working together: A handbook for parents of children with special needs in school.* Manitoba Education. https://www.edu.gov.mb.ca/k12/specedu/parent/pdf/workingtogether.pdf

This 34-page handbook, created by Manitoba Education in 2004, was created for parents of children with special needs in schools. One can expect to find information about how schools work in partnerships with parents to best serve their children. Everything from identification and assessment to planning and programming is explained in detail within this handbook. An entire section focuses on ongoing communication between families and schools throughout a student's education and suggests ways in which questions and issues may be addressed. Finally, there is an additional resources and references section in which parents can find helpful forms and reading materials relevant to Manitoba education.

Videos

San Bernardino Unified School District. (2017, October 4). *Relationship building: parent/teacher communication* [Video]. Youtube. https://www.youtube.com/watch?v=LTKOhxE4LNc

This 2017 YouTube video, posted on the San Bernardino Unified School District channel, discusses the importance of trust and communication in parent-teacher relationships. Multiple teachers from this school district speak about how they stay in contact with parents, form stronger relationships, and gain their trust. Some teachers call multiple parents every day to inform them about positive things their child has done, others are mindful of responding to parent emails as promptly as possible, and sending parents newsletters prior to the beginning of school so that they can understand how your classroom works.

Professional Articles

Aguilar, E. (23, September 2011). *20 tips for developing positive relationships with parents.* Edutopia. https://www.edutopia.org/blog/20-tips-developing-positive-relationships-parents-elena-aguilar

This article highlights twenty key ways in which educators can develop positive relationships with parents. Aguilar explains that the role of an educator can be one with many responsibilities to students and parents. Thus, the relationship between a teacher and a parent is a crucial one for the overall success of the child, as both adults are key people in the child's life. Aguilar touches on points such as learning parent names, being honest with your intentions, communicating often and in various forms, and leading with positive talking points. She also explains that the role of language is vital; whenever necessary educators should find a translator and be very mindful of the words used. Aguilar packs a lot of helpful information for communicating effectively with parents into this article.

Buckmann, S., & Pratt, C. (1999). *Supporting students with asperger's syndrome who present behavioral challenges*. Indiana Institute on Disability and Community. https://www.iidc.indiana.edu/irca/articles/supporting-students-with-aspergers-syndrome-who-present-behavioral-challenges.html

Steve Buckmann and Cathy Pratt present this article explaining methods for supporting students with Asperger's syndrome, in particular those who demonstrate behavioral difficulties. Through their experiences and generalized strategies from the applied behavior analysis arena, the authors were able to contain their findings for effective supports for students with Asperger's syndrome and behavioral challenges. Providing positive behavioral support through a functional analytic approach is the one approach that is highlighted. This approach contains strategies such as person-centered planning, team meetings, systematic interviews, and direct observations. Buckmann and Pratt discuss differing strategies and suggest to take a highly individualized approach to providing behavioral interventions and supports to students with Asperger's syndrome.

Education Corner. (n.d.). *Teaching students with Asperger's syndrome*. Education Corner: Education That Matters. https://www.educationcorner.com/teaching-students-with-aspergers-syndrome.html

This article, created by Education Corner, focuses on teaching students with Asperger's syndrome. This article narrows in on teaching students with Asperger's syndrome in the least restrictive environments. Topics such as student sensory processing, obsessive focus, low frustration threshold, and executive functioning gaps are emphasized in this article within the context of teaching. This website can be particularly useful for those working with or dealing with learning with Asperger's syndrome, as it provides practical strategies and techniques for teaching and learning for students with Asperger's syndrome.

London, R. A. (June 2016). *Family engagement practices in California schools*. Public Policy Institute of California. https://www.ppic.org/content/pubs/report/R_616RLR.pdf

This report outlines engagement strategies, the research approach utilized, findings on district plans for family engagement, measures for family engagement outcomes, and finally, conclusions that may be drawn from the research. This study finds providing resources and opportunities for family engagement, using effective communication practices, sharing responsibility and leadership, and creating a welcoming environment are four key engagement strategies. Two contextual issues relevant to and important for family engagement are: (1) capacity building for both parents and school staff and (2) attention to cultural and linguistic differences between school staff and families.

Scholastic. (n.d.). *Understanding Asperger's in the classroom.* Scholastic. https://www.scholastic.com/teachers/articles/teaching-content/understanding-aspergers/

This article provides a window into classrooms and understanding them as they pertain to students with Asperger's syndrome. The article encourages educators to dig a little deeper into understanding why a student with Asperger's syndrome may become scared or resistant to an activity. Scholastic's article helps readers to understand "rules" that students with Asperger's syndrome may create for themselves, as well as why they may think classroom rules do not apply to them. Keeping lines of communication open is emphasized both between parents and educators, and educators and students alike.

Websites

Autism Speaks Canada. (n.d.). *Asperger syndrome.* Autism Speaks Canada. https://www.autismspeaks.ca/about-autism/what-is-autism/asperger-syndrome/

This website provides information about autism. It provides readers with basic and detailed information regarding behaviors associated with Asperger's syndrome, how it is diagnosed, and what kinds of services or supports are available for those with Asperger's syndrome. This webpage also addresses how the understanding of Asperger's syndrome has evolved over the years.

Asperger's Society of Ontario. (n.d.). *Asperger's society of Ontario.* Asperger's Society of Ontario. http://www.aspergers.ca/

This webpage provides a portal into the many different platforms available on this website. This site is a tool for learning about what Asperger's syndrome is, along with what the Asperger's Society of Ontario is all about. Through the map feature, users are able to find resources in their local areas all around Ontario. Furthermore, individuals are able to access the Asperger's Society of Ontario's blog, media library, services and calendar of events.

American Federation of Teachers. (2007). *Building parent-teacher relationships.* Reading Rockets. https://www.readingrockets.org/article/building-parent-teacher-relationships

This article is available for reading on the Reading Rockets website and focuses on the theme of building parent-teacher relationships. The article discusses how the benefits of strong parent-teacher relationships are three fold, having positive effects on parents, teachers and students alike. A variety of forms of communication are mentioned; parent conferences, weekly or monthly folders of student work sent home, phone calls, emails and curriculum nights are just a few examples. The components of effective communication strategies that are detailed are: initiation, timeliness, consistency and frequency, follow through, clarity and usefulness of communication. This is a powerful resource for educators navigating the terrain of creating positive parent communication and relationships.

Chapter 11

An Accident and an Injury

CASE 3: ELEMENTARY SCHOOLS

Crosscutting Themes: Collaboration, Relationships/Trust, Parents/Caregivers/Family.
Leadership Competencies: Policies and Procedures, Values Inclusion, Professional Learning, Embodies Professional Standards, Collaboration.

Sofia Perez is a resource teacher at Lexington Elementary and teaches students in the development education classroom. This classroom is specially designed for students with special education needs.

Students in this classroom face challenges in communication, cognition, and mobility. Some students are also hearing and vision impaired. Having a classroom dedicated to students with these special education needs allows them to get the support they require while still being a part of the school community. Not all of the public elementary schools in the area have developmental education-specific classrooms, so the staff at Lexington are very happy to offer this unique resource to students and their families. There are three paraprofessionals who also work in the classroom alongside Sofia. Sofia loves her job tremendously, and although there are days that are exhausting, she finds her work to be very rewarding.

However, an incident recently occurred with one of Sofia's students, Philip, that made her reflect on her commitment to working with some of the most vulnerable students in the school. Philip is eleven years old and is nonverbal. He communicates entirely through gestures and his communication system on his iPad.

He was diagnosed with a neural disorder where the connective tissue between the two halves of his brain was damaged at birth. He tends to become

Figure 11.1 **Inclusive Classroom.** *Source*: https://www.istockphoto.com. Credit: zoranm.

aggressive and violent when he doesn't get his way. He is quite large for his age, much larger than the other eleven-year-olds at the school. One of the paraprofessionals in the classroom, Jalen, remains with Philip at all times to prevent him from hurting himself and others. Jalen often takes Philip to the school's sensory room where he is able to work on calming down without others nearby. The sensory room is a perfect place for many students to work on calming down. Having a space where Philip can go to calm down really helps him get through the day.

A few weeks ago, Sofia was going about her regular routine with her class. It was time to take the students to the school gym for their daily physical activity. On the way to the gym, Janeene Yager's grade three class was also in the hallway heading to the library. As the two classes were passing each other, Philip was startled by a loud noise when a grade three student threw a book on the ground. Philip reacted to the noise and accidentally knocked another student, Desmond, in the nose with his elbow. Desmond's nose started to bleed and, in just a few seconds, blood was all over the hallway floor. Some of the other students began screaming at the sight of so much blood, and one little boy from Janeene Yager's class looked like he was going to faint. Sofia, who was also starting to feel sick to her stomach from the sight of so much blood, immediately told Janeene to take her students to the library.

"We don't need anyone getting blood on them and we certainly don't need anyone fainting. We need to clear this hallway *immediately*," Sofia said. "I'll take Desmond to the office."

Figure 11.2 Student Using Assistive Technology. *Source*: https://www.istockphoto.com. Credit: monkeybusinessimages.

Sofia then directed Jalen to take Philip back to the classroom. She could see that Philip didn't fully understand what was going on. He had a confused look on his face and also looked horrified by the amount of blood on the floor.

Sofia walked Desmond to the school office to get some help. Miguel, the school principal, was in his office when the two arrived. Seeing Desmond's state, he immediately got an icepack for Desmond to put on his nose to stop the swelling, but the blood didn't stop. It appeared that his nose had been broken.

"He needs to go to the emergency room," Miguel finally said. "He's lost quite a bit of blood. I'm going to call his mom."

Within minutes, Desmond's mom, Cheryl, stormed into the school. She immediately went to her son and began asking him what happened. Before taking him to the hospital, Cheryl made a few comments under her breath—but loud enough for those close by to hear—about how she knew one of the "dev ed" kids would do something like this. And then, as she was halfway out the office door, Cheryl turned to Sofia and Miguel and said, "Students like Philip should be somewhere else and not in a regular school. He should be among kids *like* him *only*." She then proceeded to march out of the school with her son.

Sofia and Miguel looked at each other, both feeling overwhelmed and not knowing what to do next.

Questions to Consider:

1. What are your next steps with the parents? How do you solve this problem?
2. How can you help parents to see the benefits of an inclusive school community? To what degree do you see the value of congregated classrooms? Do you see them as part of "full inclusion?" Why or why not?
3. What routines could be put into place in order to avoid a situation like this from happening again?

Expert Opinion:

I believe the school has begun the journey to becoming more inclusive. However, there is still a long way to go. I can clearly see that Lexington Elementary has good intentions as it has a dedicated classroom to support students with special educational needs. Unfortunately, separate classes could do more harm both to students who are in the classes and to those who are not in the classes. Students in resource classrooms recognize how they are different from others which can negatively impact on their self-concept. Students without special needs may fear the unknown and may decide to stay away from the students in the resource class.

It is possible, Miguel, the school principal is not fully aware of the ill effects of having a special class on campus. The school needs to fully embrace inclusion philosophy rather than partially accept it.

The school will need to change a few things and conduct a series of workshops for the staff to fully understand the inclusion model. The school needs to understand inclusion should be the foundation to provide high-quality education to all. The school needs to create broader awareness among the community members and parents about how inclusion can assist in creating an excellent school.

I will invest heavily in the professional learning of everyone at the school including the principal. A key focus of professional learning will be for each member of the school to recognize the value of inclusive education and how everyone in the school will benefit if they could include all learners. A major focus of the PL program will be on understanding "why," "what," and "how" of inclusion. The school must recognize that inclusion is the only way to provide high-quality education to all learners. The school must recognize that inclusion is the way to achieve excellence.

I will also highlight the need for the school to recognize that creating inclusive schools takes time and one should not expect that it will be without any challenges. The school cannot ignore parents', students', and educators' concerns about inclusion. The school should invest in understanding their concerns by conducting surveys/focus group interviews. The professional learning program should be informed by this data and should empower

Figure 11.3 Teaching and Learning in an Inclusive Classroom. *Source*: https://www.istockphoto.com. Credit: kali9.

the leadership team and educators to address the concerns identified by the surveys/focus group interviews. Lastly, inclusion is not possible in schools where the staff is not well supported and where they don't collaborate. I would advise the principal to find out ways that each member of the staff could be supported in their efforts to make the Lexington Elementary—an excellent and inclusive school. Small teams could be formed which can work on making school an inclusive workplace.

References:

Ainscow, M. & Sandill, A. (2010). Developing inclusive education systems: the role of organisational cultures and leadership. *International Journal of Inclusive Education*, 14(4), 401–416, doi: 10.1080/13603110802504903.

Billingsley, B., McLeskey, J. & Crockett, J. (2019), Success for all students: leading for effective inclusive schools. In J. Crockett, B. Billingsley, & M. Boscardin (Eds.) *Handbook of Leadership and Administration for Special Education* , 2nd ed., Routledge. pp. 306–332.

DeMatthews, D., Billingsley, B., McLesky, J. & Sharma, U. (2020). Principal leadership for students with disabilities in effective inclusive schools. *Journal of Educational Administration*. https://www.emerald.com/insight/0957-8234.html

Kunc, N. (1984) *Being realistic, isn't realistic*. https://www.broadreachtraining.com/integration-being-realistic-isnt-realistic

Sharma, U., & Desai, I. (2008). The changing roles and responsibilities of school principals relative to inclusive education. In Chris Forlin and Ming-Gon John Lian

(Eds.), *Reform, inclusion & teacher education: towards a new era of special education in the Asia-Pacific region*, pp. 153–168, Routledge.

Name: Umesh Sharma
Position: Professor and Academic Head
Institutional Affiliation: Monash University

Resources

Videos

Edutopia. (2017). *The sensory room: Helping students with Autism focus and learn* [Video]. Edutopia. https://www.edutopia.org/video/sensory-room-helping-students-autism-focus-and-learn

This video touches on key topics such as creating safe spaces for students, physical therapy, and self-regulation through sensory breaks. When designing a sensory room it is important to consider: carpeting the floors, putting shades on harsh lighting, incorporating exercise balls and yoga mats, offering different stations to calm or energize students, and offering full body tactile stimulation. Educators in the video mention that the purpose of a sensory room is to allow students a healthy and safe space.

KGW News. (2019, February 4). *Classrooms in crisis: Outbursts plaguing Oregon classrooms* [Video]. YouTube. https://www.youtube.com/watch?v=Om7yVbuap9k

This YouTube video is a newscast focusing on the outbursts and disruptive behaviors in Oregon classrooms. A panel of teachers from Oregon schools are interviewed in regards to aggressive, violent, and disruptive behaviors they have witnessed in their own or others classrooms. One teacher remarks that she does not believe the students wish to hurt someone, whether that be staff or fellow classmates, they just do not know how to communicate their feelings in any other way.

Academic Articles

Shultz, T. R., Able, H., Sreckovic, M. A., & White, T. (2016). Education and training in Autism and developmental disabilities. *Parent-Teacher Collaboration: Teacher Perceptions of What is Needed to Support Students with ASD in the Inclusive Classroom*, 51(4), 344–354.

34 teachers participated in this qualitative study to understand teachers' perceptions of helpful parent involvement and advocacy strategies. Focus groups and interviews were used as research methods. Teachers emphasized the need for parental collaboration with the school team and parental advocacy and also provided examples of advocacy strategies. Examples included information-sharing networks, Circle of Friends, and IEP information sheets or booklets to help teachers in understanding their children.

Professional Articles

Phillips, M. (2012, November 27). *Parents and teachers: Turning conflicts into partnerships.* Edutopia. https://www.edutopia.org/blog/parent-teacher-conflicts-into-partnerships-mark-phillips

This 2012 article by Mark Phillips revolves around transforming parent and teacher conflicts into positive partnerships. Phillips speaks from years of personal experience as a high school teacher and a teacher educator. Phillips emphasizes that educators must remain calm, truly listen to the parents, and put themselves in the shoes of their student's parents when dealing with conflict. Typically, parent-teacher conflict arises from control issues, differences in values, or different perceptions of the student, according to Phillips. The author dives deep into topics such as roles, expectations, communication, compromise, perceptions and realities, to gain a better understanding of the parent-teacher partnership.

Guetzloe, E. (2006, March). *Practical strategies for working with students who display aggression and violence.* Child and Youth Care-Online. https://www.cyc-net.org/cyc-online/cycol-0306-guetzloe.html

This article focuses on working with children or students who display aggressive or violent behaviors. Strategies to prevent aggression that are outlined include: reducing access to possible victims, establishing reasonable norms and expectations, avoiding confrontation, minimizing competition, using nonverbal signals or reminders, providing constant supervision, and providing desirable backup reinforcers. Guetzloe also discusses functional assessment, which is a prescriptive approach to determine what function an aggressive or violent behavior serves for the student. Finally, a variety of practical strategies and supports are detailed for those working with students demonstrating aggressive or violent behaviors.

CBC. (2019, February 17). *'I felt helpless': Teachers call for support amid 'escalating crisis' of classroom violence.* CBC Radio. https://www.cbc.ca/radio/thesundayedition/the-sunday-edition-for-february-17-2019-1.5017616/i-felt-helpless-teachers-call-for-support-amid-escalating-crisis-of-classroom-violence-1.5017623

This article outlines the experience of educators across Ontario when it comes to student aggression and violence. Educators state that incidents of student verbal and physical violence targeting staff and classmates have exhausting impacts on them. Multiple educators quoted in this article explain their hesitation to report these incidents as not much is done by the school board and union in response in the past. In an Elementary Teacher's Federation of Ontario (ETFO) poll in 2016-17, 80% of educators reported incidents of violence to be increasing. Some Ontario teachers have been provided personal protective equipment including a Kevlar jacket, neck, shin, and wrist guards, helmets, and spit guards.

Rauhala, J. (2018, September 20). *Building relationships with teachers.* Edutopia. https://www.edutopia.org/article/building-relationships-teachers

Johanna Rauhala is the author of this 2018 article written for Edutopia, which discusses how parents and guardians may positively build relationships with teachers. Rauhala discusses writing thank you notes to teachers at the beginning of the school year to offer opportunities to connect, provide support, and share information with your child's teacher. The author mentions it is important to mention your child's strengths and challenges, along with your openness to receive information and communication throughout the school year from the teacher. Tone, respecting the roles, and giving genuine gratitude are key aspects of forming a positive relationship with teachers that are highlighted in this article.

Websites

Autism Canada. (n.d.). *Autism explained*. Autism Canada. https://autismcanada.org/autism-explained/

This webpage was created by Autism Canada to educate individuals about what autism is. This webpage explains that autism is a neurodevelopmental disorder which impacts brain development, and outlines the most common problems experienced by those with autism. Furthermore, the concept of autism being a spectrum disorder is described, along with commonly co-occurring medical conditions. This webpage is also the hub from which users can click to different pages to learn about the history of autism, early signs and characteristics, diagnosis, co-occurring conditions, and screening tools.

SECONDARY SCHOOL SPECIFIC CASES

Chapter 12

The Incident in Mr. Mooney's Science Class

A Case of Student Advocacy

CASE 1: SECONDARY SCHOOLS

Crosscutting Themes: Advocacy, Relationships/Trust.
Leadership Competencies: Values Inclusion, Contextual, Lived Experience of Students.

Casey is a grade ten student at Emerson Secondary School, where I've been the vice principal for three years. Casey was diagnosed with autism when he was four years old. He is verbal but often has difficulty expressing himself. At times, he becomes aggressive when he gets overwhelmed or upset, which makes it difficult for him to participate in regular classes. However, Casey was successful in completing most of his grade nine courses through regular classrooms although with support. At the beginning of the grade ten year, we paired Casey with a great paraprofessional, Mr. Lu, for morning classes. Mr. Lu is very attentive to Casey's needs. Casey's morning classes include an hour in Mr. Mooney's Science class. Mr. Lu has told me that Casey demonstrates a real aptitude for science and loves to work with his peers in the class for different activities.

Casey has had a bit of trouble, however, when experiments involve chemical reactions and small explosions because it's frightening to him. One morning in the fall, Mr. Mooney did an experiment in front of the class where he made an egg explode with hydrogen gas. The loud noise visibly upset Casey, causing him to run out of the classroom and down the hall. Mr. Lu had to chase him down the hall. After that incident, we asked Mr. Mooney to notify Mr. Lu when he was going to do something in class that might upset Casey so that Mr. Lu could bring him outside of the classroom for a couple of minutes.

Figure 12.1 Students in Science Class. *Source*: https://www.istockphoto.com. Credit: monkeybusinessimages.

It's now the middle of the school term and Casey has been doing really well in class. Of course, he has good days and bad days, but Mr. Lu is usually able to calm him down and we have a designated quiet room in the school that Casey can use to de-stress and take a break from class if it becomes too much. But last Tuesday was a really hard day for Casey. The Science class was dissecting frogs with scalpels and scissors. Mr. Lu was using the scalpel on the frog that Casey had been given to examine and dissect. One of the other students in the class, Jared, made a rude comment to Casey—something along the lines of being "too dumb" to dissect his own frog and needed a "babysitter" to help him all the time. The comment, understandably, upset Casey. He started yelling at Jared and tried to approach him. Casey also began swearing at the other students and threatened to "hunt them down and hurt them all."

Mr. Lu had come to my office at the end of the day to talk about what happened and what was said between the two students. We agreed it would be best to take Casey out of the class for a week because we thought his classmates would be startled and upset that Casey threatened to be aggressive with them. We knew that Casey's parents would not be happy about this since they wanted their son to be with his peers, but we needed to ensure that the other students were able to learn in an environment free from the threat of harm. We went to talk with Mr. Mooney's class to check in to see how the students were doing and notify them that Casey wouldn't be joining them for the next week in class.

In the classroom, I apologized to Mr. Mooney and to the class for the disruption. Then one of the students, Julie, raised her hand.

"This is obviously Jared's fault and he should be apologizing. What he said to Casey was *so* rude."

I glanced at Jared, who was sitting in the back of the classroom. He rolled his eyes at Julie's comment.

"I'm not here to have a conversation about who's *fault* this is, Julie," I said. "I just wanted to de-brief with you all and ensure that everyone is okay. We are here to ensure that you all feel safe at school."

Julie continued. "We are *fine*, Mrs. Owen. I think we're all more concerned about Casey. We want to make sure that *he's* okay. We know that he has his good days and bad days. I'm not concerned about my safety or anything."

I was surprised. "Thanks Julie," I told her. "I really appreciate your concern for Casey."

Another student, Will, piped up. "It's okay that Casey got upset. I think we all agree that we want Casey to stay in our class."

Looking around the room, I saw other students nodding their heads. Surprised at the students' responses, I left the Science class and let Mr. Mooney continue on with the dissection unit.

Figure 12.2 Student Comforting a Bullied Student. *Source*: https://www.istockphoto.com. Credit: fstop123.

Later when I was reflecting on my classroom visit with Mrs. Harrison, the school principal, I told her,

> You know, if Casey was only in class once in a while, the students would have probably reacted differently and might define him more by his bad days and difficult behavior. But because he's with them every day, they see the good times too. They see that he works hard to understand and to communicate with people.

The next day, Mr. Lu stopped me in the hall. He told me, "You know, in all my years being a paraprofessional, I've never seen students stick up and advocate for a classmate the way that Mr. Mooney's Science class stood up for Casey. It was so cool."

I couldn't help but feel proud of the students and staff members at the school. Despite Casey's difficulties, everyone wanted to ensure that he was successful and included at school. I should have figured that this happy feeling wouldn't last for long. Two days after the incident in the science class, my phone rang. It was Jared's mom, Mrs. Flemming.

"I heard that there was an incident in Jared's Science class with another boy. I hear that my son was attacked. Why wasn't I notified about the incident? I'm *not* okay with this."

I told Jared's mother that I understood her concerns.

"I assume that this autistic boy *won't* be staying in the classroom, correct?" she interrupted me.

I told her firmly that Casey *would* be staying in the class. "Mrs. Flemming, we do everything we can to ensure that students with special education needs are included here . . . so Casey will continue to be in Jared's Science class."

"But that's not okay!" she retorted. "Why is everyone so concerned about this autistic boy and not concerned about *my* son? What about *my* son's safety? What about *his* success?"

Oh dear, I thought. *How do I respond to this?*

Questions to Consider:

1. How would you respond to Mrs. Flemming's concerns?
2. Mr. Mooney does not seem to play a large role in supporting Casey's success in his class. How can high school teachers, often specialists in their fields, be encouraged to support all students, particularly those who may learn in alternative ways?
3. Mrs. Flemming referred to Casey as "that autistic boy." How do you respond when people have negative attitudes about students with special education needs or use language that might be offensive?

4. What is your role as a school administrator in helping to foster advocacy for students with special education needs in your school? What strategies do you use to help students develop self-advocacy skills?

Expert Opinion:

As a mentor coach for new school administrators, and "hindsight being 20/20," all social-emotional and behavioral incidents in a school are learning opportunities. In Casey's case, this is an opportunity for reflective leadership regarding decision-making, implementing preventative strategies, and engaging parents/guardians in strengthening a safe, caring and inclusive school culture.

Reflectively: consider the investigation of this incident as an exercise of "connecting the dots." Each dot represents one of the parties involved. Each one must be seen and heard. Through active and unbiased listening, and by providing equitable opportunity for each party to share their experience, either verbally or in writing, you can determine how each party interacted with each other to bring about the present situation.

When you do this, the investigation slows down because leaders build capacity one conversation at a time. As a result, the punitive and reactive decision made in this case would have been replaced by a data-informed

Figure 12.3 Teacher Listening to Student. *Source*: https://www.istockphoto.com. Credit: SDI Productions.

decision based on all the dots' details. For example, if I were to ask you to list all the parties involved in this situation, you would find that some voices are completely missing including the classroom teacher. In fact, I am wondering how the students, Casey and Jared, are doing?

Secondly, there is much celebration over how "comfortable" Casey's peers are with him in the classroom. However, researched models and strategies of inclusive learning conditions suggest an expansive model is needed to foster respectful and reciprocal social, emotional, and peer-to-peer mental engagement. Such engagement can be hindered by overly attached one-to-one support. In addition, the classroom teacher is responsible for the learning environment and they must get to know all their students while setting and enforcing 'ground-rules' for respectful interaction in the classroom.

Third, as a school administrator, be careful about interjecting yourself into the situation. Your goal is to empower your teachers to handle these situations by reminding and resourcing them about inclusivity and learning. Furthermore, this also presents a critical opportunity for the school administrator to reflect on their own misconceptions and inconsistencies regarding inclusivity that played out in the situation. I wonder if you noticed any as you read through the incident?

Lastly, the voices that must be heard long before the phone rings in your office are those of the parents and guardians particularly of those students who are involved in such an incident. Believing that parents are doing the best they can with what they have and what they know, an invitation must be extended by the school administrator to meet with Jared's mother for further discussion. Beyond the immediate parents, today's technology affords a strategic opportunity to educate, report to, and support all families. All this takes time, and it does mean that other administrative tasks must be prioritized in order to fully invest in cultivating a safe, caring and inclusive school culture through reflective leadership.

Name: Lisa Devall-Martin
Position: Professor & Former Principal
Institutional Affiliation: Redeemer University

Resources

Videos

San Bernardino Unified School District. (2018, February 16). *Differentiation within the inclusion classroom model.* YouTube. https://www.youtube.com/watch?v=7G_PuCIpaaM

This eight-minute video walks teachers through a segment of their professional development series focusing on differentiation with the inclusion model. The video has teachers of specific subjects showcasing strategies for differentiation, using a two-team teaching model allows these classes to plan and integrate ideas into the classroom setting. Showcasing the two-team model, the teaching styles are compared from use of manipulatives, space in the room and classroom management strategies. Finally, differentiation is explained by showcasing in their lesson, what strategies they implement in the class to help the students succeed. This is explained in red (struggling, need teacher help), yellow group (I need a quick touch base to be okay), and green group (I've got this). They also use assessment and differentiation to specifically help each students' individual needs.

The Understood Team. (n.d.) *4 benefits of inclusive classrooms.* Understood.org. https://www.understood.org/en/learning-attention-issues/treatments-approaches/educational-strategies/5-benefits-of-inclusion-classrooms

This video is attached to an article which both explain an inclusive classroom and how general educators and special education teachers work together to meet the needs of students. The video shows examples and strategies that prove the benefits of giving special education students the support they need while in the general education classroom as all students benefit from an inclusive classroom. The article also focuses on family worries when their child is identified and the importance of explaining collaboration and the mission of inclusion to support all students.

Academic Articles

Griffin, D., & Galassi, J. (2010). Parent perceptions of barriers to academic success in a rural middle school.(Report). *Professional School Counseling,* 14(1), 87–100. doi: 10.1177/2156759X1001400109

This journal article details a study on parent perceptions of barriers to academic success. This article insightfully explores how parents communicate with students and schools to create these perceptions. This article worked to identify school barriers as well as school and community resources to overcome these barriers. There were six common barrier identified which are able to be explored and used to improve student success in the classroom and community.

Jacobs, D. S., (2019), Safety and consent for kids and teens with autism or special needs: A parents' guide. *ProtoView,* 2019(51). Ringgold Inc.

This piece is a guide for parents with children on the autism spectrum, primarily ages 5–12, to explore and understand personal safety and issues of consent. This text is written for caregivers to learn about healthy friendships, body awareness, personal empowerment and how to tell when something is wrong. This text would be helpful for parents to understand strategies such as role-playing games and lessons which are geared toward helping children on the spectrum thrive while acknowledging and understanding they are often vulnerable. There is also a description of warning signs of abuse and examples of how to talk to children about personal safety and autonomy in this parent guide.

Murry, F. (2005). Effective advocacy for students with emotional/behavioral disorders: how high the cost? *Education & Treatment of Children*, 28(4), 414–429.

This article written by Francie Murry explores special issues and severe behavioral disorders in children, social advocacy, and the involvement of school administration, child psychiatry, and mental health services in the United States. This research focused on advocacy behavior and found that teachers and administration are lacking advocacy due to fear of punishment. This journal article suggests advice and steps for teachers to become effective advocates for their students with special needs. These steps include maintaining loyalty to the individuals they serve despite potential conflict, seeking to change the status quo, representing individuals while working collaboratively with others, and working to correct and/or improve identified problematic areas.

Obiakor, F., Harris, M., Mutua, K., Rotatori, A., & Algozzine, B. (2012). Making inclusion work in general education classrooms. *Education & Treatment of Children*, 35(3), 477–490. doi: 10.1353/etc.2012.0020

This journal article focuses on the educational treatment of children, specifically the treatment of students with special needs. The article identifies a phenomenon that stakeholders, teachers or educational professionals often downplay the capabilities of students and the student's willingness to live a "normal" life. This results in placements, which default to exclusion in the name of "student success" where peer-to-peer contact with other students with disabilities is prioritized over a general classroom education. This article explores how educators can make inclusion work in general classrooms, emphasized how important an expansive peer-to-peer experience benefits all students, and how to truly support students with special needs, goals, and needs while removing biases. This article describes teaching strategies for inclusion as well as general guidelines to maintain engagement. Further, there are case studies to bring these principles to life.

Professional Articles

Barrett, D. (n.d.). Determination and partnerships: Keys to successful inclusion for secondary students. *Inclusive Education*. https://www.edweek.org/ew/articles/2018/10/17/the-important-role-principals-play-in-special.html

This article is by Donna Barrett who is an accomplished educator and school administrator in Alberta. This article explores stories and lessons learned in the process of including students with developmental disabilities in middle and high schools. The article identifies where families and school staff can advance inclusive education for all. With strong support and leadership, the process of learning to support students helps teachers identify and meet the needs of students. This article shares a case study which breaks down the family and school interactions, how to build inclusion with these relationships and their learning. Specifically, a focus on inclusion in field trips and extra-curricular activities informs the "look ahead" of transition to high school and lessons learned of the many elements that contribute to quality inclusive practice in schools.

Samules, C. A. (2018, October 16). The important role principals play in special education. *Education Week,* 38(9), 26–28. https://www.edweek.org/ew/articles/2018/10/17/the-important-role-principals-play-in-special.html

This article was written by Christina Samules who researched the role of principals in special education. This resulted in dissecting the principal role where there are multiple areas of expertise such as policy and regulations, a leadership role as well as support. The article explores learning on the job, how principals need to know the families, gather data, and make connections with teachers and students. This learning revealed gaps in principal training in regard to special education and what professional development opportunities there are to help with these. Research suggests seeking out parent and school relationships to improve the flow of communication, to learn more and best support the student needs. The advice is to continue to learn, and choose the options and communication that is best for the students' success.

The State of Victoria. (2009, April). Addressing parents' concerns and complaints effectively policy and guides. *Education Victoria Government.* https://www.education.vic.gov.au/Documents/school/principals/management/parentsconcerns.pdf

This professional document created by the Department of Education and Early Childhood Development in Victoria, Australia recognizes that parent involvement is crucial to children's development and learning. By fostering positive relationships, school partnerships are stronger. The document walks through relevant policy such as the concerns and complaints policy, advice for schools when developing policy, guides for positive relationships, dealing with complaints, and understanding aggressive reactions as well as the blame cycle. The document is thorough with definitions and strategies to implement. It also walks through some professional development on improving listening skills, saying "yes" and "no" with confidence, managing a request for an apology, as well as encouraging fair play in negotiations.

Websites

Autism360. (2016, February 4). *ADHD and Autism in the classroom.* Autismag. https://www.autism360.com/adhd-and-autism-in-the-classroom/

This website is a resource for both parents and teachers to learn more about attention deficit disorder and autism in the classroom. This article explores why children experience frustrations in the classroom due to many stimuli such as peers, sensory and the need to balance with coping mechanisms. With specific goals and positive reinforcement such as meaningful rewards can help children focus on behavior and the positive repercussions. There are helpful links such as teaching strategies, managing difficult behaviors, and visual aids for learning. The article then details specifically some examples of problems in the classroom setting and what educators or parents can do with a three-part success plan, positive classroom settings, and classroom strategies to maintain focus and concentration for students with special needs.

Autism Society (2020). *About the Autism society.* https://www.autism-society.org/about-the-autism-society/

This website is created by the Autism Society of America and describes how they have worked to advocate and improve lives of all affected by autism over the past 50 years. This website provides historical background on strategies and skills needed to treat individuals to the highest of dignity and maximize their quality of life. The website sites how this society began, how to get involved such as the national conference on autism as well as information on their referral team. Finally, the webpage explains the Autism Society's Panel of Professional Advisors (PPA) which sets the standards for policy and governing practices.

Autism Society Newfoundland and Labrador (2003). *Strategies for classroom management.* .https://www.autism.nf.net/service-provider/resources-for-educators/strategies-for-classroom-management/

This website focuses on strategies for classroom management. This website walks through the importance of structured and predictable environments, a daily visual schedule, understanding aspects which students experience frustration and how to plan relocation opportunities and areas. Then the website explores providing opportunities for meaningful contact with peers who have appropriate social behavior; this specifically helps those struggling with appropriate behavior model. Other considerations are to plan for transitions, prepare for student change, and understand the impact of sensory factors. These factors are broken down by the senses with key questions to consider. This resource is ideal for teachers to understand and adapt to an appropriate learning environment for their specific student needs.

Conners, H. (2016, December 2). *'Inclusion' is the classroom challenges teachers are too afraid to talk about, educator says.* CBC.ca. https://www.cbc.ca/news/canada/nova-scotia/nova-scotia-teachers-classrooms-inclusion-work-to-rule-1.3879240

This CBC article from 2016 focuses on inclusion being the elephant in the room when thinking of classroom working conditions and frustrations teachers face. It is noted that inclusion does not want to be addressed as a problem, but demands have increased, and more resources, and conversations are needed if we don't want kids to fail. Part of inclusion is meeting student strengths and needs, and that teachers start this profession to see students succeed, inherently we need to embody the learning for all structure to support student success and inclusion. Awareness is needed for this topic to improve resources and conversations.

Dubec, R. (2018). *Foster inclusion in the classroom.* Teaching Commons Lakehead University. https://teachingcommons.lakeheadu.ca/foster-inclusion-classroom

Lakehead University has a forum where Dr. Rhonda Dubec submitted this resource on fostering inclusion in the classroom. This webpage includes nineteen strategies explained under five specific categories. These categories are how to include diverse content, creating an inclusive environment, encouraging growth mindset, striving for equality of access to instruction and assistance, and how to use feedback to refine and improve your methods. Under each of these categories are tips and suggestions to help instructors broaden and expand their understanding of their own discipline and what they hope to accomplish in teaching.

Lakhani, K. (2016, June 21). *How to support a child with Autism in the classroom.* Autism Speaks. https://www.autismspeaks.org/blog/five-ways-teachers-can-support-students-autism

This website includes a letter from Kamini Lakhani who founded Support for Autistic Individuals in 2004 in Mumbai, India. She is a mother of a child with autism and shares a story of a fourth-grade teacher looking for advice on a student with autism. She speaks to hearing the teacher's perspective, and wrote a letter to encourage and support teachers with advice. She includes five immediate steps to best support children with autism. Then she speaks to the perspective from another teacher explaining that the teaching role is so important to impact a child's life, when we work with new strategies and positively engage with children, you grow, they grow and the influence ripples from peers and staff alike.

Tompkins, A. (2018, June 25). *Principal hotline: I'm buried in parent requests. What do I do?.* WeAreTeachers. https://www.weareteachers.com/buried-in-parent-requests/

This website has a segment called "Principal Hotline" which is a principal's perspective on common topics in the education system. The advice given is to reflect on the district's policy regarding parent requests, as well as a clear outline on how parents can go about requests for their child's specific learning situation. The article also notes transparency is key, as parents want to know their children are cared for, listen, use your best judgment and always breathe, remember you're not alone in handling these requests.

Chapter 13

Overheard in the Staff Room

CASE 2: SECONDARY SCHOOLS

Crosscutting Themes: Communication, Relationships/Trust, Agency/Efficacy
Leadership Competencies: Values Inclusion, Embodies Professional Standards, Professional Learning, Advocacy, Human Resources.

Paisley is a grade eleven student here at Waterby High School, where I'm the principal. Paisley has dysphasia, a condition that impacts her ability to speak and understand language. Paisley's parents pulled her out of a neighboring high school in the middle of grade nine because she was struggling. They implemented a home-schooling system with a speech-language pathologist and sometimes a psychologist to help Paisley continue to learn and grow in her home environment rather than a school environment. Paisley's parents had determined that if they saw real improvement in Paisley's abilities and felt that she was ready to enroll back in a high school environment, they would do so because they wanted her to establish some friendships while still in high school.

Last May, I got a call from Paisley's parents indicating that they would like to register Paisley at Waterby for grade eleven. After a meeting with Paisley, her support team, parents, and school board personnel we determined a plan to re-register her in Waterby and extend her schooling beyond her regular graduation time if necessary.

It was a more difficult transition than I had anticipated. The new teachers, students, environment, and routines meant a need for more communication with Paisley and her family than what any of us had imagined. I found that I was regularly checking in with teachers to ensure that Paisley was doing okay.

At times there were daily meetings with special education staff at the school as we worked in a highly responsive and flexible way to meet Paisley's needs.

Paisley was extremely bright and especially loved animals and nature. We thought it would be good to enroll her in an academic-stream biology class, so she was exposed to some more challenging course material.

By February, Paisley was doing so well in the class that we decided to scale back some of the special education support that she had been receiving at the school. After this change was implemented, things still seemed to be going well. I eased my regular visits to her classroom, and began meeting with the biology teacher, Mrs. Shah, monthly instead of weekly to discuss her progress. Everything was going so well—or so I thought. One afternoon I was in the staff room heating up my lunch in the microwave when I heard two people enter the room. I couldn't see who had come in because the kitchen area is behind a wall. I couldn't help but hear the conversation the two individuals were having.

They were complaining about their students—how students don't listen in class, don't apply themselves, and aren't going far in life. I couldn't believe what I was hearing. I had never heard teachers say such rude things about students before. I was appalled that teachers at the school held such negative attitudes about students.

Then the two individuals began talking about Paisley.

Figure 13.1 Teacher Hearing Her Coworkers Talking. *Source*: https://www.istockphoto.com. Credit: FangXiaNuo.

Figure 13.2 Principals' Influence on Teachers. *Source*: https://www.istockphoto.com. Credit: tampatra.

"I can't believe the school let Paisley in," one of them said. "We don't have the resources to help her."

"I agree," the other staff member said.

> I try to support her but how can I communicate with a student who can't talk? It's ridiculous. I have *other* students to worry about. The administration clearly doesn't understand. They think inclusion is the be all and end all.

I felt my face go warm at the sound of "the administration."

"They've forgotten what it's like to be in a classroom with students with special needs. Those students need to be in a *separate* class where they can get the help they need," the other staff member said.

"I agree. But what can I do? I can't tell Sue that I don't want Paisley in my class, right? Whatever. I just hope Paisley doesn't take another biology course so that I don't have to deal with her next year."

I realized that the person talking was Mrs. Shah, Paisley's biology teacher. I had no idea that Mrs. Shah was struggling with teaching and supporting Paisley. Every time I talked to Mrs. Shah, she said that everything was fine. Paisley was doing well academically and was even making friends in the class. I thought that Paisley was a valued member of the school community—but it turns out I was wrong.

The microwave suddenly beeped. The staff members immediately stopped talking, realizing that they weren't alone in the staff room. I quickly thought about what to do. Should I stay in the kitchen area until the two teachers left? Should I make a run for the door? I decided to step into the large common area. I glanced at the two individuals: Mrs. Shah and the grade ten mathematics teacher, Ms. Redford. They both looked shocked to see me.

"Hi," I said. "I think we should talk about the comments I just heard."

Questions To Consider:

1. How would you respond to the comments from the two teachers?
2. How can you build an inclusive school culture, particularly when teachers might resist inclusive initiatives?
3. How can you support staff members who have negative attitudes about their students, including students with special education needs?
4. High schools tend to be large organizations with diverse, often competing, needs. As a principal, how would you offer a rationale for why you might support the allocation of resources to support students with special education needs instead of other competing needs?

Expert Opinion:

This case clearly highlights the importance of four main categories of school principal's roles in an inclusive school: (1) a role in promoting inclusion (making known the foundations and principles of inclusion while being receptive to resistance and divergence in order to establish a constructive dialogue); (2) a role in professional development of the school staff (knowledge, skills and awareness of effective inclusive practices); (3) a role in the implementation of inclusive practices (implementation, consistency of actions and conditions to inclusive practices); and (4), a role in the regulation of actions (assessment and reassessment of the school staff needs as well as the measures to be taken in the process of assessing the measures put in place in order to maintain a climate conducive to inclusive practices) (Thibodeau et al., 2016). Furthermore, the school administration would also have a certain influence on the attitude of teachers toward inclusive education, in particular by adopting its values (Rousseau et al., 2019).

The case shows, on the one hand, a certain lack of transparency in the dialogue of Mrs. Shah, dialogue which differs according to her interlocutor. On the other hand, the case shows a courageous and relevant reaction from the school principal by explicitly naming the need to discuss the comments heard in the teachers' lounge. Indeed, in the present case, both the roles of promoting inclusion (which opens the door to dialogue) and of regulating actions (which opens the door to the assessment of the measures put in place) are called upon. As such, a clear vision of inclusion and the values associated with it, that is, values of social justice, equity and democracy requires transparency, honesty, accountability, concern, moral courage and activism from the school leader (Thibodeau et al., 2016).

A mentor could certainly invite the principal to build on the recognition of what is experienced at school by remaining attentive and understanding the concerns of staff members, but also by emphasizing their strengths. A mentor could also invite the school principal to approach Mrs. Shah using a nonjudgmental, principled discourse, such as "do no harm to others." This can help to put into perspective and verbally express attitudes and behaviors that it would be desirable to stop or modify. For example: "When you act this way, it leads to the following consequence in the student's daily life." Again, to do this, a dialogue leading to the emergence of a compromise where everyone has the opportunity to come out a winner is to be prioritized.

Finally, certain lines of thought could allow an in-depth analysis of the case and the actions to be taken to resolve it:

- How did the school principal initially approach the teacher to ask her (or inform her) to welcome Paisley into her biology class?
  - Does the school principal know the teacher's educational approaches?
  - Did the school principal engaged Mrs. Shaw upstream to develop strategies and target the best conditions aimed at maximizing Paisley's participation in the classroom?
- How did the school principal engage the staff in planning for Paisley's return to school?
  - How have the staff (teachers and specialists) been used in planning for Paisley's return?
  - Is there a collaborative relationship between the biology teacher and the special education staff surrounding Paisley's inclusion? For example, co-planning or problem-solving practices.

References:

Larochelle-Audet, J., Magnan, M.-O., Doré, E., Potvin, M., St-Vincent, L.-A. et Gélinas Proulx, A. (2020). Diriger et agir pour l'équité, l'inclusion et la justice sociale : boîte à outils pour les directions d'établissement d'enseignement. Observatoire sur la formation à la diversité et l'équité. *Repéré à* : http://collections.banq.qc.ca/ark:/52327/bs4027379

Rousseau, N., Point, M., Desmarais, K. et Vienneau, R. (2017). Conditions favorables et défavorables au développement de pratiques inclusives en enseignement secondaire : les conclusions d'une métasynthèse. *Revue canadienne de l'éducation*, 40(2), 1–29.

Rousseau, N., Thibodeau, S., St-Vincent, L.-A., Point, M. et Desmarais, M.-É. (2019). Le leadership de la direction d'école : son influence sur la mise en place de pratiques plus inclusives au secondaire. *Revue ERADE*, 2(1), 26–42.

St-Vincent, L.-A. (2017). *L'agir éthique de la direction d'établissement scolaire. Fondements et résolution de problèmes.* Québec: Presses de l'Université du Québec.

Thibodeau, Gélinas-Proulx, St-Vincent, Leclerc, Labelle et Ramel, 2016. La direction d'école : un acteur crucial pour l'inclusion scolaire. Dans Prud'homme, L., Duchesne, H., Bonvin, P., et Vienneau, R. (dir)., pp. 57–70. De boeck.

Name: Lise-Anne St-Vincent & Nadia Rousseau
Position: Professors
Institutional Affiliation: Université du Québec à Trois-Rivières

Resources

Books

Dempster, K., & Robbins, J. (2017). *How to build communication success in your school: A guide for school leaders.* Routledge

The books by Karen Dempster and Justin Robbins, gives a step-by-step process of how to build effective communication in schools. The book includes strategies and planning materials to get the best teachers, improve leadership and management skills, work with parents and what to do in a crisis. These key topics are important stepping stones for any school leader to help create an effective school environment that is centered around communication.

Videos

Katherine Hampsten. (2016, February). *How miscommunication happens (and how to avoid it)* [Video]. TED-ed. https://www.ted.com/talks/katherine_hampsten_how_miscommunication_happens_and_how_to_avoid_it?language=en

This video features Katherine Hampsten on TED-ed and can help answer some questions about why miscommunication happens. Communicating with teachers as a school administrator can be difficult and complicated, so better understanding why and how miscommunication happens may help solve a small amount of that problem. The end of the video also includes a few practices on how to improve communication and have less miscommunication.

Academic Articles

Clark-Howard, K. (2019). Inclusive education: How do New Zealand secondary teachers understand inclusion and how does this understanding influence their practice? *Kairaranga*, 20(1), 46–57. ISSN 1175-9232

This article examines how forty-four secondary school teachers truly feel about inclusive education. While the teachers believed that inclusive education is important, they also felt unprepared and that teachers who were specially trained would do a better job. There are also a number of barriers that the teachers who took part in the study identified as affecting special education students' achievement.

Sider, S., Maich, K., & Morvan, J. (2017). School principals and students with special education needs: Leading inclusive schools. *Canadian Journal of Education,* 40(2), 1–31. Retrieved from http://journals.sfu.ca/cje/index.php/cjerce/article/view2417/2433

While this entire document is a great resource, look specifically at the "School culture and leadership" section starting halfway down on page 16 and finishing on page 18. This section of the study talks about how it is not just the teachers who create an inclusive school culture, the custodians and secretaries and other support staff also come in contact with students with special education needs and therefore also need to help create an inclusive school climate. The document also talks about advocacy for the student on behalf of the principal to create that inclusive school culture.

Professional Articles

Inclusive education Canada. (2013). *School principals leading the way to inclusive schools: Implementation steps for moving forward.* Inclusive Education Canada. https://inclusiveeducation.ca/wp-content/uploads/sites/3/2013/07/School-Principals-Leading-the-Way-to-Inclusive-Education.pdf

This PDF presented by Inclusive Education Canada was created for principals to help them implement inclusive education more effectively in their schools. The document includes a number of flow charts to help with understanding what inclusive education is, how to implement it and different levels of support. This comprehensive document is a quick overview of what public education is and why it is important that it is inclusive and how principals can make it inclusive.

Websites

LeadToInclude. (2021). *Supporting principals and school leaders as they develop inclusive school environments.* https://www.leadtoinclude.org/resources

This is the website for the Lead to Include research team, two of whom are the authors of this book. The website hosts a lot of great resources for principals and those responsible for their professional development. There are five "choose your own adventure" cases that have branching scenarios for decisions. There are also a wide variety of refereed journal articles, professional articles, podcasts, and websites to support inclusive school leadership.

Meador, D. (2019, January 29). *How principals can provide teacher support.* Thought Co. https://www.thoughtco.com/suggestions-for-principals-to-provide-teacher-support-3194528

In Derrick Meador's article on how principals can support teachers, he offers the techniques to try out. Many of the techniques that Meador recommends are similar ways in which teachers support their students. He says to have their back, be consistent and encourage them to bring problems to you, among other things.

LD @ School (n.d.) *Resources*. https://www.ldatschool.ca/resources/

The LD @ School website has a vast amount of information on learning disabilities to help educators, administrators, and parents be better informed about students with learning disabilities. There are resources, online modules and an educators' institute which can be accessed for a fee, while the resources and articles are all available free of charge. Using the search function, allows for specific resources to be found.

Chapter 14

Truly Inclusive?

CASE 3: SECONDARY SCHOOLS

Crosscutting Themes: Communication, Relationships/Trust.
Leadership Competencies: Lived Experience of Students, Professional Learning, Problem-solving, Embodies Professional Standards.

Zahra's Perspective

My name is Zahra, and I'm starting grade eleven at Bayview High. Six years ago I was diagnosed with a learning disability that causes me to have a hard time with my "cognitive processing," but I'm not totally sure what that means. It takes me a really long time to write papers, and I don't always understand what the teacher wants from me. I use an iPad in my classes, which helps speed up my writing process, and I do practice activities and quizzes on it. All of my teachers and the school principal, Mr. Laird, have been pretty nice. They've always been accommodating and have let me use the iPad in all my classes.

In grade nine, everyone thought it was *so* cool that I was allowed to use an iPad in class. I think some of the other kids were jealous of me. Looking back, I think it honestly helped me to make a lot of friends. But now that I'm starting grade eleven, I feel like the iPad sets me apart from everyone else. I feel like the iPad totally labels me as the "student who needs extra help" and singles me out from my classmates.

I've lost some friends over the past couple of years because everyone knows I have a disability. I guess people don't want to be friends with someone who has a disability. It really sucks to lose friends.

Figure 14.1 A Student Feeling Like They Do Not Fit In. *Source*: https://www.istockphoto.com. Credit: skynesher.

I've tried telling my parents that I don't need the iPad anymore but the conversation always ends with me slamming my bedroom door and shouting some choice words at my parents because they say I have to use it.

Mr. Laird's Perspective

I have been the principal at Bayview for the past four years. We pride ourselves on our excellent special education program. We have two classes for students with special education needs and have two paraprofessionals in each of the classes to provide extra specialized care to students. Many of our students with special education needs are in regular classes and may receive occasional support from one of our special education teachers. Our students have access to some of the best assistive technology in the region. For example, many of our students with disabilities have their own devices such as iPads and Chrome Books, which I'm particularly proud to offer.

I'm also proud that these students are a part of our school community; they attend assemblies, sports games, and holiday events. Bayview is truly an inclusive school!

Yesterday, Mrs. Carr, a grade eleven English teacher, mentioned to me that one of her students with a learning exceptionality had sworn at her during class and had run out of the room crying. The student was also refusing to use

Figure 14.2 Student Using Assistive Technology. *Source*: https://www.istockphoto.com. Credit: zoranm.

her support iPad. Mrs. Carr wanted some advice about how best to approach the situation.

Zahra's Perspective

Yesterday in my English class the teacher, Mrs. Carr, announced, "By Wednesday, everyone must hand in an essay featuring an alternative ending of Macbeth. Be creative." And then, as an afterthought, Mrs. Carr said, "Except Zahra, just send it to me by email by Friday night if you can. But don't stress if you can't get it done."

I was so embarrassed that she singled me out so obviously—no teacher had done that before. I could feel my face turning red like a tomato as the other students turned to face me.

"I'll get it done," I muttered. I was ashamed that she brought attention to the fact that I need more help than my classmates.

Then one of the guys, Kyle, muttered, "Or maybe go to the class for *disabled* kids and stay there." Some of the other students laughed at his comment.

My heart was racing. I couldn't take it. I screamed at Kyle and Mrs. Carr and began swearing up a storm. Then I ran out of the classroom, crying. I went straight to the girl's washroom to hide. I wondered if anyone would come and find me, but no one did. Not even Mrs. Carr. I ended up staying in the washroom until the bell rang for the end of the day and then caught the bus home.

Mr. Laird's Perspective

Zahra came into my office very emotional and told me how embarrassed she was when Mrs. Carr singled her out in class the day before. My heart went out to her. I understood why she was so embarrassed. She told me that she didn't want to use her support iPad anymore. "The iPad shows the other students that I have a disability," she complained. "I don't want to be singled out anymore."

I told Zahra that she didn't need to use the iPad if she didn't want to. She looked relieved. She then went on to say that she didn't feel like she belonged at the school. She told me that she had hid in the washroom after the incident in Mrs. Carr's class and no one had come to find her. "It showed me that no one cares about me at this school," Zahra cried, tears streaming down her face. "No one even cared to check up on me to see if I was okay. Not even my own teacher."

I was shocked by Zahra's words. I had always thought that Bayview was an inclusive community for students with special education needs. But this was the first time I had actually sat down with a student and heard their perspective on what it is like to be a student with a special education need at the school. *I've been wrong this entire time*, I thought, feeling defeated. *How can I help students like Zahra know that they're a part of this school?*

Questions To Consider:

1. If you were Mr. Laird, how would you support Zahra? What would your next steps be?
2. What would be your approach to talk with Mrs. Carr about her actions?
3. How can you build an inclusive culture in a high school environment? How can you show students with special education needs that they are a part of a school community?
4. What are some examples of effective inclusive education practices that you have seen in high schools?

Expert Opinion

This case study highlights how easy it is for an administrator to see the surface layer of their school culture and belief system and be content. In reality it is the role of the school principal to continually assess practices in their school to determine areas of strength to build upon as well as identify areas that do not appropriately meet the complex needs of students and replace them. Principal Laird believed Bayview to be a very inclusive school for students with special education needs. Now, he is questioning his view of the school culture. His assessment of the nature and degree of inclusivity at his school was based on very superficial criteria suggesting he may lack a depth of understanding of special education and school inclusivity. It also indicates that inclusivity is not part of his ongoing school improvement plan. What if any intentional and very purposeful steps are the principal taking as a school leader to ensure a continuous move toward school inclusivity?

A strong school leader is always working with their staff and students on a continuous plan for improvement and growth. While this principal may be focused on other areas of school improvement, equity and inclusion must be at the inner core of what school administrators do if they are genuinely working to improve student achievement and close gaps.

After reviewing his school improvement plan a beginning point for Principal Laird may be to strategically select a group of staff and students to go on an equity walk through their school. A great deal about school culture, beliefs, and what a school values can be learned through observing the intentional and unintentional messages portrayed on the walls of the hallways, common spaces such as the library and cafeteria, and the classrooms of a school. It would be important to have clear criteria of what are indicators of inclusion and what things around their building give a non-inclusive or exclusionary message?

This case raises the question of how do we prepare vice principals and principals to lead truly inclusive schools? Special education is discussed during principal's qualification courses; however the focus is mainly on the legal requirements of a principal in the area of special education. In reality, unless a principal seeks it out there is limited mandatory professional development for administrators in this area. Research indicates that specific leadership practices including building a school vision for special education, ongoing professional development, and shared leadership are intentional principal actions that will help move a school toward inclusivity.

This case illuminates the need for all administrators to have a deep understanding of special education needs and the importance of an inclusive school. Once they have gained the knowledge they require further professional development to enable them to create that environment is necessary.

Name: Carolyn Salonen
Position: Principal
Institutional Affiliation: Waterloo Region District School Board

Resources

Books

Pawlas, G. (2013). *The administrator's guide to school-community relations*. Routledge.
George Pawlas created this book not only as a piece of educational literature, but also an interactive book. The book itself includes examples of community projects, school brochures, school videos, and parent engagement. All of these resources ultimately show how to bring your school and the wider community together.

Videos

Denver Academy. (2012, October 16). *How are you smart? What students with learning disabilities are teaching us* [Video]. YouTube. https://www.youtube.com/watch?v=OdqaUcq7YVQ
The Denver Academy is a high school dedicated to helping all students achieve their full academic potential. The video itself follows four students and their teacher as they use different techniques for students who have a learning disability. The strategies introduced in the video are used with high school students and so are age appropriate.

Iowa Student Learning Institute. (2016, February 26). *It makes us feel stupid: School from a special education student perspective* [Video]. YouTube. https://www.youtube.com/watch?v=WQ1BjgI55YE
The video shared by Iowa Student Learning Institute is all about seeing school from the perspective of a student with special education needs. By seeing what students with special education needs need from their teachers and schools, everyone can be more prepared to help them. The video not only shares how students feel but also calls to action others who can make a difference in their education.

Academic Articles

Robinson, K. (2018). Four secondary teachers' perspectives on enhancing the inclusion of exceptional students. *Exceptionality Education International, 28*(1), 1–21.
The study by Kyle Robinson sought to understand how secondary school teachers include students with special education needs in their classroom. The study found that these four specific teachers not only looked to certain learning and assessment practices that would best support these specific students, but which supported all their students. This study helps to understand that educators support all of their students in what they need, not just those identified as needing support.

Professional Articles

Cunningham, T. (2020). *How do I choose between the different types of assistive technology to make sure my students have the tools they need to succeed?* LD@school. https://www.ldatschool.ca/choose-assistive-technology/
Knowing what assistive technology to use for students and how to use can be a serious problem in the classroom. This article written by Todd Cunningham helps to

fix just that problem. On the LD @ school website, this article uses a case study with solutions to help understand how to use assistive technology in the classroom for students with learning disabilities. There is also a section explaining the benefits of different types of assistive technology as well as frequently asked questions.

Perras, C. (2015). *Learning disabilities and mental health.* LD@schools. https://www.ldatschool.ca/learning-disabilities-and-mental-health/

This article by Cindy Perras talks about the risk of mental problems for those that have a learning disability. The article includes facts as well as links to other resources, like the Ontario Ministry of Education Supporting Minds document, and the ABCs of Mental Health by SickKids. With all the links to other places in the article it also provides the reader with information on each link and an overview of signs of mental health problems among adolescents.

Websites

Ontario Teachers' Federation. (n.d.). *Learning disabilities.* TeachSpecEd. http://www.teachspeced.ca/?q=node/695

This website presented by the Ontario Teachers Federation shares different teaching strategies for learning disabilities. The strategies can be geared toward anger management, assistive technology, self-advocacy skills, or self-esteem to name a few. By clicking one of the strategies provided, the next page presents specific techniques to help improve the specific behavior that the student is exhibiting.

COMMUNITY SUPPORTS

Chapter 15

Involving Community Programs
The Case of Aki

CASE 1: COMMUNITY SUPPORTS

Crosscutting Themes: Parent/Caregivers/Family, Advocacy.
Leadership Competencies: Policies and Procedures, Embodies Professional Standards, Communication, Problem-solving, Lived Experience of Students, Contextual.

I was in many different teaching and administrative roles before I began my position as vice principal of an elementary school in southern Manitoba, Canada. I am Indigenous myself and when I first began teaching, I was a resource teacher at a small school board in a far northern town in the province. Perhaps it was really a village. In any case, I facilitated workshops for teachers on Indigenous knowledge to equip my teachers with the tools needed to support Indigenous students in their classes and to incorporate Indigenous teaching methods.

The school I'm at now also has a significant Indigenous population. Many of these students have also been identified with special education needs. I try to help staff members understand why it is important to include Indigenous teachings and approaches in their lesson plans while also ensuring that their lessons are differentiated to include all our students with special education needs. Some staff members feel ill-equipped to bring in Indigenous knowledge because their own understandings are so limited. I always try to reassure the teachers that even though they don't know everything, trying, learning, and starting where they are is better than not including any indigenous aspects at all. I also encourage the staff to reach out to their community and see if they can find Indigenous people to come in and talk to our students.

Figure 15.1 Traditional Loom Weaving. *Source*: https://www.istockphoto.com. Credit: Natalia Plankina.

One of our grade five students, Aki, has posed some particular challenges. She transferred to our school last year in the middle of grade four. Aki seems to display signs of what looks like some sort of extreme social anxiety. It was very challenging for her to adjust to a new school and all the new routines that come with this kind of change. She seems to be extremely nervous around people and is very self-conscious. She seems to be isolating herself from other kids in her class, so she doesn't have many friends. She also has a very hard time coming to school in the mornings.

One morning I witnessed Aki crying and screaming at her mom, Megis, in the school parking lot. Aki clearly didn't want to leave her mom and her mom told me this happens almost every morning—and nobody helps. Eventually, Megis had to basically pry her daughter carefully out of the car and carry her into the school as Aki screamed and struggled to get down.

The school team, which includes Jill, the special education resource teacher, and I, often meet to discuss ways to help support Aki. She is allotted two breaks during the school day where she is able to go to the resource room to read for 15 minutes. She is an avid reader, and we found that independent activities, like reading, really seem to help to calm her anxious feelings. She also has the option to go to the library during some of the nutrition breaks to find books to read.

A few weeks ago, an interesting situation arose with Aki's mother. She met with Jill and I and expressed her concerns about Aki's anxiety. She told us that she is really worried about Aki since she didn't seem to have any friends at school. Megis also said that Aki often tries to hide in the house so that she doesn't have to go to school. She wants her daughter to "be like everyone else" and have a positive experience at school, but Megis wasn't sure how to help her daughter. And she wasn't sure anyone else did, either. She went on to say that her family is Indigenous. She acknowledged all of the hard work that our school has accomplished over the years in terms of creating a positive environment for Indigenous peoples. But she said that she wanted Aki to feel like she could embrace her culture in her class and she hoped that this might "bring her out of her shell."

As Megis was talking, I started to wonder if we should connect with an outside organization to provide help for Aki. I immediately thought of Lesterwood, a local organization that provides help to children with special needs. I knew that Lesterwood had a specific program for students with severe social anxiety. I wondered if the program might be a good fit for Aki. I also learned a number of the staff members at the organization were indigenous and might be able to help Aki embrace her heritage.

"Have you ever heard of Lesterwood?" I asked Megis. She shook her head.

> It's a great organization for kids with special needs. They actually have a program that might be beneficial for Aki. The program helps kids cope with their social anxiety and gives them different strategies to use when they start to feel anxious. A number of kids from the school go there.

Megis immediately wanted more information. "Where is this organization? Does the program run after school? Who should I contact?" she asked. I didn't know all of the answers, so I looked up Lesterwood's website and jotted down some contact information on a sticky note for Megis to take home.

Two days after our team meeting, I got a phone call from Megis. She sounded defeated. "You never told me that there is a fee to attend programs at Lesterwood," she said. "I can't afford to send Aki there. I was so excited about this possibility but I don't have the money."

I was about to respond, but Megis didn't give me a chance.

"Can the school help me cover the fee?" she asked quickly. "I don't like to ask for charity, but I am desperate here. Aki needs help. *Please*? Can you please help me with this?"

Questions to Consider

1. How do you feel about the principal's suggestion of a community program when the family was seeking support in the school?
2. How would you respond to the question Megis raises at the end?

Figure 15.2 Student Not Wanting to Leave Parent. *Source*: https://www.istockphoto.com. Credit: fstop123.

3. What community supports exist in your local community to which you can connect local families?
4. How can you support a student with what seems to be social anxiety?

Expert Opinion

School can be a challenging setting for children who are uncomfortable in social situations. After all, most activities at school—formal and informal—involve some kind of social interaction. The information, in this case, suggests that social interactions are a prominent source of struggle for Aki, however, I have a number of concerns about the school response, and I am not convinced that it is in Aki's best interests to attend a special school.

My first area of concern is the principal's communication to Megis about a "program (that) helps kids cope with their social anxiety." The implication in this statement is that the principal has decided that Aki suffers from a kind of mental illness called social anxiety. Because educators spend so much time with children throughout the school year, they are in an excellent position to note behaviors and signs of distress that seem outside the norm. However, the principal has offered a diagnostic opinion by assuming that Aki's distress is caused by social anxiety. Diagnosis is a licensed act only allowed by certain regulated mental health professionals. These licensed professionals have several years of post-secondary education and specialized training that allows them to make diagnoses. Although Aki *may* suffer from social anxiety, there are many different types of anxiety disorders, and a number of mental health disorders with overlapping symptomology. Only a mental health professional can and should determine if Aki's mental health challenges warrant a diagnosis, and if so, what that diagnosis is.

Educators can avoid diagnosing the struggles of students by communicating objectively about behavior seen and heard and resisting the temptation to *interpret* that behavior. In this situation, the conversation with Aki's mother might be an opportunity for the principal to say,

> I have seen Aki's struggle to leave you to come into the school. I have also found that Aki seems nervous around people, self-conscious, and has difficulty making friends. It sounds like you and I are seeing very similar issues.

This statement lets Megis know that the school staff are aware of Aki's struggles and concerned about her well-being, without suggesting that Aki suffers from a mental health disorder.

Another area of concern is in regards to potential missed opportunities to connect with Megis prior to this conversation. Efforts to support struggling students will be much more effective when there is a strong home-school connection and a positive working relationship among all people. Aki's continued struggles to settle into her new school are a signal to staff to build a trusting and open relationship with Megis, thereby laying the foundation to create a team to support Aki's school needs. This foundation also increases the likelihood of more positive outcomes when difficult conversations are required. Witnessing Megis having to pry her daughter out of the car is one such example. A follow-up phone call would have been helpful, first as an opportunity to offer a listening ear to a mother who was likely very distressed by this experience, and second, as an opportunity to invite the mother to a meeting to generate ideas for what can be done to help Aki (rather than waiting for Megis to approach the school).

In terms of generating ideas for assisting Aki, a philosophy of inclusive education invites all parties to think about ways in which the school environment can be reimagined to meet the needs of students. First, however, there needs to be shared communication of what everyone is seeing and experiencing, what is working, what is not working, what changes everyone wants to see, what is feasible and what is not. Had this conversation taken place, Megis' ideas regarding bringing more of Aki's indigenous culture into the classroom might have received the time and attention they deserve. It also would have clarified that solutions involving any kind of significant financial expenditure are not realistic for either the family or the school.

In this scenario, the conversation moved immediately to a solution generated by the principal, and the solution offered by the school located the problem solely within Aki. The suggested solution was to remove Aki from the school so that she can learn to "cope with . . . social anxiety." Even allowing Aki to use the library to "calm her anxious feelings" involved isolating Aki from her peers. Although seemingly effective in the short term, this response did not help Aki feel more comfortable, happy and engaged in the classroom.

To support the creation of solutions using an inclusive approach it is helpful to imagine the end goal—Aki happily waving goodbye to her mother and running into the building to be with her friends, in a school where she knows her education will fit within her culture, and her culture will be celebrated and nurtured. Once the student, family and school develop a shared vision of a positive future, they can work backward to determine what needs to be done to reach this goal. Certainly removing Aki to Lesterwood is unlikely to reach this goal, although individual or family counseling may assist along the way. Allowing Aki to isolate herself in the library does not help her reach the goal either. However, there are a number of other approaches that might bring everyone closer to the desired outcomes, such as using dim lighting in the classroom, introducing more quiet and calm time in the classroom, bringing more books and activities with an indigenous focus into the classroom, and pairing Aki to work occasionally with another student with a calm and quiet temperament. As Aki's confidence and comfort grows, new activities can be introduced, such as joining another student for an outdoor activity at lunchtime.

In summary, we best serve our students suffering from any kind of mental distress by refraining from making assumptions about the nature of that distress, by building a strong working relationship with the family in which everyone's input is welcomed and valued, and thinking creatively about how to reimagine the school environment so that a shared vision of success is realized.

Name: Carolyn FitzGerald
Position: Assistant Professor
Institutional Affiliation: Wilfrid Laurier University

Resources

Videos

Montgomery County Public Schools TV. (2018, June 15). *FYI... Parent engagement and MCCPTA advocacy* [Video]. YouTube. https://www.youtube.com/watch?v=e6gFQiuByDY
This 2018 video can be found posted on the Montgomery County Public Schools TV YouTube channel. The president of the Montgomery County Council of Parent-Teacher Association, Lynne Harris, describes how parents can get involved and

advocate for their child. She mentions that parents have their own skill sets and passions when it comes to school engagement and that they should play to those when navigating how they can participate in the school community. For example, a parent may be passionate about student wellness or nutrition or special education, and many more issues. Harris also suggests that parents, students and teachers engage collaboratively to better benefit the school community.

Academic Articles

Burke, M., Meadan-Kaplansky, H., Patton, K., Pearson, J., Cummings, K., & Lee, C. (2018). Advocacy for children with social-communication needs: Perspectives from parents and school professionals. *The Journal of Special Education,* 51(4), 191–200. doi: 10.1177/0022466917716898

The journal article focuses on advocacy for children with social-communication needs. This article includes perspectives from parents and school professionals. Parents often advocate for special education services, this paper explores this advocacy from an interpersonal exchange standpoint. Parents and school professionals reported similar advocacy strategies, which yielded positive outcomes for children with disabilities. Some parents experienced challenges and felt that school professionals were negatively perceiving parent advocacy, whereas, in fact, school professionals positively perceived parent advocacy. This leads to a conversation on communication and family-school partnerships are explored with future research such as parental approaches, content of IEP meetings, volume and type of requests, as well as perceptions associated with advocacy strategies.

Coyle, S., & Malecki, C. (2018). The association between social anxiety and perceived frequency and value of classmate and close friend social support. *School Psychology Review,* 47(3), 209–225. doi: 10.17105/SPR-2017-0067.V47-3

This study examines the relationship between social support from close friends and social anxiety. This article defines social anxiety, and how it is seen in school. There is a discussion on gender differences, social support as students with higher anxiety often have more negative peer relationships, sources of support, and the importance of considering the aspects of a student's perception of support and the social validity of behaviors from their peers. Frequency of support was negatively correlated with social anxiety which means it is important to keep support moderated in comparison to the perceived importance.

Moghtader, L., & Shamloo, M. (2019). The correlation of perceived social support and emotional schemes with students' social anxiety. *Journal of Holistic Nursing and Midwifery,* 106–112. doi: 10.32598/JHNM.29.2.106

The authors indicate that students with higher perceived social support experiences lower social anxiety. It is important to adapt emotional schemes to help students understand and act on their anxious feelings. An ineffective emotional scheme causes individuals to misunderstand their emotions, or interpret them negatively, augmenting anxiety, adapting emotional schemes involves early intervention strategies, parental and teacher supports. Anxiety is often heightened with test taking and self-regulation, showing that participants looked to support from their parents, teachers and classmates.

Professional Articles

Council of Ontario Directors of Education. (n.d.). *Building partnerships for the future: Engaging parents of students with special needs.* Ontario Directors. http://www.ontariodirectors.ca/CODE_Webinars/files/CODE_Parents_EN.pdf

A three page brochure which supports the belief that positive parents involvement with students with special needs leads to student success. The key elements are described as student achievement, leadership, relationships and communication, school and system climate, and the whole child. These elements are explained further with the "what," "so, what" and the "now what" to provide strategies and options to fulfilling the partnership matrix.

Niblett, B. (2017, April). *What works? Research into practice, facilitating activist education.* http://www.edu.gov.on.ca/eng/literacynumeracy/inspire/research/tips_activist_educators.html

An article written by Blair Niblett which explores social and environmental justice in the classroom to practice and promote achievement, equity and well-being. This professional article explores why schools need activist, what activist educators look like which is designing the environment, ideas and actions. Additionally, the article explores what can teachers do with promoting achievement, equity and well-being through activist education. Finally this article shares the importance of activist education and how it engages students intellectually in learning tasks.

Toulouse, P. (2013, February). *Fostering literacy success for first nations, métis and inuit students.* What Works? Research into Practice.http://www.edu.gov.on.ca/eng/literacynumeracy/inspire/research/WW_Fostering_Literacy.pdf

Dr. Pamela Toulouse wrote this article focusing on literacy success. She focused on a bilingual approach and individualized programs to make real-life connections. It is also critical for educators to embrace a respectful bilingual approach as cultural and community nuances are embedded in these dialects. Literacy methods need to represent this uniqueness. She goes on to list practices which would benefit students such as engaging and motivating resources and real-world connections. It is important to foster an environment of confidence and showcase the students' world views, personal identity, and experience.

Hasan, S. (2018, August). *Social phobia factsheet for schools.* KidsHealth.https://kidshealth.org/en/parents/social-phobia-factsheet.html

A professional resource from Kids Health which outlines resources for parents, this article outlines what teachers should know about social anxiety, some examples of what students with social phobia may experience, as well as what teachers and parents can do to help their student/child. At the end of the article there are more suggested articles for parents, kids, and teens to explore.

Websites

Anxiety Canada. (n.d.) *Social anxiety disorder.* https://www.anxietycanada.com/articles/social-anxiety-disorder/

This website is a resource for those to understand how students with social anxiety disorder experience difficulties in school or home. This website explains how anxiety impacts students at school from the early years all the way to high school and beyond. There is a downloadable coping strategies resource accessible.

Canadian Teachers' Federation. (2021, May 3). *Mental health.* https://www.ctf-fce.ca/?s=mental+health&x=0&y=0.

The Canadian Teachers' Federation compiled a list of resources, activitiesm, and supports that educators can use to support the mental health of their students. Under this website, there is a redirect to articles which challenge mental health stigma in classrooms, mental health resources, exploring mental health in the classroom, how society benefits when you support students' mental health, and more articles on the Canadian Teachers' Federation website.

Hurley K. (2018, September 26). *Classroom accommodations to help the anxious child at school.* Psycom.https://www.psycom.net/classroom-help-anxious-child-at-school/

The article written by Katie Hurley 8 is a parents' guide to getting your children support which is needed for their success. The article explores anxiety disorder through definition, along with ways to help kids such as physical and mental health. An explanation of anxiety and learning explains the difficulties children face and then what accommodations can be explored and implemented to help students feel less anxious in schools such as more time, modified tests, a scribe for notes and preferential seating.

Ontario College of Teachers. (2018, November 8). *Professional advisory: Supporting students' mental health.* Ontario College of Teachers https://www.oct.ca/Home/Resources/Advisories/Mental%20Health

This website offers very clear guidelines as to the roles, responsibilities and limits of educators working with students suffering from mental distress. Specifically discussing supporting students mental wellness, the Ontario College of Teachers provides insights to the realities of mental health disorders provided by the World Health Organization, defines the role of teachers and professional standards and responsibilities. Finally, the article explores policy, and advice for supporting student mental health as well as prompting teachers to use a self-reflective framework to improve their practice (included).

Ontario Ministry of Education. (2020, May 7). *Special needs support.* Children.govon.ca.http://www.children.gov.on.ca/htdocs/english/specialneeds/index.asp

This website provides resources and services for mental health, rehabilitation, coordinated service planning and various exceptionalities such as autism, developmental disabilities, and fetal alcohol spectrum disorder. This website also provides links to financial and respite supports as well as various other supports and services for specific populations.

Chapter 16

The Case of Sahar Said

CASE 2: COMMUNITY SUPPORTS

Crosscutting Themes: Communication, Parents/Caregivers/Family, Advocacy.

Leadership Competencies: Contextual, Fosters Relationships, Professional Learning, Differentiated Leadership, Collaboration.

Greenhaven School has experienced an influx of Syrian refugee students in the past two years. This new population of students has made Greenhaven a more diverse environment which has, of course, come along with other changes.

Greenhaven's principal, Stan Russel, tends to focus his attention on helping staff members adjust to their changing school environment. Stan believes that, as the school population diversifies, so should the school's policies, events, and even their goals. His staff members have shown some resistance, however, to these new changes—both to the changes themselves and to the direction of the changes. Many of the teachers have taught at the school for over ten years and they appear to be the ones that are having more difficulty adjusting. Stan's approach to these struggles is to implement extra professional development, both during and after school hours. Stan's priority is that the teachers adapt their teaching approaches to best meet the needs of the changing population of students.

One of these new students, Sahar Said, is struggling with her transition to a new school, a new town, and a new country. Sahar often appears to become extremely angry. She shows agitation to the point where she yells, screams, and throws objects violently at anyone near to her. Each time such aggression occurs, her teacher, Jenny Ling, calls the special education resource teacher,

Figure 16.1 Diverse Students Reading Together. *Source*: https://www.istockphoto.com. Credit: FatCamera.

Eric Fisher, to take Sahar out of the classroom and help her calm down. Sahar's behavior has become quite a disturbance for the classroom environment and Jenny is concerned about the rest of her students who deserve a peaceful environment for learning.

During school-based team meetings, Eric has shared stories that Sahar has told him about her life in Syria and also in Lebanon when her family was living there as refugees. Eric is worried that Sahar's emotional issues and her behavior are both the result of trauma she has experienced. The school team has also considered the impact of Sahar's home life on her behavior. She is the eldest child in a family of seven. Her mother, Leila, is six months pregnant as well, so the family will soon be welcoming a new baby. Sahar's father is trying to find work, but hasn't been successful, so finances are tight. The whole family lives in a cramped, two-bedroom apartment—which seems difficult—even though they regularly share that they are grateful to be safe and together.

One morning, Stan stopped by Jenny's classroom to connect with her, as he tries to do with every teacher every week—at least once. During this drop-in visit, Jenny voiced that Sahar was disturbing other students and was even frightening some of them with her extreme behavior. Jenny even admitted that she was a little frightened when Sahar started up with her anger and aggression.

"Stan, I want to do everything I can to help Sahar and to help her adjust to this school," Jenny said.

I want her to feel welcome, but I am finding it increasingly difficult. Sahar keeps interrupting my lessons. I feel like I can't stay caught up with the curriculum, or even get to it at times. I worry about how this will impact the other students in the classroom. The violence worries me and, frankly, I'm exhausted. Everyday I'm dealing with screaming, throwing, and more. I have always loved teaching, but these days I find myself dreading going to work. I want to help Sahar, but I just don't know if this is the right environment for her. What kind of ideas do you have? Would there be a way to get her transferred somewhere else? Maybe another school would have better—or more—resources that would benefit Sahar?

Stan took a minute to think about his response, rather taken aback. He knew how exhausting this situation was for Jenny and he didn't blame her for feeling this way. But he didn't appreciate Jenny's idea of transferring Sahar elsewhere. He has heard other schools administrators discuss having certain difficult students transferred so that they were no longer their problem. But Stan thought, *If we all did that, then where would the student have to go?* He was not a fan of school exclusion as problem-solving. He explained his thoughts to Jenny, who looked unsatisfied with his response. As the days passed, she continued to express her frustration and exhaustion while hinting at the possibility of Sahar moving to another class or even school.

While contemplating this situation over a very early morning coffee the next week, Stan suddenly thought of the local family and children services branch, which provides assistance to children and their families going through tough times. He wondered if Sahar could get help from this service. Maybe she could get connected with a counselor to work through some of the trauma she experienced. As soon as the clock struck a reasonable hour, Stan called Sahar's parents to discuss this possible support. Sahar's mom, Leila, answered the phone.

"Hello Mr. Russell," Leila said, her English speaking skills still hesitant, "Nice to hear from you."

"Hi," Mrs. Said. "I am calling today because I wanted to tell you about a community organization that might help Sahar," Stan began. "It's called family and children services. They offer counseling to children and other support programs to help them with their behavior."

Leila cut Stan off. "Counseling? My daughter does not need counseling."

"Well, Sahar's teacher has noticed some behavior that is concerning. When Sahar gets angry in class she sometimes throws things. It might be helpful if Sahar got some extra help."

"No!" Leila cried. "No! My daughter is fine! She does not need help!" And with that, Sahar's mother hung up the phone.

Questions To Consider:

1. How would you respond to a similar situation? What could the principal have done differently while engaging with Sahar's mother?
2. What might you tell a teacher, like Jenny Ling, who expresses her frustrations about a student with special education needs? How do you support a teacher who doesn't want to include a student and who does not feel responsible for that student any longer?
3. How would you create an inclusive environment in a school that experiences such a drastic change in its student population? What types of local community—or other— supports might you seek to help support this growth?

Expert Opinion:

The main ideas that transpired for me in this case were two-fold: Sahar's personal circumstances dictated the way teachers saw her in the class, and her teachers, namely Jenny, were more interested in getting her transferred to another school than in finding out about her problems and how to help her succeed.

This case is typical of situations where school staff hastily jump to conclusions based on personal biases and lack of judgment. If the Syrian refugee context is removed and the student's name is Sarah Whiteside, the treatment she received would have been different. Most likely, the three steps below would have been first in mind:

1. Jenny and Eric would document all the incidents and keep a good record of the different behaviors exhibited by Sahar.
2. Sahar's teachers would have informed Mr. Russel, the school principal, and contacted her parents multiple times about any disturbances and achievement issues.
3. After the first two steps, Mr. Russel and his staff would have explored with Sahar's parents the possibility of considering a written request to refer Sahar to an Identification, Placement, and Review Committee (IPRC). The IPRC would decide then whether Sahar has special needs, and if so, what type of educational placement is appropriate for her to be successful.

One central issue in this case is the deficit mindset that informs all the interactions and discussions regarding Sahar's situation. From the principal to the most experienced teachers, no one seems to see the influx of Syrian refugee students as an asset that can enrich the culture of the school. Additionally, judgment is made based on Sahar's home life and her family's socioeconomic status, with seven children and a baby on the way, without taking into account any comparative cultural considerations. The school team just established the cause and effect relationship irrespective of the views coming from the family. That very fact is the opposite of the notion of inclusion that rejects perceptions of differences as deficits favoring those of understanding and honoring diversity (Zaretsky et al., 2008).

At the beginning of the case, Mr. Russel showed some promising signs of great leadership as a school principal. He understood the need to focus his attention on helping his staff adjust to their changing school environment through professional development. That is very commendable for a principal. He demonstrated that he understood that teachers needed to adapt their teaching approaches to their changing student population and not the other way around. However, all this glimmer of hope was evaporated due to the way the call with Sahar's mom, Mrs. Leila Said, was handled and ended abruptly.

In terms of school leadership, Mr. Russel may have attempted to develop people by focusing on professional development.

However, he fell short by not considering some other aspects of his role that would have been instrumental in supporting Sahar as well as her teachers. These aspects are the "four broad categories of practices identified in research summaries: setting directions, developing people, redesigning the

Figure 16.2 Teachers Engaging in Professional Learning. *Source*: https://www.istockphoto.com. Credit: Rawpixel Ltd.

organization, and managing the instructional (teaching and learning) programme" (Leithwood et al., 2006, pp. 18–19). While he opposed the transfer of Sahar to another school, there was no real plan to set directions and redesign the organization to address the needs of Sahar as well as the other Syrian refugee students in the school.

Stronger leadership features in these difficult cases are needed to reach better outcomes. If the approaches at the school were better thought out, that would have avoided to have a poor phone conversation that didn't help Sahar's situation.

Involving available community stakeholders toward achieving educational goals for the Syrian refugee students would have been very helpful to bridge the gap between the school and Sahar's family. The case highlights some real disconnection between the school team and the family. It also begs for the following questions:

a) How do schools assess the real needs of children and their families when there are cultural distances between school teams and the people they serve?
b) How do school leaders decide on community resources that are best suited to support children and their families?

References:

Leithwood, K., Day, C., Sammons, P., Harris, A., & Hopkins, D. (2006). *Successful school leadership: What it is and how it influences student learning*. Research Report 800. London, UK: Department for Education.

Zaretsky, L., Moreau, L., & Faircloth, S. (2008). Voices from the field: School leadership in special education. *Alberta Journal of Educational Research*, 54(2), 161–177.

Name: Jhonel Morvan
Position: Former Curriculum Manager at Ontario Ministry of Education; current Superintendent
Institutional Affiliation: Conseil scolaire catholique Nouvelon

Resources

Video

CBC News: The National (2016, May 30). *Struggling to adapt: One Syrian refugee family's story*. [Video]. YouTube. https://www.youtube.com/watch?v=6CFYoJQKM7A

A part of a news special, this video tells the story of a Syrian refugee family as they begin living in Canada, learning English, and sending their children to Canadian schools. This video provides insight into some of the struggles faced by Syrian refugee families, as they must adapt to a whole new country, schooling system, and way of life. The family of nine has seven children, and their struggles and successes in school are documented in this video.

Today. (2017, March 2). *How one high school is welcoming refugee students | TODAY*. [Video]. YouTube. https://www.youtube.com/watch?v=rMGVJu_M-dc

This YouTube video details a high school which has taken in many Syrian refugee students and one way in which they made the transition into American schooling more welcoming. The teachers and students are shown in open circles with native-American and Syrian refugee students, creating a safe space for open communication about where they come from and the rights and norms that they are familiar with. Students and teachers are welcoming the Syrian refugee students by acting as an educational support system, ready to receive information and share it.

Academic Articles

Ennab, F. (2017). *Being involved in uninvolved contexts: Refugee parent involvement in children's education*. Canadian Centre for Policy Alternatives Manitoba. https://www.policyalternatives.ca/sites/default/files/uploads/publications/Manitoba%20Office/2017/04/Refugee_parent_involvement.pdf

Fadi Ennab is the author of this 2017 policy research piece written for the Canadian Centre for Policy Alternatives Manitoba. Fadi explains that parent involvement from refugee parents is crucial for academic success and community development. The author also recognizes that refugee families have unique social needs, and schools may not always provide the culturally sensitive supports that they require. Fadi finds that there are numerous barriers to parent involvement, such as psychosocial barriers, lack of school supports, lack of communication, lack of diverse staff and culturally sensitive training. Recommendations include educators considering parent experiences to avoid misunderstandings, having more accessible and inclusive schools, and advocating and offering more supports.

Thomas, R. L. (2016). The right to quality education for refugee children through social inclusion. *Journal of Human Rights and Social Work*, 1(4), 193–201. doi: 10.1007/s41134-016-0022-z

Thomas explains that the needs of refugee children may be complex due to traumatic experiences, disrupted education, and having to adapt to a new culture. Furthermore, the role of schools is key for refugee children as schools help them find a sense of safety and maximize their learning potential, determining the future for these young refugees. Finally, Thomas suggests strategies that facilitate a larger effort toward social inclusion of refugee children. Through more efforts for social inclusion, refugee childrens' well-being is being taken into consideration and they are allowed to become an integral part of society.

Professional Articles

Carrier, C. (n.d.). *Teacher support for refugee children in Canada.* British Columbia Teachers' Federation.https://bctf.ca/uploadedFiles/Public/SocialJustice/Programs/GlobalEd/Teacher%20Guide%20PDF.pdf

This portable document format file, written by Chris Carrier, is available on the British Columbia Teachers' Federation website. This document was created to be a form of professional development or orientation for educators receiving refugee children into regular classrooms for the first time. Key concepts discussed in this document include culture shock, English language learners, cultural practices, checking for comprehension, adapting curriculum, problematic assumptions, fear, and stress. Some activities and strategies are provided at the end of this document for reducing stress.

Childminding, Monitoring, Advisory and Support Canada. (2015). *Caring for Syrian refugee children: A program guide for welcoming young children and their families.* Childminding, Monitoring, Advisory and Support Canada. https://cmascanada.ca/wp-content/uploads/2015/12/Supporting_Refugees/Caring%20for%20Syrian%20Refugee%20Children-final.pdf

This program guide for welcoming young refugee children and their families was written by Childminding, Monitoring, Advisory and Support Canada (CMAS Canada) in 2015. This program is laid out with an introduction, information about the refugee experience, tip sheets, and resources for further information. Within the refugee experience section, readers may find insights into how both refugee children and parents may be feeling as they transition to living in Canada. Key topics that CMAS touches on include, but are not limited to, anxiety, depression, post-traumatic stress disorder, "overprotective" parents, and difficulty focusing or absorbing information.

Social Sciences and Humanities Research Council of Canada. (2017, October). *Supporting refugee students in Canadian classrooms.* Cities of Migration. http://citiesofmigration.ca/wp-content/uploads/2018/04/What-Works-Monograph_Supporting-Refugee-Students-in-Canadian-Classrooms_Oct.-2017.pdf

This monograph, created by the Social Sciences and Humanities Research Council of Canada, was written in 2017 for the Cities of Migration website. This article mentioned that Canadian educators may be ill-prepared to support refugee students coming to terms with war, violence, trauma and interrupted schooling. Social support has been shown to be one of the highest mediators for refugee children and adolescents undergoing a transition into Canadian schooling. Furthermore, the loss of social networks along with familial stressors can have a large impact on social challenges these children face. Professional development for educators, collaborative multi-level settlement programs for refugee families, and developing partnerships between education and government agencies serving refugees can help refugee students overcome socio-psychological challenges that they face.

Websites

The Canadian Safe School Network. (n.d.). *Welcoming refugee children to the classroom*. The Canadian Safe School Network. https://cssn.me/welcoming-refugee-children-to-the-classroom

This webpage, on The Canadian Safe School Network website, contains information on welcoming refugee students into the classroom and improving immigrant parent involvement. In regards to parents the authors recommend making it clear that parent involvement is encouraged, securing a translator for school events, making all communications home clear to parents, and asking parents who are involved in the school community to "buddy up" with the immigrant parents. Along with this, the article provides strategies for; overcoming language barriers, creating welcoming environments, and discussing the issues in Syria with your classroom.

Madden, M. (2019, September 9). *For Syrian refugee children, back to school brings major challenges*. Concern Worldwide US. https://www.concernusa.org/story/syrian-refugee-children-back-to-school/

Madden sheds light on the stories of many parents and children, who are Syrian refugees. She highlights the value of education and parent engagement in their childrens' education. This article shares real-life stories and struggles, in order for readers to gain a deeper understanding of some of the hardships refugees face. Furthermore, it explains that parents may want to be engaged in their children's education, but there are many barriers that are present in their lives.

Chapter 17

"She Won't Go"

CASE 3: COMMUNITY SUPPORTS

Crosscutting Themes: Advocacy, Communication, Collaboration.
Leadership Competencies: Lived Experience of Students, Problem-solving, Advocacy, Professional Learning, Agency, Values Inclusion, Collaboration.

My school, Fishermann Secondary School, is a unique place to be a vice principal, in my opinion. It's a fairly large, urban school, with just over 1,600 students from a set of very diverse backgrounds. Many of our students have special education needs. I've been at the school for only a short while and I've already experienced a very challenging situation related to a diagnosis in one of our complex adolescents. Let me tell you about it.

One of our grade ten students, Alexander, is diagnosed with bipolar disorder and also experiences anxiety, both of which have been managed through medication for most of his late childhood and early adolescent life so far. The school is aware of Alexander's medical history and the staff have been involved in supporting his parents while his psychiatrist established the correct medication, which was a long and rocky process in itself. This process happened during Alexander's first year at Fishermann when his doctors had him trying a variety of medications to see what worked best. During this time, Alexander really struggled to pay attention in class. He often skipped classes due to what his parents referred to as intense anxiety. He struggled through periods of time that he referred to as dark depression and extreme happiness. This emotional rollercoaster took a toll on his academic performance and social life. Since I am responsible for the special education leadership at our school, I worked quite closely with Alexander's teachers during this bumpy time to support him. By the end of grade nine, Alexander was finally on a medication that was working for him, and at the beginning of grade ten, he had settled into a decent school routine. We saw huge improvements in his grades and social life at school.

But Alexander's mom, Tara, came into my office a few months ago to chat about her son's progress. During our conversation, she *completely* threw me for a loop. She explained that Alexander had decided to have sex reassignment surgery. He was beginning his transition to become female. The school was to call him "Alexis" from now on and use female pronouns with him. I told Tara that we, as a school, would do everything we could to support Alexis during her time of transition.

I was, however, concerned with the situation as I thought about all the struggles that she had faced due to her bipolar disorder and anxiety. I had never worked with a transgender student before—that I knew about—so this was a fairly novel situation for which my reading had not totally prepared me.

Over the past few months, as Alexis has started to transition, we have noticed that her mood swings have intensified. Some days she has so much energy that she is difficult to control in the classroom environment. Other days, it appears like she doesn't have any energy at all. I even found her sleeping in the hallway near her locker one afternoon. At that point, I decided to call Tara to discuss my concerns. When we spoke, Tara expressed her gratitude that I had reached out. She had been meaning to give me a call but just hadn't had the time with everything that was happening. She explained

Figure 17.1 **Identities.** *Source*: https://www.istockphoto.com. Credit: LemonTreeImages.

to me that Alexis has read articles online about the hormonal treatments she is receiving and had learned that the treatments could be less effective if taken with other medications. Alexis then made the rash decision to stop taking her mood-stabilizing medications. Tara explained that she didn't even know if the website that made those claims was accurate or related to her daughter's specific medications. They were on a waiting list to get back to see the specialist doctor to learn more about the facts of this very complicated life transition. As the weeks passed without her medication intact, Alexis' behavior became more and more unmanageable. Her teachers have struggled to keep her in the classroom and her grades have suffered significantly—once again.

It was at that place that I recognized I was at a breaking point. I knew the school didn't have the resources needed to support Alexis. We needed outside help. More help. Better help. I began looking up community support organizations that help people living with mood disorders and found one. I called the organization to ask about the programs they offered. After I had learned about the program consisting of outpatient community groups, I was convinced that it would benefit Alexis. I immediately called Tara to tell her about the organization. She really liked the idea and kept saying how grateful she was to have me as an advocate for her child. I gave her the contact information for the organization and left it in her hands to register Alexis.

A week went by and I received a phone call from Tara. "She won't go," she said. "Alexis won't go to the support program. She says she doesn't need it."

Tara continued. "Alexis isn't making good decisions right now. She isn't taking her medication, she refuses to get any sort of help for her behaviour, she's not thinking clearly. I don't know what to do but something, *anything*, needs to be done." Tara began crying over the phone. "Honestly, I worry that she might be a danger to herself right now. I'm worried that she might try to take her life."

Questions To Consider:

1. What is the most immediate issue here? How would you follow up with this significant concern?
2. What would you say to Tara, who is worried about the student's well-being?
3. What community organizations are there that can support children as they navigate a mood disorder? What about children who undergo sex changes?
4. To what degree can a school get involved if a student refuses to take his/her/their medication?

Figure 17.2 Group Discussion. *Source*: https://www.istockphoto.com. Credit: SDI Productions.

Expert Opinion:

After reading the case, I reflected that although the school indicates an inclusive model in place, the student did not seem to have an inclusive voice regarding their education and accessing community services. From the vice principal's perspective, the student's team involves the mother and the vice principal. The vice principal works closely with the teachers and then, reports back to the mother. From my work in Inclusive Education, I would recommend that this student be provided with a school team to advocate for what is best for his education. Meetings should take place regularly, involving the administration, parent, teachers, community agencies and more importantly, the student. Everybody at the table advocates for the student's educational and community interests to enhance his educational experience.

While the student is transitioning from male to female, the vice principal sets up a few community services that may interest the student. Although as a school leader, this was a proactive idea, the reason I believe it would not work out is that the student was not part of the plan. Research for various services to help the student with the transition, along with other mental health issues require a team effort and the student requires to see how it would benefit their wellness. The community liaison advocate should be part of the student's team. Being included in all aspects of your own life is important for success to occur.

The vice principal in charge of special education diligently provided the resources that were available. He found community services for the student to attend. The intention was good. However, I would recommend that the vice principal branch out to colleagues within the board or district for possible examples on how a similar situation may have been previously handled with a degree of success.

Name: Lillian Scibetta
Position: Instructor
Institutional Affiliation: Brock University

Resources

Books

Manitoba Education and Training. (2017). *Supporting transgender and gender diverse student in Manitoba schools.* Manitoba Education and Training. https://www.edu.gov.mb.ca/k12/docs/support/transgender/full_doc.pdf

Manitoba Education and Training published this policy document regarding supporting transgender and gender diverse students. This document pertains to increasing understanding of trans and gender diverse identities and gender expression, legal and policy frameworks, creating affirming schools, and providing guidelines for supporting and affirming students. A whole school approach to integrating trans and gender diverse students is outlined here along with multiple provincial and international support services available to the public.

National Centre for Transgender Equality. (2017). *Model school district policy on transgender and gender nonconforming students.* National Centre for Transgender Equality. https://transequality.org/sites/default/files/images/resources/trans_school_district_model_policy_FINAL.pdf

The purpose of this document is to foster an educational environment that is safe, welcoming, and free from stigma and discrimination for all students, regardless of gender identity or expression, to facilitate compliance with local, state and federal laws concerning bullying, harassment, privacy, and discrimination, to ensure that all students have the opportunity to express themselves and live authentically. Language, commentary and resources are modeled throughout this district policy. Key topics include correct terminology explanations, bullying, harassment, names, pronouns, student transitions, working with parents, and professional development.

Videos

BP Children. (2011). *Webinar Series 1* [Video]. Vimeo. https://vimeo.com/22245908 #embed

This is the first video in a four-part webinar series focusing on teaching children with bipolar disorder. The segments focus on; understanding your students with bipolar disorder, how bipolar disorder affects learning, development and school, interventions and strategies for your classroom, and tackling tough topics. This particular webinar revolves around seeing the world through the eyes of students with bipolar disorder, and getting a better understanding of how they function.

GLSEN. (2017, November 13). *How to support transgender students* [Video]. Youtube. https://www.youtube.com/watch?v=kq19QdOfH1Y

This YouTube video details how to support transgender students. Children and adolescents speak from differing perspectives within this video to educate viewers on what it means to be a person and student who is transgender, what school is like for a transgender student, and how schools can support transgender students. The individuals in the video provide concrete examples of what they feel has not been handled well by the schools they are in, and what can be done by administrators and staff at schools to better support students who are transgender, like themselves.

Academic Articles

Gelfer, J. I. (1991) Teacher-parent partnerships: Enhancing communications. *Childhood Education*, 67(3), 164–167, doi: 10.1080/00094056.1991.10521602

Gelfer emphasizes that both parents and teachers must view their roles as interdependent in a child's development. Parent-teacher communication can help in providing useful information for parents in helping support their children in school and in the home. Researchers have found that parents want to know what happens to their children while at school and what they can do to help their child at school and at home. Gelfer provides ways for teachers to support their students and parents to support their child, including teachers helping parents learn about resources available to them, including parents in assessing, implementing and evaluating their child's development, and strengthening their ability to provide a positive home environment.

Professional Articles

Egale Canada Human Rights Trust. (n.d.). *Preparing students for the transition of a transgender or gender diverse peer*. Government of Newfoundland and Labrador. https://www.gov.nl.ca/eecd/files/k12_safeandcaring_pdf_preping_students_diverse_peer.pdf

This document outlines the ten steps an educator is recommended to take when they find out a student has decided to affirm their gender identity in their class. The goal is to prepare the student for this transition, minimize potential for bullying or harassment, and equip the classroom students to be strong friends and allies. The beginning steps include modeling a positive attitude, teaching the basics, using affirmative language, and negotiating any slip ups in affirming identity. These are followed by discussing what constitutes as transphobic bullying, reaffirming school's safe learning community for all, stating your availability, and promoting opportunities for self-selected allies.

Child & Adolescent Bipolar Foundation. (2007). *Educating the child with bipolar disorder*. Child & Adolescent Bipolar Foundation. https://www.dbsalliance.org/pdfs/BMPN/edbrochure.pdf

This 12-page document contains information on; what bipolar disorder is, the commonly associated behaviors that come along with it, how it affects cognition and learning, strategies for teaching children who have it, handling changing moods, and using social stories to rehearse new situations. This document is dense with practical strategies and accommodations that can be utilized when teaching children with bipolar disorder.

Websites

Canadian Mental Health Association. (n.d.). *Bipolar disorder*. Canadian Mental Health Association. https://cmha.bc.ca/documents/bipolar-disorder/

The Canadian Mental Health Association has created this webpage to shed some light on what bipolar disorder is. On this page one can find information about this mood disorder, symptoms that could point toward one having this disorder, statistics about those most affected by bipolar disorder, and what can be done if one does have it. Medication, counseling, support groups and self-help are outlined ways to deal with bipolar disorder. At the bottom of the webpage, a list of clickable resources for more information and help can be found.

National Institute of Mental Health. (n.d.). *Bipolar disorder in children and teens*. National Institute of Mental Health. https://www.nimh.nih.gov/health/publications/bipolar-disorder-in-children-and-teens/index.shtml

This webpage, created by the National Institute of Mental Health, is directed at parents, guardians and key adults in the lives of children and teens with bipolar disorder. It provides background information on the disorder, possible causes, prevalent symptoms, and commonly co-occurring issues. Readers can also find information on how the process of diagnosis works, where to go for help, treatment options, and what individuals can expect from the treatment. Some ways for adults to support a child with bipolar disorder outlined include: being patient, encouraging talking, paying attention to triggers and mood changes, and sticking to a treatment plan.

HealthLink BC. (n.d.). *Bipolar disorder in children: school issues*. HealthLink BC. https://www.healthlinkbc.ca/health-topics/ty6942

This webpage recommends working with a child with bipolar disorder to create an individual education plan (IEP) that takes into account their specific needs. Potentially helpful school accommodations are available through this webpage. Some of these accommodations include: reducing homework, extending deadlines, having a later start to the school day, providing small class size, and having a designated and knowledgeable staff member for the student to meet with if needed. At the bottom of this page, readers can click to access related information and resources.

BP Children. (n.d.). *Teachers*. BP Children. https://www.bpchildren.com/teachers

This webpage focuses on the role of a teacher when working with children with bipolar disorder. The page is formatted in a question and answer way, with questions such as: how does bipolar disorder affect a child in the classroom, what accommodations may be helpful, and can a child with bipolar disorder also be gifted? Following this, a bank of resources can be found; these provide information on key topics such as brain abnormalities, cognitive dysfunction, level of stability/flexibility in school and many more.

Transequality: National Centre for Transgender Equality. (n.d.). *What are my rights at school?*. https://transequality.org/know-your-rights/schools

The National Centre for Transgender Equality has created this webpage for transgender students to learn their rights regarding federal and state laws and the U.S. Constitution. This webpage outlines the eight specific rights students who are transgender have within a school environment. Some of these include; the right to be treated according to your gender identity, the right to be called the names and pronouns that match your gender identity, and the right to present yourself according to your gender identity. One section of the webpage explains what students may do if they are being discriminated against, and another provides information about which laws protect transgender students from discrimination at schools.

SCHOOL BOARD SUPPORTS

Chapter 18

Supporting T.J. and Mr. Garcia

CASE 1: SCHOOL BOARD SUPPORTS

Crosscutting Themes: Relationships/Trust, Communication.
Leadership Competencies: Policies and Procedures, Collaboration, Human Resources, Professional Learning, Advocacy.

I've been the vice principal at South Forks Elementary School for almost a year now. I love working here and I have to attribute that to my staff. We work well as a team and all strive to ensure that each staff person feels supported. From my experience as an educator, the teachers and paraprofessionals often work with students with special education needs who need to debrief the most and receive the most support.

Our school board has a tiered system to support students with special education needs. The system is supposed to help us identify students who need various levels of support. One boy in our grade five class at South Forks, T.J., has been at Tier 1 for most of his time at the school. At this tier, students are included in the general classroom with support primarily provided by the classroom teacher. However, due to T.J.'s recent struggles in class, we switched him to Tier 2, which offers increased, individualized support to students. In his case, T. J. received support from a special education teacher for one or two classroom periods a day. Tier 3 supports are the most intensive, often with specialized, long-term one-on-one supports.

The administration decided to make the transition because T. J. has become increasingly aggressive and hostile in class. His teacher, Mr. Garcia, has resorted to removing him from class, which happened far too often for my liking. In the last few months T.J.'s behavior has got so bad that he hasn't been to class at all, and one of our paraprofessionals has worked with him individually in a separate classroom.

The school principal, Geraldine Rhodes, and I have tried to talk to Mr. Garcia about pulling T.J. out of class on such a regular basis. In one of our meetings, I told Mr. Garcia, "We want T.J. included in the class so that he doesn't miss out on valuable relationships with his peers."

In response, Mr. Garcia exclaimed, "It's just so frustrating! He argues with everything I say and refuses to do the things I ask of him. Then, he starts lashing out when he gets frustrated. I'm so tired of it."

We were aware that T.J. had some family history that contributed to his difficulties, which caused us to believe that some other issues were at play as well. I had met with his foster care coordinator early in the year and she shared that T.J. had moved around to a few different homes in recent years, and she thought it had the potential to take a toll on him mentally, physically, and socially. I also guessed it was tough for him because over the last few years, the administration at South Forks had been in transition. Principal Rhodes and I had been brought in of September of last year. I think that if the prior administrators had ensured that T.J. remained in the classroom, he wouldn't be struggling as much as he was now.

As part of T.J.'s transition to Tier 2, we consulted our school board personnel in the special education department. A behavior specialist from the board office and a psychologist were brought in to observe T.J.'s in-class behavior and interactions with other students and Mr. Garcia. They also completed a battery of diagnostic assessment, after which the psychologist determined that T.J. had pronounced learning disabilities and oppositional defiant disorder, indicating that he struggled with obeying and listening to authority.

Geraldine and I sat down with the behavior specialist and the psychologist to discuss how to support T.J. We agreed that it was imperative for him to stay in class—perhaps not all day, but at least for the morning. It was obvious that his self-esteem was plummeting and his marks weren't improving. I had also personally witnessed his embarrassment when the resource teacher came in to remove him from class. All of these factors were causing T.J. to feel excluded at school.

When Geraldine and I sat down with Mr. Garcia to discuss our wishes for T.J.'s new education strategy, he was extremely concerned. "I have 26 other students who need my attention too," he told us. "How am I supposed to support T.J. at the same time?"

We told Mr. Garcia that we could bring in a paraprofessional to assist him for parts of the day and give T.J. the individualized support he needs. But Mr. Garcia wasn't convinced.

"I worry for the safety of my other students if T.J. is in the class," he said. "And, frankly, I worry about my own safety. T.J. can get very aggressive. I worry that something horrible is going to happen if he stays in the room."

The meeting had to end before we came to any conclusion, as Geraldine and I had a meeting at the board office that we needed to attend. A week later, Geraldine came to my office, looking defeated, as she said that she had received a message from the teachers' union about Mr. Garcia's concerns with T.J. The school superintendent had also been contacted and was requesting a meeting with Geraldine.

"This isn't good," Geraldine sighed. "This situation is getting out of control. What do we do?"

Questions To Consider:

1. If you were in the principal or vice-principal's shoes, how would you respond to this situation?
2. What do you do to support teachers who may not feel like they can properly support students with special education needs? What is the process in your district to access supports from the school board?
3. In your district, how do assessments of special education needs take place? What resources are available at the school board office to support principals and teaching staff in schools with regard to students with special education needs?
4. How do you respond when the safety of teachers and other students becomes an issue? What is the communication process for alerting superintendents of issues involving students or teachers?

Expert Opinion:

As an educator of more than thirty years, I come to my position from the lens of a classroom teacher, school counselor, school-based administrator, and district-based administrator. One must be aware of their philosophy of education and acknowledges that there are multiple perspectives on every case study.

Teachers and educational assistants need support and encouragement of both colleagues as well as the school leaders. The leadership of the school needs to find time to de-brief and to listen to what new staff is experiencing and feeling. Books like "Mentoring Matters" by Bruce Wellman and Laura Lipton are great resources for developing a practical guide to working as a school team.

Response to Intervention is a great format to provide support to needed students. It requires the involvement of a school-based team and the collection of data to determine how to move forward with our complex cases.

Figure 18.1 Teacher Completing a Checklist. *Source*: https://www.istockphoto.com. Credit: Eva-Katalin.

To access Tier 3 support, schools would have to share information with the district team to access behavioral supports of district consultants (teachers, counselors, and psychologists) and further behavioral supports. The data could include individual educational plans, positive behavioral support plans, employee safety plans, and school-based team minutes. The school-based team must explain the supports and strategies tried before the district team becomes involved. The school team is required to "own" their student and not necessarily see the district team as a way of removing the student from their home school. School staff and district staff must work together with the student, the family, and the community supports. Often the district team recommends an integrated case management meeting (ICM). These meetings bring together everyone involved in assisting the child's learning, including parents and community support such as behavioral interventionists and mental health clinicians. Parents can also bring advocates to this meeting if they deem that needed. ICMs are opportunities to have meaningful consultations with families and a circle of support for the student to form and work together.

With district involvement, additional strategies could be considered to work successfully with this student. Of course, removing a student from his regular class is not a long-term strategy that our district would support. We would look at all options, such as trying to determine antecedents to his behavior, what lagging skills this student might need help with and also building the capacity of the teacher to use strategies and interventions instead of having the student removed. We might have a short term intensive behavioral support person (STIBS) work within the class, assisting the teacher and student. STIBS are support staff trained in social-emotional learning, which could benefit this student as well as the rest of his peers.

Of course, these are complex cases and require patience and targeted support. As a school district we do not believe students should be segregated or restrained; however, our behavioral support staff are trained in CPI (crisis prevention institute training) which has been proven to work in deescalating situations, and we also have many staff trained in Positive Behavioural Intervention Strategies (PBIS). Also, we presently are training staff in the low arousal program to impact positively on the culture of a school. It is always a last resort that we might need to remove a student from a class or a school due to safety concerns for staff and students. When that happens, we have extensive information collected and parental permission to consider a district program to provide intensive targeted support for the agreed-upon period. Parents must be in support of this process and need to be informed that this is program is being offered to hopefully help the student acquire the skills to successfully return to a mainstream class and his home school. When working with a teacher, we actively listen to them, so they feel heard, we validate their concerns and reinforce the importance of educating all our students, and

Figure 18.2 **Teacher Making Observation Notes.** *Source*: https://www.istockphoto.com. Credit: DGLimages.

we then provide the training and capacity building to assist them in moving forward. We do that through our district consultants and our behavioral support staff.

Name: Douglas Louis Matear

Position: District Principal of Alternate and Alternative Education
Institutional Affiliation: Vancouver School Board

Resources

Books

Cooper, V. (2005). *Support staff in schools promoting the emotional and social development of children and young people.* National Children's Bureau.
The book explores how children and young people require one-to-one support when facing barriers to learning at school. This one-to-one support is integral to their social and emotional development. The book provides strategies on what school can do to effectively involve support staff, services and reduce barriers for not only children but also the barriers that support staff face. These strategies enable children to make the most of their education. The book also includes a checklist for effective practice of provisions of support.

Academic Articles

Boyle, C., Topping, K., Jindal-Snape, D., & Norwich, B. (2012). The importance of peer- support for teaching staff when including children with special educational needs. *School Psychology International,* 33(2), 167–184. doi: 10.1177/0143034311415783
The focus of this article is peer support for teaching staff (including teaching staff, school administrators and supports such as psychologists, education assistants, and more). A study of forty-three teachers was completed to understand the themes related to inclusion. It was found that there were positive attitudes toward inclusion, but it was integral that the management team was on board to create successful inclusion. With peer support they were able to more readily include students with special needs.

Obiakor, F., Harris, M., Mutua, K., Rotatori, A., & Algozzine, B. (2012). Making inclusion work in general education classrooms. *Education & Treatment of Children,* 35(3), 477–490. doi: 10.1353/etc.2012.0020
This article provides a different perspective of what inclusion in the general classroom looks like, and how it deserves to be re-evaluated to prioritize the needs of the learners. The article states to improve normalcy in their lives, instead of looking to separate classrooms or services, students should be educated with their peers without disabilities in environments which are inclusive. The article also offers a

discussion on how special educators can make inclusion work even with concerns over the practicality of all learners being in the classroom.

Professional Articles

Bennett, S. (2009). *What works? Research into practice: Including students with exceptionalities.* ETFO-OTS. http://etfo-ots.ca/wp-content/uploads/2013/08/Including-Students-with-Exceptionalities.pdf

Written by Dr. Sheila Bennett from Brock University, this document explores how educators develop and maintain inclusive environments for students with exceptionalities. With a growing number of students considered at risk (not yet identified as exceptional) there is a higher need for inclusion in the classroom which emphasizes education for all. Considering planning for all learners helps to remove berries and improve inclusion in regular classrooms.

Inclusive Schools. (2015, August, 20). *The principal's responsibilities in supporting quality instruction.* https://inclusiveschools.org/the-principals-responsibilities-in-supporting-quality-instruction/

This resource explains how principals play a key role in the delivery of quality instruction from monitoring instructional strategies, effective support, and to guide teachers when needed. Principals are seen as a leader so effective communication and trust is necessary. Principals are the catalyst for effective collaboration with a great deal of work, planning and trust into the process. Suggestions for principals include conducting surveys to determine topics for professional development, ideas to improve good teaching practices, and ways to identify which current practices are successful.

Ontario Ministry of Education. (2007). *Shared solutions: A guide to preventing and resolving conflicts regarding programs and services for students with special education needs.* Edu.gov.on.ca. http://www.edu.gov.on.ca/eng/general/elemsec/speced/shared.pdf

Shared Solutions is a document which contains a tear out sheet for solutions on the go for teachers oriented around preventing and resolving conflicts specifically with programs and services for students with special education needs. This involves reaching a shared solution, and key questions to help involve the student. The document also shares that students are best served when conflicts are resolved promptly, without negative feelings, and with minimal stress from all parties. This helps to teach students positive strategies to help them with conflict resolution in the future.

Tranter, D. & Kerr, D. (2016). *Understanding self-regulation: Why stressed students struggle to learn.* Edu.Gov.on.Ca. http://www.edu.gov.on.ca/eng/literacynumeracy/inspire/research/ww_struggle.html

This is a document for teachers written by Dr. David Tranter and Dr. David Kerr to explore and support self-regulation for students. Children who experience chronic stress experience difficulty matching their state of arousal with the demands of the classrooms. The article defines self-control as a muscle and that students can be coached with their meta-cognitive skills such as their working memory, inhibitory control, and cognitive flexibility to explore social, emotional and cognitive tasks.

The article goes on to explain the continuum of regulation and define type of arousal, which impact student success in the classroom. The article finally suggests strategies for the classroom and to remember that self-regulation is about responding to stress and managing one's state of arousal.

Websites

Davies, L. (2006). *Oppositional defiant disorder in children.* Kelly Bear. http://www.kellybear.com/TeacherArticles/TeacherTip68.html

Leah Davies has created a straightforward article, which describes oppositional defiant disorder (ODD) in jot notes. The article also explores conduct disorder, and how it is often a more severe form of ODD, but is not always developed by children with ODD. Davies explains that intervention needs to be early to be able to assist students. She also shares her thoughts for teachers with students identified with ODD.

Davies, N. (2016, January 7). *Oppositional defiant disorder in the classroom.* Headteacher-update. http://www.headteacher-update.com/best-practice-article/oppositional-defiant-disorder-in-the-classroom/112142/

Dr. Nicola Davies explores ODD and how teachers may support students with the condition. This article is backed with medical references as well as quotes explaining the source/triggers for ODD such as stress. She then states that teachers must understand ODD to be able to employ effective strategies. Dr. Davies dives into strategies which can create a successful learning environment conducive to all learners. There is also a list of potential interventions to explore for classroom management in the form of programs, strategies, and games to promote student buy in. An important aspect is the shared success stories from using these strategies.

Dusenbury, L. (2012). *Creating a safe classroom environment.* Education World. https://www.educationworld.com/a_curr/creating-safe-classroom- environment-climate.shtml

This website is a comprehensive look at tips summarized from a training DVD that Dr. Dusenbry developed called "Best Practices in Classroom Management." The emphasis is on creating a classroom that is organized and that teachers are promoting learning with interactive approaches such as small groups and cooperative learning. Finally, Dusenbury prompts a reflection on the school environment itself to ensure that supervision and positivity are in place to make students feel welcome.

Moshman, R. (n.d.). *Supporting kids with oppositional defiant disorder in the classroom: What teachers need to know.* Classroom Management. https://www.boredteachers.com/classroom-management/teachers-need-to-know- oppositional-defiant-disorder-odd

This website defines oppositional defiant disorder, the symptoms, and how a teacher can best support child such as working on a behavior plan, documentation, positive reinforcement, keeping a calm demeanor with clear and consistent rules, and consequences for everyone. Finally, the website cites the importance of working with the parents and creating connections to support students. Students often are experiencing emotions and have difficulty processing them, in situations of heighted stress, model moving forward. The article ends with resources from a school psychologist.

Teaching Students with Emotional & Behavioral Disorders. (2009). *Oppositional defiant disorder in the classroom – Strategies & advice.* Bright hub education. https://www.brighthubeducation.com/special-ed-behavioral-disorders/26631-strategies-for-teaching-children-with-oppositional-defiant-disorder/

This website briefly explains ODD in the classroom, a focus on prevention, how to establish expectations, providing praise, and finally natural consequences. Written collaboratively, this site helps to explore strategies such as a focus on prevention to help the child overcome frustration, or avoid frustrating tasks and promote coping mechanisms. The article also emphasizes that though students may act as though they do not care for others, praise is important with positive reinforcement to create accountability for actions along with natural consequences.

WeAreTeachers. (2019, April 2). *What teachers need to know about students with ODD (oppositional defiant disorder).* https://www.weareteachers.com/students-with-odd/

This website provides a perspective piece from a teacher trying to support a student with ODD in the classroom. The article then explains ODD and how it is different from a child simply arguing. The article also explains what ODD "looks like" in children and the frequency of behavior to help teachers understand. Treatments are discussed as are resources for teachers on how to help.

Chapter 19

A Case of School Board Funding

CASE 2: SCHOOL BOARD SUPPORTS

Crosscutting Themes: Relationships/Trust, Advocacy, Legal/Legislative.
Leadership Competencies: Advocacy, Fosters Relationships, Embodies Professional Standards, Legal Requirements, Communication.

I became the new principal of Wilson Avenue Elementary School just a few months ago. It was a big adjustment for me to move from Hillcrest Elementary where I was the principal for over seven years. Wilson Avenue is an inner-city school with nearly 300 students, although the population has been decreasing for many years.

At one point, Wilson Avenue had 700 students. Hillcrest, on the other hand, is seemingly in the middle of nowhere. It has about 400 students, the majority of whom live on farms. My commute to work was usually pretty slow because there are so many slow tractors on the roads!

One of the reasons that I switched to Wilson Avenue was because it has a large number of students with special education needs. I started my career in education as a paraprofessional and worked individually with students with special education needs. Special education is near and dear to my heart.

When I was hired at Wilson Avenue, the administrative assistant was almost apologetic as she explained to me that Wilson has more than 100 students with a variety of special education needs. She said, "It got to be too much for the last principal. That's why he quit. Couldn't handle all the stress. Parents, the board, teachers, they were always trying to tell him how to do his job." But I wasn't one to be apprehensive. I looked forward to a new challenge.

Figure 19.1 Principal Budgeting for Special Education Resources. *Source*: https://www.istockphoto.com. Credit: Yok_Piyapong.

A big part of my job as principal and something that I really value is having a strong relationship with the school board, especially the superintendent for our school district. I've had nothing but positive experiences with superintendents and school boards until I started at Wilson Avenue. I feel like our school superintendent, Kate Arsenault, isn't all that interested in Wilson Avenue. Last week I sat down with Kate to talk about resources for our students with special education needs, particularly assistive technology and classroom furniture. There are few accessible classroom tables, chairs, and computers. And many of our chalkboards are too high, which means that some of our students in wheelchairs are unable to reach them and participate in some classroom activities. I'd really like to replace all chalkboards with interactive whiteboards—and get some iPads to help our students with particular learning challenges. There is so much technology out there that we can use to support our students' learning!

When I told Kate about my requests, she shifted uncomfortably in her seat. "Cam, I understand your requests," she said cautiously. "But let me explain something to you. You've heard all about the government budget cuts to public education. These cuts are devastating our already-low fund for accessible equipment and resources. And . . ."

Kate paused, not making eye contact with me.

"And one of the reasons I wanted to meet with you today was to let you know that the board is thinking of closing Wilson Avenue Elementary School."

I was shocked. "What?" I stammered.

"*Please* don't repeat that. It certainly isn't final," she said quickly.

"Okay," I said. "How come I'm just learning about this now, Kate?"

"The board has just started talking about it. But a decision could be made pretty quickly depending on what our government funding is for next year. So . . . what I'm trying to tell you is that we can't allocate new resources to schools if they are going to close."

That night, I tossed and turned. How could the board close Wilson Avenue? I knew it was a small, older, inner-city school and the board was experiencing budget cuts, but *close* the school? It was the only public elementary school in this section of the city. And refuse to provide necessary equipment for students with special education needs? I had to find a way to fix this. The next day at our staff meeting, I proposed that we rally as a community and have a fundraiser for special education equipment at Wilson Avenue. The teachers were all extremely hesitant. The grade two teacher, Miss. Laroche, piped up and said, "How is a rally going to change anything? We've never had proper equipment or resources here at Wilson Avenue because the board doesn't care about us. We're a small, urban school. Nothing is going to change."

"No!" I exclaimed. "It's our job to advocate for these students. This has to change." I noticed that some in the staff meeting seemed to be nodding their heads in agreement while the others either avoided eye contact or appeared to smirk. In the end, we decided to defer a decision to the next month's staff meeting.

A week later, I was at my desk looking through educational regulations and trying to find legal materials to counter the board decision. I had to show that the board had an obligation to provide equipment to students with disabilities. Suddenly my phone rang. I looked at the caller ID and saw that someone from the board office was calling. Sighing, I picked up the phone.

"Hello?"

"Cam. It's Kate."

"Oh, hi Kate," I said.

"Have you seen the newspaper?" she snapped.

"No, I haven't. Why?"

"Look online. The paper has published a *scathing* article about how the school board won't fund resources for students with disabilities at Wilson Avenue. It's bad. And somehow information about the possibility of Wilson Avenue closing was leaked."

"Oh no," I said. *This is going to be a nightmare*, I thought.

"Do you have any idea how the information was leaked? *You* were one of the only people outside of the board office who knew that information," the superintendent said in an accusatory tone.

I was annoyed with her tone. "Kate, I don't know. I didn't tell anyone."

"Well, a meeting has been called at the board office with our communications officer this afternoon. We need you at the meeting. This is going to be bad for all of us."

Questions to Consider:

1. There is clearly some tension between the principal and superintendent. What are the consequences of a poor relationship between a principal and school board representatives? Why might issues related to special education contribute to tense relationships between school and board personnel?
2. What would you suggest Cam do in preparation for the meeting at the board office? What advice would you provide to him for the meeting itself?
3. What strategies could be implemented to improve the relationship between the principal and the superintendent?
4. What obligations do school boards have to provide resources for students with special education needs in your state/province?

Expert Opinion:

This case highlights the importance of the principal superintendent relationship, the need to have our most vulnerable students at the forefront of decision-making and for school boards to develop and implement strategic plans that identify their priorities.

School boards have a responsibility to provide an inclusive, safe, and accessible learning environment for all students. It is apparent that the school principal in this case study is a true advocate for students with special education needs, as well as students who reside in low socioeconomical communities, and part of the entry plan is to identify the needs of the school in the hope of receiving additional resources.

The challenge this case presents is that in addition to inadequate resources and the limitations of the physical building to provide an accessible learning environment, the school is also facing the possibility of being closed. As a school principal there will be times when you don't agree with the direction of the school board and the decisions being made. The decisions may appear to be inequitable and not in the best interest of students and school communities; however, it is at this time that your relationship with your superintendent

Figure 19.2 Superintendent and Teachers Meeting. *Source*: https://www.istockphoto.com. Credit: shironosov.

is paramount. This is not a time as a school leader to make decisions based on emotions, but rather allow yourself the time to develop a plan that includes board priorities, which also aligns with the needs of your school community and then share this with your superintendent prior to engaging other stakeholders. These challenging circumstances provide an opportunity for the principal to further enhance a relationship with the superintendent.

Recognizing that the school may be closing, the principal still needs to develop a plan for the upcoming school year that includes resource enhancements, based on the needs of the students and that it is supported by school data. By developing a well thought out plan it provides a forum for the principal and the superintendent to engage in a discussion, which could lead to a mentoring conversation where the superintendent would be able to give the principal some suggestions when sharing the plan with the school staff and community. This also provides an opportunity for the principal to share their vision for the school, show that their advocacy is supported with evidence and also ensure that the superintendent knows that the principal understands their role within the organization while at the same time striving to meet the learning and well-being needs of the students and school community. In essence this approach would allow the superintendent and the principal to further develop a productive working relationship, which ultimately benefits the school community and the district.

Within a broader educational community if we truly place our special needs and vulnerable students as a priority then why aren't funding models differentiated in a way that supports inner-city schools and prioritizes neighborhood schools for those who most need this connection?

Name: Scott Miller
Position: Superintendent, Student Achievement and Well Being—Special Education
Institutional Affiliation: Waterloo Region District School Board

Resources

Academic Articles

Mason, V. (2013). *Challenges to instructional leadership practices: Superintendent and principals' experiences.* Library and Archives Canada.

This study was conducted to examine the relationships between superintendents and principals. It was found that the goal of these relationships is to effectively practice instructional leadership. Five challenges were identified from vision/mission, teaching and planning time, managing classroom instruction, student success/progress, and positive atmosphere. It was found that more professional development is needed in these areas to improve these challenges. Oftentimes, more emergent issues such as stakeholder input, working with reluctant staff members, and financial limitations were burdens on these professional relationships. This study revealed recommendations that could improve these relationships, but that focused not only on the principal and superintendent but also on policy-makers, and trustees and community stakeholders. This document continues to define the roles and leadership expectations of principals and superintendents and identifies three leadership practices: moral leadership, transformational leadership and instructional leadership. A combination of these three needs to vary for every individual relationship to ensure the school and respective teachers are best supported and communicated with. Final findings were that superintendents and principals need more opportunities to focus on instructional leadership duties to optimize the school working dynamic.

Teutsch, F., & Gugglberger, L. (2019). Analysis of whole-school policy changes in Austrian schools. *Health Promotion International,* 35(2), 331–339. doi: 10.1093/heapro/daz006

The article identifies how one's health and happiness can be impacted by their environmental, organizational, and social factors. In recognition of this it is integral to provide children and adolescents with the opportunities and resources to build a strong foundation for their health later in life. It is at the core of the school's process of teaching and learning to prioritize well-being as well as academic outcomes. Many policies are changing to impact the way people interact with each other, and these policies depend on the conditions at the school level from morale, access to resources such as technology, physical activity and social health. To ease the changing of policies or to positively implement change, leaders need to be able to share and explain data which lead to the decision-making in order to include all of the components of a school-wide change to prioritize students' health, specifically psycho-social health and well-being.

Vyas, B. (2020). *Perspectives of the superintendent and principal: Leadership for technology integration.* ProQuest Dissertations Publishing.

This dissertation focuses on leadership styles and theories but more specifically focuses on the demands of effective educational leadership. Vyas focuses on creating school community and culture, mastering strategies for collecting and using data, leading people and the curriculum, managing policy and governance and finally collaboration between principals and superintendents. These collaborations are what foster cohesive decision-making. Finally, they focus on technology and technology integration in teaching. There are barriers such as funding, training and consistent implementation while the benefits for special education, as well as prioritizing strategies to benefit all students through diversifying instructional methods.

Professional Articles

Baker, L., Diggs, L., & Royal, M., (2019, February). *The evolving relationship: Principals and their supervisors.* National Association Secondary School Principals. https://www.nassp.org/2019/02/01/the-evolving-relationship-principals-and-their-supervisors/

This professional article focuses on principal leadership, coaching, and instruction as a priority over operations. They also focus on evaluating school culture to understand that what is going on outside of the classroom is just as important as what goes on inside the classroom. Finally, they focus on crisis management.

Ontario Ministry of Education. (2012, October). *Parent engagement.* Capacity Building Series K-12. Edugains. http://www.edugains.ca/resourcesLIT/ProfessionalLearning/CBS/CBS_ParentEngage.pd

This professional article focuses on a call to action of parent's engagement to ensure that schools can become a positive place to teach, learn, and grow. The impact of community and parent support to the success of school's is integral not only for student success but for advocacy for schools when policy changes threaten to impact their success. To successfully engage parents and garner their support, schools must reach out to parents who may not feel included or who's children are experiencing challenges with the curriculum to build positive family-school partnerships to improve attitudes to school and enhance students' future success. When parents and teachers are united and maintain positive relationships, they can discuss and share input for important conversations such as how community engagement can enhance the school and classroom.

Ontario Institute for Education Leadership. (2013, September) *The Ontario leadership framework.* Edugains. http://www.edugains.ca/resources21CL/SchoolLeader/SettingDirections/OLF_User_Guide.pdf

This document outlines school and system leadership and acts as a guide for putting Ontario's leadership framework into action. This document helps to break down and navigate the leadership maze, as a leadership roadmap is needed to understand that school leaders, and system leaders are integral to the growing body of professional knowledge to improve student achievement and well-being. The document breaks down the traits of effective leaders, characteristics of effective organizations and common leadership language used to facilitate effective dialogue, professional learning, and collaboration. This document is integral to understanding the leadership framework and the key concepts of leadership, management, authority and the importance of sharing leadership purposefully. The consistency of instructional leaders and supervisory officers creates a common chain of command for leadership questions and focusing on growth-oriented and collaborative approaches. This document prioritizes five core leadership capacities which are setting goals, aligning resources with priorities, promoting collaborative learning cultures, using data, and engaging in courageous conversations.

Websites

Autism Support Network. (2017). *Advocacy roadmap*. Autism Support BC. https://autismsupportbc.ca/advocacy-roadmap/

Autism Supports British Columbia has created an advocacy roadmap on how to communicate with school districts. In the classroom there are many funding needs for students with autism and this website walks parents and advocates through how to document, follow up, and ultimately have the conversations to create change, achieve funding, and support for students.

Litvinov, A. (2017, July 16). *School funding facts, Pt. 3: How to advocate for public school resources*. Education Votes National Education Association. https://educationvotes.nea.org/2017/07/16/school-funding-facts-pt-3-advocate-public-school-resources/

This website is part three to a series of school funding facts. The first two parts describe four essential facts about school funding, how to share this with networks and persuade policy-makers when necessary. There are suggestions of what to avoid in conversations such as misleading words, and not to simply say what isn't working, and to come with a plan.

Peel District School Board. (n.d.). *Special education programs and services*. Peel Schools. https://peelschools.org/parents/specialed/Pages/default.aspx

This website focuses on special education programs and services in the Peel District School Board, one of Canada's largest school systems. It describes specifically which students receive support, how they identify these students requiring support, as well as how special education programs and support are delivered. The website goes into depth on special education resources for the special education team, service animals, and the important role of technology in the classroom.

Chapter 20

Wandering Off: A Case of a Safe Arrival Program

CASE 3: SCHOOL BOARD SUPPORTS

Crosscutting Themes: Communication, Advocacy.
Leadership Competencies: Policies and Procedures, Legal Requirements, Collaboration, Advocacy.

I have served as an elected trustee on our district's school board for the past two years. My son, Hayden, attends one of the local public elementary schools, so I ran for the trustee position because I am invested in public education for my son and for other kids in the community.

In my role, I work with other trustees to approve policies and bylaws for the school board. Our main priority is to ensure that the needs of all students are met. It's a really rewarding position.

One morning, my phone rang. It was Jayden Fairchild, principal of Sunview Elementary, the school my son attends. I respect Jayden and think he is doing a great job at the school, especially in implementing inclusive classrooms.

"Hi Jayden," I said. "How are you?"

"I'm doing well, thanks. I would like to share something with you and see if I can get your help," he replied.

"I'm happy to help. What's going on?"

"Well," Jayden began.

"We have a *situation*. Yesterday one of our students with autism, Kayla who is in grade xix, wandered off school grounds in the morning. A woman who lives down the road from the school found Kayla and called the police. We didn't even know Kayla was missing until the police showed up with her."

Figure 20.1 **Presentation.** *Source*: https://www.istockphoto.com. Credit: monkeybusinessimages.

"Oh dear," I said, thinking through the implications of a student wandering off. "How long was she off school grounds for?"

"I'm not exactly sure. But probably over an hour," Jayden admitted, sounding defeated.

"Wasn't a teacher on duty?"

"Yes," the principal responded.

"But the teacher didn't even know that Kayla had been dropped off, so she didn't know that she was missing. When Kayla's mom heard about what happened, she was very upset. It was horrible. But she dropped off her child without ensuring that a teacher knew Kayla was there."

I sighed, wanting to move the conversation to figure out some next steps. "How can I be of help?"

"We need to implement a safe-arrival program at the school for students with special education needs," Jayden said. "I know other schools in other districts have similar programs. It would mean that each child's parent or guardian stay with them until the teacher comes to meet them on the tarmac."

"My thought is that this would ensure a safe transition between home and school. It might prevent a situation like this from happening again."

"Sounds like a good idea. I'm actually surprised the board doesn't have a program like this in all schools by now."

Figure 20.2 Safe Student Arrival. *Source*: https://www.istockphoto.com. Credit: jarenwicklund.

"I agree. What would be the process to start a program like this? As well as a policy about safe arrivals for students with special education needs?"

I thought for a moment. "Well, I think we should begin by having a meeting with you, me, and Helena," I said, referring to the school superintendent. "I also think we need to gather more information on what happened with Kayla. Then we can start talking about what a policy and safe-arrival program might involve."

Jayden and I talked for a few more minutes about when we might meet. I thought we were about to finish the conversation when Jayden said,

> There's one other thing. I worry that Kayla's mom is going to go to Helena about this and try to blame the situation on me. It just wouldn't surprise me if she escalated this. She's like that.

I understood Jayden's concerns. I told him that he should meet with Kayla's mom to talk about the situation and what time teachers go on duty in the mornings to supervise students arriving at the school. Jayden and I finished the conversation and both hung up. I sat in my office with many thoughts running through my mind. On the one hand, I was thankful that nothing happened to Kayla when she wandered into the neighborhood by the school. On the other hand, I was concerned that this situation might happen again. *We need to do more*, I thought. *We obviously need better gates and fences around the school grounds. What about Jayden's idea about a safe-arrival program for our students with special education needs? And what about Kayla's mom? What if she goes to the media about this?*

My head was spinning. I knew this situation was far from over.

Questions To Consider:

1. What can be done to ensure the safe arrival and departure of students with special education needs? What policies and procedures are in place in your school to support safety?
2. Can you identify the processes in place in your school that support the safety and security of all students, particularly students with special education needs?
3. If you were to do a risk analysis at your school, what would you discover? Consider the risk assessment with particular consideration for a student with autism, a developmental disability, or is physically disabled. What unique risks must you consider due to specialized needs?

Expert Opinion:

As most cases go, there are many multifaceted aspects and players in this likely scenario. The most prominent topics include the following: transition planning and supports, IEP (individual education plan) team collaboration, general school safety procedures, and last but surely not least of these, parent trust. Starting with the first two, this case highlights a lack of preparation and consideration around the transition needs and supports for Kayla by the IEP team. Historically transition has been thought of as preparation for a student's move from secondary school to adulthood. This often included school-based experience and instruction focused on employment, community living, and further education for high school students with exceptionalities. However, the concept of transition has expanded to include all to or from activities such as from class to class, recess to lunch, or from primary to secondary education. This shift in thinking is especially beneficial for students with autism as unplanned or unsupported transitions both small and large can be a source of confusion and anxiety and in some cases lead to problematic response behaviors. Transition needs and supports should be sufficiently considered and addressed in the student's IEP. This case highlights an overlooked transition support need. It will be up to the IEP team, including Kayla's parents, to ensure that transitions are sufficiently discussed and when needed, appropriate and well-supported plans are put in place to ensure a safe and productive learning experience.

While the attention on a safe arrival program for students with exceptionalities could be a good start to the discussion, the broader issue here is related to transition and ensuring that all students with an IEP receive appropriate supports in this area. Additionally, this case brings about the need to discuss and debrief the general school and/or board procedures related to school incidents with specific inclusion on missing students. Updates to the procedures as well as staff training may be needed to ensure the safety of all students regardless of exceptionality.

The final issue in this case relates to trust. Parents place an enormous amount of trust in schools; this is often more difficult and potentially consequential for parents of children with unique needs. A trusting relationship between schools and parents is incredibly important for student success. In the immediate, it would be helpful to ensure that there is an honest and open conversation with the parent regarding the facts of the case as well as the path for moving forward. In this case, it is clear that the IEP team missed a critical support need for Kayla. Ensuring that this is a collaborative discussion with the IEP team will enable a collaborative resolve with essential input from the multiple stakeholders working to support Kayla. Also, this effort helps to reiterate and strengthen the collaborative and interdisciplinary nature of supports for students with exceptionality.

Name: Jordan Shurr
Position: Associate Professor of Special Education
Institutional Affiliation: Queen's University

Resources

Academic Articles

Winton, S. (2011). Managing conduct: a comparative policy analysis of safe schools' policies in Toronto, Canada and Buffalo, USA. *Comparative Education*, 47(2), 247–263. doi: 10.1080/03050068.2011.554088

This article focuses on comparing school districts and their safe school policies in Buffalo, USA and Toronto, Canada. The author found that there are local, state/provincial, national, and international factors that impact local safe school policies. When it comes to policy-making and involving students, it was suggested to take in to account what a "safe learning environment" needs in terms of local, state/provincial and national levels. The focus needs to move away from unfairly punishing students and creating barriers to relationship building to supporting students and keeping human rights at the forefront of decisions.

Pelletier, J., Laska, M., Nanney, M., & Pratt, R. (2018). Cross-sector collaboration on safe routes to school policy advocacy and implementation: A mixed methods evaluation from Minnesota. *Journal of Transport & Health*, 9, 132–140. doi: 10.1016/j.jth.2018.04.004

This article focuses on improving active ways to promote physical activity and cardiovascular fitness among children. There is a broader need for policy and environmental changes to be able to ensure the safety of children from physical dangers such as high traffic and ensure safe arrival and drop off. Local communities developed teams including public health, education, city planning, and law enforcement to implement comprehensive safe routes to school. Cross-sector collaboration was crucial to ensuring that all of these partnerships worked collaboratively for the safety of children on their way to and from schools. The article explains the steps needed for such a policy change and how to engage community partners such as law enforcement and public safety to support these policy changes and student safety.

Professional Articles

Australian Government Department of Social Services. (2017). *Disability advocacy*. Department of Social Services. https://www.dss.gov.au/disability-advocacy-fact-sheet

This document compiled by the Australian government focuses on disability advocacy, and why it is important. Advocacy is defined in this context as acting, speaking or writing to promote, protect and defend the human rights of people with disabilities.

Royal Botanical Gardens. (2019, March). *Health and safety risk assessment*. KEW. https://www.kew.org/sites/default/files/2019-03/Risk%20assessment%20for%20visiting%20schools%20Kew%202019.pdf

This document was created by the Royal Botanical Gardens and outlines the health and safety protocols for school visits. This document is integral to ensuring the schools can maintain safety of children. This is an example of effective risk assessment protocols to be followed when implementing new policies. The document also outlines further action needed to reduce risk. These are outlined for each possible risk, keeping in mind students with physical and developmental disabilities and their needs. This document is expansive and identified many health and safety assessment points to ensure that the operations are as smooth and safe as possible for all participants from students, administration and teachers.

EduGains. (n.d.) *Special education advisory committee*. Ontario Ministry of Education. http://www.edugains.ca/newsite/SpecialEducation/prolearnfac/seac.html

This is a website which links to many professional articles focusing on the Special Education Advisory Committee (SEAC). This site focuses on supporting learning and building positive relationships. There is a discussion on SEAC effective practices and strategies for parent engagement in special education programs. There is a description of the framework of support that is a general guide that schools follow outlining the roles of supervision and support from the classroom educator, school leader, system leader and professional learning facilitator.

Websites

Chandler K. (2015, September 9). *Support services for children with special needs*. KidSpot. https://www.kidspot.com.au/school/primary/learning-and-behaviour/support-services-for-children-with-special-needs/news-story/911e36a9cb6680a16fe168fe9e0971d3

This website provides a resource for parents and teachers to understand more about children with a variety of disabilities as well as behavioral difficulties. This website specifically sources resources in Australia that support parents and schools through health information, advocacy, specific school support with student support programs and school education along with well-being support.

John Adams Elementary School. (n.d.). *Drop-off and pick-up procedures*. ACPS.k12. https://www.acps.k12.va.us/Page/1561

John Adams Elementary School has safe drop-off and pick-up procedures for their school. This is accessible on their website and outlines specifically what morning drop off looks like, which entrances students may use, and where parents should say goodbye and pass off their child. This type of policy is a fantastic way to ensure that all individuals involved in the process are on the same page and able to execute safe arrival and dismissal of students.

SCHOOL TEAMS

Chapter 21

Caught Between a Rock and a Hard Place

CASE 1: SCHOOL TEAM

Crosscutting Themes: Parents/Caregivers/Family, Relationships/Trust, Collaboration, Agency/Efficacy.
Leadership Competencies: Values Inclusion, Fosters Relationships, Collaboration, Professional Learning, Problem-solving.

I have been a high school administrator for about twelve years now and have changed schools almost every four years. Because I have moved around a lot, I have realized how important it is to create strong relationships with *everyone* in the school—from students to staff to parents.

Forming these bonds can make your life as a principal or a vice principal much easier. I have also learned that each and every school is unique. My last school had many students with special education needs. I was able to build close relationships with my staff fairly easily, and our team became very strong as we supported our students with special education needs. We all had worked hard to build trusting relationships. But it's not always so easy to build relationships with a school team. At my current school, Lincoln High, I have had to put a lot of time and effort into building strong relationships with staff. It has been a bit of a frustrating process to be honest, but I am pushing through it because having a strong team is a crucial part of creating an inclusive environment.

Unlike my last school, the staff at Lincoln are a bit more reluctant to some of my "inclusive" ideas. They have a different vision of what inclusive education for students with special education needs should look like. As a mid-sized high school of approximately 1,700 students there are certainly many students with special education needs. We have a number of congregated

Figure 21.1 Principal Talking to All Staff. *Source*: https://www.istockphoto.com. Credit: M_a_y_a.

classrooms where those students with intensive or developmental needs are taught. We also have a congregated class for students with significant learning disabilities. Those classrooms are in a separate wing of the school.

I would much rather see many of these students integrated into other classrooms as much as possible. I have had push back on this from some of the staff because they view these students as problematic and a distraction to other kids. I realize that it takes trust, strong relationships, and lots of communication in order to support the staff and help them along this journey of inclusive education.

When I first arrived at Lincoln, the school was in a tense situation: a parent had reported to the school superintendent that their child's needs were not being properly accommodated. This situation happened over a year ago, but the school was still dealing with the repercussions. The student in question, Sam, was in grade ten when his parents had involved the superintendent. Sam needed extra support with reading and writing, as he was working at a grade seven level at the time. He also had difficulties concentrating on school work, so his Individual Education Plan included extra support from paraprofessionals, a desk space for increased concentration, and extra breaks throughout the day as needed. Sam's parents felt that his English teacher, Mr. Hagerty, was not giving him enough time to complete his reading and writing assignments. Sometimes he didn't understand how to complete assignments because the

Figure 21.2 Experienced Principal Mentoring a New Principal. *Source*: https://www.istockphoto.com. Credit: gradyreese.

instructions were wordy or used vocabulary that was beyond his comprehension. Sometimes he didn't even start assignments because he assumed he wouldn't finish them.

Sam's parents were worried about their son. They had had a number of conversations with Mr. Hagerty about Sam's progress but nothing seemed to change. The administrative team did not seem to take their concerns seriously. Eventually the parents made a call to the school superintendent.

When I came to the school, everyone was on edge because the school was being watched and monitored by the superintendent in an attempt to ensure that Sam's needs were being met, as well as the other students with specialized needs in regular classrooms. I could understand why many teachers were concerned with my hope to provide more opportunities for the inclusion of students with special education needs.

One day, Sam's new English teacher, Julia Gomez, stopped me in the staff room. She told me that she was feeling completely overwhelmed by having Sam in her class. She knew about the situation with Mr. Hagerty last year and didn't want Sam's parents to call the superintendent on her. She was doubting if she was the right person to teach Sam. I assured her that she was the right person for the job and that I knew she could handle it. I asked her how I could help support her. I understood the stress she was under. Together we discussed her options and settled on her participating in some professional development workshops at the board office to support students with special education needs. I wanted her to know that I was on her team and that we could get through it together. I offered to help act as a buffer with the relationship with Sam's parents. I decided to organize a team meeting with Julia and the head of the special education department to talk about supports for Sam. I also called Sam's parents to include them in the meeting. It was going to take a team effort to help Sam.

A week after my conversation with Julia, she stopped by my office to chat again. She was at her breaking point. She said that Sam's parents had called her the previous day and had complained about her teaching methods. Julia was feeling scrutinized. And she was continuing to feel very anxious that the parents were going to call the superintendent. The parents had also complained that they weren't being involved in conversations about their son. I told Julia that I *had* reached out to Sam's parents to invite them to a team meeting, but I had never heard back from them. Obviously there had been some miscommunication. Although it was possible that they had left a message on my answering machine and I hadn't seen it—I was a bit behind with answering my phone calls, but I didn't admit that to Julia.

Julia went on to tell me that she didn't think she was receiving enough support. I thought I had handled the situation really well and gave her more than enough support. I admit that it had been an extremely busy time since our initial conversation, but I did all that I could for her. She said she wanted extra support in the classroom for Sam. She wanted one of the paraprofessionals at the school to attend the English class with Sam and assist him. If that wasn't possible, Julia wondered if it was best for Sam to be in the congregated classroom for students with significant learning disabilities for parts of the day where he could get more individualized help with his reading and writing. She ended the conversation by telling me that things needed to change or else she feared that she may need to go off on stress leave. She said her stress was negatively impacting her work and her home life. I felt terrible.

Now as I reflect on the situation and decide what to do, I feel caught between a rock and a hard place. On one hand, I feel very strongly that students with special education needs should be in regular classes with their peers. I'm always telling staff that students should be kept in the regular classroom as much as possible. I didn't want to seem like a hypocrite if Sam is taken out of the English class. On the other hand, I see that Sam may not be getting the individualized support he needs. I also see the stress that Julia is under. I know Sam can be challenging to have in the classroom. And I know that his parents are extremely difficult to work with—they are obviously willing to go to the board level to get their complaints heard. I need to help both Sam and Julia. But how? What do I do?

Questions To Consider:

1. What should the principal's next steps be? What questions or concerns do you have about the steps that have been taken thus far?
2. Why is it important to work as a team to help students with special education needs and staff members? What advice would you provide to a principal who is "going at it alone" in working to re-shape the culture of the school?
3. How would you support Sam at school? How would you engage his parents?
4. What are the unique challenges and opportunities that high schools avail for working as a team in supporting students with special education needs?

Expert Opinion:

Principals who value the relationship of *all* members of a school community are a gift to any school. In fact, inclusive program delivery, staff collaboration, and parental engagement are important responsibilities of a principal in an inclusive school (Cobb, 2015), and a key to all these obligations is relationships. While the principal expressed support for relationships, in the case of Sam, the principal appeared to have failed at the above duties: the principal appeared unaware of Sam's IEP; there seemed to be little, if any, collaboration among staff members at the school, and the principal did not include Sam's parents in the arranged meeting, a potentially significant issue since Sam's parent had already expressed that their concerns were not being heard at the school level.

The situation is, unfortunately, not unique. Lincoln's principal appeared to mean well and supportive of inclusion, a crucial role when attempting to meet the needs of students with exceptionalities (Billingsley et al., 2014). However, most administrators have little formal education in special or inclusive education prior to landing positions as principals with many educational leaders reporting that most of the learning in these areas take place on the job (McHatton et al., 2010; Sider et al., 2017).

Like many principals, Lincoln's could greatly benefit from coaching and mentorship.

Because they involve *active* learning, these two methods of professional development are generally considered far more effective than workshops, the activity the principal assigned to support Julia (Boyle et al., 2004; van Veen et al., 2012). In Sam and Julia's case, it would appear the principal could benefit from mentorship around how to support students with exceptionalities *and* how to support teachers in meeting the needs of exceptional learners.

Since time in this appears to be short, meeting with Sam's case manager or the head of the special education department to gain quick access to Sam's strengths and needs would be a good first step, along with examining Sam's file with information on his IEP. Supervision of curriculum delivery is the responsibility of principals (Cobb, 2015), and since IEPs fall under curriculum, Sam's IEP is something the principal needs to have an understanding of.

Other questions also arose. The principal had been a high school administrator for more than a decade. In previously questioning the principal's skillset, it is also worth pondering what approaches to inclusive education the school district finds adequate. Furthermore, while administrative support for teachers is invaluable in ensuring teachers can do a good job (Kipps-Vaughan et al., 2012), it does not change the fact that teachers frequently report being ill-equipped to teach in inclusive classrooms and meeting the needs of all learners (Dickenson, 2017). While the principal expressed support for Julia when she voiced her insecurity about being able to teach Sam, referring her for workshops and not providing the supports Sam's IEP outlined raised further questions around how the needs of students with exceptionalities at Lincoln, as well as at other schools in the district, are met.

References

Billingsley, B. S., McLeskey, J., & Crockett, J. B. (2014). *Moving toward inclusive and high-achieving schools for students with disabilities.* https://www.azpromisingpractices.com/PrincipalLeadership_InclusiveAchieving.pdf

Boyle, B., While, D., & Boyle, T. (2004). A longitudinal study of teacher change: what makes professional development effective? *The Curriculum Journal,* 15(1), 45–68. doi: 10.1080/0958517042000189470

Cobb, C. (2015). Principals play many parts: A review of the research on school principals as special education leaders 2001–2011. *International Journal of Inclusive Education,* 19(3), 213–234. doi: 10.1080/13603116.2014.916354

Dickenson, P. (2017). What do we know and where can we grow? Teachers preparation for the inclusive classroom. In P. Dickenson, P. Keough, & J. Courduff (Eds.), *Preparing pre-service teachers for the inclusive classroom* (pp. 1–22). Hershey, PA: Information Science Reference.

Kipps-Vaughan, D., Ponsart, D., & Gilligan, T. (2012). Teacher wellness: Too stressed for stress management? *Communique,* 41(1), 1, 26–28.

McHatton, P. A., Boyer, N. R., Shaunesy, E., & Terry, P. M. (2010). Principals' perceptions of preparation and practice in gifted and special education content: Are we doing enough? *Journal of Research on Leadership Education,* 5(1), 1–22. doi: 10.1177/194277511000500101

Sider, S., Maich, K., & Morvan, J. (2017). School principals and students with special education needs: Leading inclusive schools. *Canadian Journal of Education,* 40(2), 1–31. http://journals.sfu.ca/cje/index.php/cjerce/article/view2417/2433

van Veen, K., Zwart, R., & Meirink, J. (2012). What makes teacher professional development effective? A literature review. In M. Kooy & K. van Veen (Eds.). *Teacher learning that matters: International perspectives* (pp. 3–21). Routledge.

Name: Anders Lunde
Position: Special Education Teacher
Institutional Affiliation: British Columbia Public School Teacher

Resources

Video

Brown, B. (2017, April 7). *Daring classrooms*. [Video]. YouTube. https://www.youtube.com/watch?v=DVD8YRgA-ck

Brené Brown focuses on understanding what impacts the way we teach and lead. She challenges educators to engage with vulnerability and learn how to recognize and combat shame. She speaks to the classroom being a place where both teachers and students commit to choosing courage over comfort, and what is right over what is easy through practicing these values such as vulnerability, clarifying values, and rising skills/ resilience. She goes on, that it's okay to experience failure, the defining moments are how you use your supports and strength to pull it back together to learn how to get back up and developing courage.

Edutopia (2019, January 14). *The power of relationships in schools*. YouTube. https://www.youtube.com/watch?v=kzvm1m8zq5g

This video focuses on how ensuring students' feel safe and supported by adults in school, and as a result, are better able to learn. The video provides insight from professionals who speak to the science of education where building long term relationships and healthy attachment fosters risk-talking, exploration and learning. This video would be helpful for promoting connections with the student with special education needs. Both elementary and high school examples are provided in the video.

Academic Articles

Billingsley, B. S., McLeskey, J., & Crockett, J. B. (2014). *Moving toward inclusive and high-achieving schools for students with disabilities*. https://www.azpromisingpractices.com/PrincipalLeadership_InclusiveAchieving.pdf

This document outlines the importance of principal leadership to support students with disabilities, what professional standards look like in regards to ethics and equity, how to improve instructional leadership with resources on positive, orderly and safe learning environments, supporting high expectations for students as well as the influence of progress monitoring in continuing these levels of support. The document is a resource guide for explaining strategies for larger topics, it also includes parent leadership and support, the importance of consistent leadership through the board and most importantly helps principals explore strategies to build inclusive schools such as shared vision, school-wide commitment and a shared responsibility for improving learning for all students.

Cobb, C. (2015). Principals play many parts: A review of the research on school principals as special education leaders 2001–2011. *International Journal of Inclusive Education*, 19(3), 213–234. doi: 10.1080/13603116.2014.916354

This article compiled by Cam Cobb from the University of Windsor focused attention on inclusive leadership, parent engagement, and special education. This article explores the work of principals and how they foster inclusion within a school community. The study resulted in three core domains: inclusive program delivery, staff collaboration, and parental engagement. The research also found that principals take on seven key roles when working to foster inclusion including visionary, partner, coach, conflict resolver, advocate, interpreter, and organizer. These roles require various approaches to leadership with this article outlines and explains challenges, and strategies/recommendations to improve principal practice.

Dickenson, P. (2017). What do we know and where can we grow? Teachers preparation for the inclusive classroom. In P. Dickenson, P. Keough, & J. Courduff (Eds.), *Preparing pre-service teachers for the inclusive classroom* (pp. 1–22). Hershey, PA: Information Science Reference.

This is a compilation of resources written by Patricia Dickenson of National University, USA. In 2017 she compiled this document which explores the responsibility teachers have for teaching students with exceptionalities as most feel they do not have the skills to effectively instruct diverse learners. The document also explores common core strategies using universal design learning, what considerations to take when instructing low socioeconomic students, math strategies, reading, spelling, and writing strategies and finally implementing effective student support teams and parents as partners in education.

Kipps-Vaughan, D., Ponsart, T., & Gilligan, T. (2012). Teacher wellness: Too stressed for stress management? *Communique*, 41(1), 1, 26–28.

This document explores how teacher wellness created more effective learning environments. This document offers levels of enhancing teacher wellness through a program they have created to develop healthy mental health practices and have these positive practices flow over to healthier and happier classrooms. The document specifically looks at how to plan, what stress management looks like, and the steps teachers can take to implement stress management programs.

McHatton, P. A., Boyer, N. R., Shaunesy, E., & Terry, P. M. (2010). Principals' perceptions of preparation and practice in gifted and special education content: Are we doing enough? *Journal of Research on Leadership Education*, 5(1), 1–22. doi: 10.1177/194277511000500101

This article explores in-service school leaders and their perceptions on how their administrator addressed necessary skills and knowledge to effectively work with children in special education and gifted programs. It was found that there is a perception that principals do not do enough for students with special education needs and that principals/administration can use courses to learn and further support teachers to create not only inclusive classrooms but an inclusive school environment.

Sider, S., Maich, K., & Morvan, J. (2017). School principals and students with special education needs: Leading inclusive schools. *Canadian Journal of Education*, 40(2), 1–31.

This article explores the need for principals to build leaderships skills to support inclusive schools. With a focus on teachers developing skills to support students with special education needs, this study explores the principal's perspective of decision-making and interactions with special education needs. The article notes that the ways in which school leaders support students with special needs serves as a key function of how teachers engage students in inclusive classrooms. There were five key themes from the associated research study:the types of training and professional learning activities principals had taken, day-to-day experiences that principals engage in to support inclusion, how principal leadership contributes to an inclusive school culture, the impact of critical incidents for principals, and personal value statements in supporting inclusive schools.

Professional Articles

Ontario Ministry of Education. (2012). *Capacity building series, parent engagement*. Edu,gov.on.ca. http://www.edu.gov.on.ca/eng/literacynumeracy/inspire/research/CBS_parentEngage.pdf

The article explores how to open the door to parents and involve them in the school, learning to listen and "lead with our ears" to identify needs and goals, and then exploring how parents can engage in school activities. Finally, the article states that trust is a large part of this process as well as listening to and supporting aspirations and efforts from both parents and students. The article concludes with tips for parent engagement.

Websites

Hoerr, T. (2017, March). *Principal connection. Connecting with students' parents*. ASCD Educational Leadership. http://www.ascd.org/publications/educationalleadership/mar17/vol74/num06/Connecting-with-Students'-Parents.aspx

This article on the ASCD website explores parent and principal connections. To begin, Hoerr asks, what can we do? Then dives into how to set the stage for parents to feel welcome and included in schools. This partnership allows for greater student support. The article also explores how to cyber-connect and tap into technology for parent communications. Finally, the fact of listening to parents when we want to involve them, take time to be a part of the conversation to see how things are going and collect data to improve your practice as a principal.

Chapter 22

A Dysfunctional School Team?

CASE 2: SCHOOL TEAM

Crosscutting Themes: Advocacy, Communication.
Leadership Competencies: Communication, Collaboration, Problem-solving, Lived Experience of Students, Agency, Policies and Procedures, Fosters Relationships, Embodies Professional Standards.

Derek's Perspective

My name is Derek and I am in grade six. I like school, but I can't hear as well as the other students in my class, so it makes it harder for me to learn. I usually can't hear my teacher's voice, so I try to look at the notes of the person sitting next to me. But sometimes this doesn't help because I can't read their writing or sometimes the other students don't even do the work. I can figure out what is going on in the lessons for the most part because the teacher writes some stuff on the whiteboard. But I know I miss a lot and then I find the assignments and test really difficult.

I don't want to tell my parents or the teacher that I can't hear in this class. It has already been hard enough for me at school because no one likes me. I am afraid if I tell anyone that I can't hear that they will make a huge deal about the situation. I don't want the other kids to see that I need extra support. My mom mentioned to me at the beginning of the year that if I couldn't hear I needed to let her know because the teacher could maybe wear a microphone. The other kids would definitely know this was for me! They have already been making fun of my hearing aids and calling me names at recess.

I do have one good friend though. His name is Eddy. He and I usually just ignore the other kids and do our own thing. I am so glad I have Eddy. I don't

Figure 22.1 Student Using Headphones. *Source*: https://www.istockphoto.com. Credit: FatCamera.

know what I would do without him. It would be helpful if I sat closer to him in the classroom because I know he would fill me in on the lessons. Eddy is really smart! He tries to help catch me up after school but doesn't always have the time.

Parents' Perspective

Our son, Derek, is in grade six this year at a new school, Deer River Elementary. Derek has a hearing impairment, which makes it difficult for him to learn in the classroom. He is not fully deaf but in both ears he hears at about 25 dB when wearing his hearing aids; other children hear at 30 dB. We think he may also have attention deficit hyperactivity disorder since he struggles to concentrate but we haven't had him diagnosed yet. We are currently waiting to see a specialist to confirm this.

I know that having a student who is hard of hearing a part of the school is new to the team at Deer River. The school doesn't have many resources to help Derek. I know from my own research that some schools provide hearing impaired students with handwritten copies of the lessons so they can follow along. I also know that some teachers wear microphone headsets to amplify their voice. But none of this has happened at Deer River.

Figure 22.2 Students Working Together. *Source*: https://www.istockphoto.com. Credit: Ridofranz.

Derek didn't tell me that he was unable to fully hear his teacher, Mrs. Fellow, in fear that he would be centered out in the classroom. He told me that he didn't want his friends to treat him differently. He didn't want to be the odd one in the class. So he went to school every day for the first three months without being able to properly hear the teacher's lessons.

It wasn't until Mrs. Fellows noticed Derek's poor marks when she was getting the midterm report cards ready in the late fall that we were notified of concerns. I thought this was really late for the school to have noticed that Derek was struggling. I wasn't too happy when the teacher called me to say that his grades were poor and that we needed to find a better solution so he could improve for the next report card. The school *knew* that Derek was partially deaf, but I guess they just assumed he would manage on his own?

A few days ago I received a phone call from the special education teacher, Stephanie Waters, who said they would like us to come into the school to be a part of a team meeting to discuss solutions for Derek. I told her that we would be able to come in as soon as possible since we were concerned about our son's well-being.

Teacher's Perspective

I was informed in the summer that I would have a student who is partially deaf join my classroom. I was nervous and my head started to spin with ideas and concerns as to how I would support the student. I am a new teacher—this is only my second year of teaching. I don't have a lot of experience teaching students who have special education needs, especially a student who is deaf. I was worried about maintaining my image as a new teacher. I was worried about looking like an amateur and asking too many questions.

When I learned that I'd have a hearing impaired student in my class, I assumed that I would have extra support in my classroom from a paraprofessional. But a couple of days before the start of school, the vice principal, Ellen, explained to me that the school had been unable to hire as many support workers as they would have liked due to recent funding cuts.

"We have to allocate those paraprofessionals to our 'high-risk' students especially those with oppositional behaviours," Ellen had told me. "But don't worry. I'm looking at getting some resources to help you and the new student. I'm looking to get you a FM microphone system to amplify your voice."

The VP's cellphone had rang in her pocket. "Ahh, I need to get this," she had said as she picked up the phone and waved goodbye to me. In that moment, I felt alone. I didn't know how to support a student with a hearing impairment and Ellen seemed too busy to really help me. I decided that I would figure it out on my own and hope for the best.

It wasn't until I began collecting the marks for the midterm report cards later in the Fall when I noticed Derek's grades. He was always busy working and never asked me any questions so I figured that he was doing alright. I had noticed a few test results that were low, but he always did well on the projects and homework I assigned the class. I guess I failed to keep track of his progress in our classroom since I was struggling with a few other students' behaviors in the classroom. It had been a particularly difficult fall since I had no extra support from the paraprofessionals or the VP who *always* seemed to be busy.

After coming to the conclusion that Derek needed extra support and clearly wasn't hearing the lessons well, I decided to reach out to the special education teacher, Stephanie Waters, for extra support. I told her that I had noticed Derek's grades slipping and thought that we needed a team meeting to figure out a proper plan for him. Stephanie agreed and arranged a team meeting, which included Ellen, myself, Stephanie, and Derek's parents. But the meeting was a total flop. First of all, Stephanie and Ellen were *both* nearly 25 minutes late to the meeting. They apologized, saying they had got caught up in other things, but I could see that Derek's parents were unimpressed.

Stephanie was supposed to lead the meeting, but didn't seem to know what the meeting was about. I saw her whisper to Ellen, "What are we talking about again?"

"*Derek*," Ellen had whispered back.

Figure 22.3 Concerned Parents Talking to a Teacher. *Source*: https://www.istockphoto.com. Credit: vm.

Stephanie didn't have an agenda for the meeting, so the conversation seemed scattered. And Stephanie did most of the talking and didn't appear to care about Derek's parent's concerns. We had only been chatting for about 20 minutes when Derek's dad looked at his watch and said, "I need to go. I thought this meeting was only going to be *30* minutes and now I'm late for work."

"Sorry about that," Stephanie said. "How about we meet again next week? We'll keep the conversation shorter. We need to create a plan to help Derek."

"Yes, I thought we were going to do that *today*," Derek's dad said, clearly irritated. "None of you seem concerned about our son." He left the room, his wife following behind him. Everyone could feel the tension in the room as the two left. I felt so embarrassed about how the meeting had gone. We hadn't come to any real solutions to help Derek. It had been totally ineffective. I wanted to show them that Stephanie, Ellen, and I were all here to support Derek but I didn't know how after such a meeting.

I hope our next meeting is more effective, I thought as I walked back to my classroom. *Derek's parents probably think that this school team is completely dysfunctional. Maybe we are.*

Questions To Consider:

1. How could Stephanie and Ellen have better supported a teacher that was new to teaching a student with a hearing impairment?

2. What made the team meeting in this case ineffective? What are some strategies you use to make school-based team meetings effective?
3. What are some possible solutions for a difficult classroom if your province or state experiences large budget cuts?
4. How might the administration have better handled the support this student needed as well as the meeting?

Expert Opinion:

When it comes to leadership, inclusion, and special education, clear and constructive communication is an essential component to working effectively as a team and creating a school culture where there are opportunities for all members of the school community to express their concerns and for their voices to be heard. In this case, poor communication and lack of effective leadership occurred on multiple levels which diminished the capacity by the school to create an inclusive and supportive learning environment for Derek and his needs.

Inclusive leadership creates the conditions and outlets for all relevant parties to have a voice in the process which in this case should include Derek, his parents, the teachers, and the school administrators. Effective communication between the parties would allow for constructive dialogue where information from multiple sources is gathered, concerns and ideas exchanged, and everyone shares their input toward creating an action plan for next steps to support Derek.

In this case, there was a clear lack of communication via check-ins by Ellen the vice principal and Stephanie the special education teacher with Derek's home-room teacher. Check-ins would have been an effective strategy to collect timely and constructive feedback about Derek's progress considering that Derek's home-room teacher is only in their second year of teaching and notified that support services of paraprofessionals were not able to be secured to help with Derek' needs directly. As well, communication between Derek's home-room teacher and his parents needed to be more constant and effective. The teacher made the assumption that everything was alright since Derek did not raise any concerns. It would have been a good idea to have informal check-ins with Derek and his parents about how things are progressing as it would have provided them with an opportunity to express their concerns. Many students feel uncomfortable sharing their concerns in a large setting in front of other students due to fear of being scrutinized or made fun of, but in a one-on-one informal setting they might open up and express their concerns.

When it came to the school team meeting with Derek's parents, there needed to be more leadership from Ella and Stephanie. The meeting needed more structure in order for it to be effective and action-oriented in identifying next steps to support Derek given that only 30 minutes was allocated for the meeting. Being late for a 30-minute school team meeting and unprepared creates barriers to building effective relationships with parents. Authentic relationships rooted in an ethics of care are key in creating a school culture where parents and students feel welcome and safe to share their concerns and experiences. In order to make the meeting more constructive, it is suggested for all parties to come prepared to share information about the student's needs and suggestions for next steps. As part of this dialogue, it should be discussed what strategies have been tried so far and what results shown as a result of the approaches and strategies already implemented. This then allows for all voices to be part of the process of creating a school support plan. This shows that the school cares and is trying multiple approaches to support Derek.

This case also highlights another important aspect when it comes to special education: that although part of the struggle is to get students to officially be identified for their needs from the appropriate professionals, the other battle is to ensure the school team works collectively and with the parents and the student to track their progress and find relevant approaches and strategies to support the student given the resources available to the school. Although increased funding can help secure resources for a school, in many schools the reality is that there is a lack of funding to secure ideal support services by professionals to support students with special needs. This should not translate into thinking that the school is not responsible or is not in a position to help the students and support their needs. Inclusion is about the embodied experience of students feeling safe and supported while at school. Hence, teachers and administrators can still work toward creating an inclusive and supportive school culture by building strong relationships with students and their parents. Small strategies such as informal check-ins with students and parents via phone calls or communication via the student planner can facilitate building relationships and minimizing miscommunication due to making of assumptions. Constant communication between multiple stakeholders allows for collection of information and constructive feedback about how the student is doing, so adjustments can be made in a timely manner to the content, environment and/or the teacher pedagogy to support the student and their identified and unidentified needs. As well, feedback for parents does not always have to be about negative events. Positive achievements should also be celebrated and shared with parents as symbolic of progress. Overall, the effectiveness of the intersection of leadership, inclusion, and special education should be assessed by how well the needs of students are supported.

Name: Ardavan Eizadirad
Position: Assistant Professor
Institutional Affiliation: Faculty of Education, Wilfrid Laurier University

Resources

Books

Beveridge, S. (2005). *Children, families and schools: developing partnerships for inclusive education*. Routledge.

This book by Sally Beveridge looks at how effective communication between school and home is always important, but becomes essential when there are special education needs involved. The book includes a background on home-school communication, a framework for how we should look at communication when trying to create inclusive schools, and strategies for effective communication with parents. The book also highlights issues of diversity and how communication may look different for different families.

Friend, M. P., & Cook, L. (2017). *Interactions: collaboration skills for school professionals* (2nd ed.). Pearson.

This most recent edition of the book was written by Lynne Cook and is geared toward those in special education. Chapter six of the text focuses on teams of educators and how they communicate and interact, while chapter 11 focuses on families and how to effectively communicate with the home. The book also has chapters on feedback, mentoring, co-teaching, and difficult interactions, to name a few.

Videos

National Deaf Children's Society. (2016, March 22). *Tips for teaching deaf children with a mild hearing loss* [Video]. YouTube. https://www.youtube.com/watch?v=jylb7TDn2Tk&t=2s

This video by the National Deaf Children's Society provides teachers with five tips for teaching students who are hearing impaired. Referencing both environmental and pedagogical changes, this video looks at all areas of how to teach a student who is hearing impaired. There are also other resources cited at the end of the video specific to elementary or secondary and resource with lesson plans.

Academic Articles

Trainor, A. A. (2010). Diverse approaches to parent advocacy during special education home-school interactions. *Remedial and Special Education, 31*(1), 34–47. doi: 10.1177/0741932508324401

This study by Audrey Trainor looks at parent advocacy for their children with special education needs. The study explains that the more a parent knows about the special education system and the opportunities available for their child the more then can advocate for their child. The study also concluded that different resources and knowledge is needed when discussing one individual student as supposed to systemic change.

Woods, A. D., Morrison, F. J., & Palincsar, A. S. (2018). Perceptions of communication practices among stakeholders in special education. *Journal of Emotional and Behavioural Disorders, 25(4)*. doi: 10.1177/106346617733716

The authors interviewed 17 special education stakeholders on home-school relationships across grade levels. The study found that the more home-school communication there is, the more satisfied parents are with the schools. The article also talks about comorbidity and includes recommendations for improving this home-school communication.

Professional Articles

Ontario Ministry of Education. (2007). *Shared solutions: A guide to preventing and resolving conflicts regarding programs and services for students with special education needs.* Edu.gov.on.ca. http://www.edu.gov.on.ca/eng/general/elemsec/speced/shared.pdf

This resource is geared toward finding solutions to problems involving students with special education needs. Appendix A on page 43 shares what the roles and responsibilities are of different stakeholders, like students, teachers, principals, parents, special education teachers, school teams, the school boards or districts and the provincial ministry of education. By understanding everyone's role in supporting students with special education needs, stakeholders are more likely to fulfill their responsibilities and the team can work together effectively.

Rosenberg, D. (2020). Finding time for new teachers to thrive. *Educational Leadership,* 77, 61–65. http://www.ascd.org/publications/educational-leadership/jun20/vol77/num09/Finding-Time-for-New-Teachers-to-Thrive.aspx

The article by David Rosenberg, a partner at Education Resources Strategies, shares a "shelter-and-develop" model. This model would be implemented by principals and other leaders to help new teachers in their transition from learner to educator. The article includes a schedule for implementing the model for both new and veteran teachers.

Websites

Bright Hub Education. (2010, March 29). *Teaching strategies for hearing impaired students.* https://www.brighthubeducation.com/special-ed-hearing-impairments/67528-tips-and-strategies-for-teaching-hearing-impaired-students/

The article highlights teaching students with hearing impairments folder and includes a long list of strategies. The webpage includes physical changes to make to the classroom, how to make regular evaluations, and visual strategies to implement. By understanding how teachers can help their students, principals are better able to guide the teachers.

Ontario Teachers Federation. (n.d.). *Self-advocacy skills.* Teachspeced. http://www.teachspeced.ca/?q=node/720

This website was created by the Ontario Teachers' Federation to help educators find great teaching strategies and practices for special education students. This specific website page provides different teaching strategies to teach self-advocacy skills to students; it looks specifically at instructional, environmental and assessment strategies. There are also extra resources at the bottom of the page.

The Understood Team. (n.d.). *Assistive technology for learning: What you need to know*. Understood. https://www.understood.org/en/school-learning/assistive-technology/assistive-technologies-basics/assistive-technology-what-it-is-and-how-it-works

This website seeks to educate the public on assistive technology. This article can help understand what different assistive technologies do, finding the right ones to use. The website has specific information for parents, caregivers, educators, young adults or employers to use more technology in their everyday lives.

Chapter 23

"No One Is Listening to Me"

CASE 3: SCHOOL TEAM

Crosscutting Themes: Communication, Collaboration.
Leadership Competencies: Values Inclusion, Fosters Relationships, Embodies Professional Standards, Differentiated Instruction, Professional Learning.

Elijah is a grade five student at Park Street Elementary. He struggles in school, especially with writing assignments because it often takes him a long time to write.

Elijah has an Individualized Education Plan (IEP) which provides him with specific accommodations to help him succeed in school. He is permitted to use voice-to-text software with his Chrome Book and is allocated extra time for tests and assignments. Sometimes, when Elijah is having a difficult day and is frustrated with writing, he lashes out at his teacher, Ms. Sebastian, and refuses to do work. The school principal, special education resource teacher, a paraprofessional, and Ms. Sebastian have met occasionally in the past to discuss Elijah's progress.

In the past month, Elijah's behavior has intensified dramatically. He gets frustrated in class a lot more and has lashed out more aggressively than before. Two weeks ago, he threw a stapler at the chalkboard and ran out of the room after the teacher confronted him about it. Ms. Sebastian is becoming more and more concerned about Elijah's behavior and worries that something else may be causing his temper and problematic behavior. She is starting to feel very stressed about the situation because it has becoming increasingly difficult to get Elijah to listen to her. She struggles with how best to handle Elijah's behavior. She has tried giving him a time-out and not letting him go

Figure 23.1 Student Focused on Their Writing. *Source*: https://www.istockphoto.com. Credit: Halfpoint.

outside for recess when he acts inappropriately in class, but nothing seems to make a difference.

One day when Elijah was inside during recess, he wandered to the boy's bathroom and wrote his name with a permanent marker all over a stall.

Another boy saw what Elijah was doing and told the school principal, Mr. Green. Mr. Green sat down with Elijah to talk about why he had decided to write his name all over the stall. Elijah denied everything. Mr. Green told him that it was better to own up to it now than to continue to lie. Elijah didn't seem to care and sat in silence across from the principal. Mr. Green informed Elijah that he was suspended for the next two days, which really upset Elijah. He began sobbing. Mr. Green called Elijah's mom, who came and picked him up.

Mr. Green decided to call a school team meeting to discuss Elijah's recent behavior. Mr. Green, Ms. Sebastian, the special education resource teacher, Mr. Buchan, and a paraprofessional, Mr. Palmer, met in the staffroom at the end of a school day. Each of the team members took time to share their experiences with Elijah since the last time they had met. After everyone finished sharing, Mr. Buchan said,

> From the sounds of it, I think Elijah may have something like oppositional defiant disorder. Do we know if he's dealing with something stressful at home? I

Figure 23.2 Concerned Teacher Meeting. *Source*: https://www.istockphoto.com. Credit: SDI Productions.

wonder if his parents have considered taking him to a doctor? Maybe getting a mental health assessment?

"I heard that his parents are getting divorced," said Ms. Sebastian. "But I honestly don't know much more than that about Elijah's home life."

"You might be right about Elijah having ODD," Mr. Palmer piped up.

I have had experience with a child who we suspected had ODD before and to be honest, even with the mental health assessment, there wasn't much extra support given. I definitely think that it should be mentioned to his parents. I think our best strategy is to come up with strategies that can help Elijah when he returns from his suspension in a couple of days.

"Yes, I really need some help," Ms. Sebastian said.

He's been a handful. I don't know how much longer I can last with him in the classroom without support. And I don't think we should be making any excuses for him by claiming he has a *disorder* of some sort. He just isn't listening and following rules. And I think he *knows* he's not behaving appropriately but thinks he can get away with it. I wonder if he should be suspended for longer than two days?

"I think two days is appropriate and is in line with the board protocols," said Mr. Green.

"I don't think he should have been suspended at all," Mr. Buchan jumped in. "This kid needs help. He needs support *at school*. Kicking him out for two days will do *nothing*."

Mr. Green cut off Mr. Buchan and said, "Elijah vandalized a bathroom stall. That merits a suspension based on the guidelines we follow."

"You're the principal. *You* know best," Mr. Buchan replied.

"Ok, let's keep this conversation focused," Mr. Green said, annoyed.

I think we all just want what is best for Elijah. Ms. Sebastian, I understand your concerns but I don't think we are making excuses for his behavior but we do need to educate ourselves and understand his behavior better in order to help him. Perhaps I will even look into bringing a specialist to help us better understand Elijah's situation.

Ms. Sebastian responded and said, "I feel like no one is listening to me or thinking about what I am dealing with. Honestly, I think I'm wasting my time here. I'm going to go." Ms. Sebastian got up from the table and walked out of the staff room. Mr. Green, Mr. Palmer, and Mr. Buchan sat awkwardly and silently, not knowing what to say. They didn't realize how upset Ms. Sebastian had been.

"Let's meet another time," Mr. Green eventually said. "Tomorrow at lunch? We need to have a game plan. Hopefully Ms. Sebastian can keep it together next time."

The three left the room, all wondering how this team would work together effectively to support Elijah.

Questions To Consider:

1. What concerns does the case raise? What discussion points are concerning? What steps have been taken that you see as helpful?
2. What next steps would you take when dealing with a case like Elijah? What is the role of the school team in determining next steps in supporting students with special education needs?
3. Do you think that a suspension is an appropriate step in a situation involving a student with a special education need? Why or why not?
4. How would you approach Elijah's parent(s)/guardian(s) about the behavior and the need for further assessment?
5. Ms. Sebastian is clearly upset and frustrated with the situation with Elijah—so much so that she left the meeting. How should Mr. Green support Ms. Sebastian? What should his next steps be?

Expert Opinion:

The attitudes and actions of the school leader and school team in this case reflect deficit-based conceptions of difference and exclusionary practices, which indicate an urgent need for a cultural shift at all levels. To illustrate, the school leader described Elijah as "not caring," team members pathologized and labeled him as likely having "ODD," and the strategies employed included time-out, removal of recess, and suspension. In order to facilitate a shift toward a more inclusive culture, that embraces diversity, the school leader in this case should deeply reflect upon his own personal values regarding inclusion, so that he can clearly articulate a vision of inclusivity. If the school leader articulates his values and beliefs regarding inclusion, he will be better able to build consensus among the school team regarding shared inclusive values (Ainscow & Sandill, 2010). A social justice framework that explores inclusion through the lens of equity and human rights may support this school leader, and the school team in understanding why inclusion is important, and compel them to take action to support a cultural change. In addition to building consensus regarding inclusive values, adopting pedagogical approaches that align with the shared vision of inclusivity such as Universal Design for Learning (UDL) (CAST; Rose & Meyer, 2002), the Three-Block Model of UDL (Katz, 2013), as well as restorative practices (Morrison & Vaandering, 2011) may further help to translate the vision into reality.

As a school leader, it is critical to establish regular, positive, proactive contact with parents, students, teachers, and community stakeholders in order to build reciprocal relationships based on trust and mutual respect. In this case, there were several missed opportunities, where the school leader could have meaningfully engaged with Elijah and his parent. Given that school leaders are role models for their staff, it is not surprising that the teachers in this case also described having limited parental contact, and little knowledge of Elijah's personal circumstances. The absence of positive, reciprocal relationships may serve to undermine the development of an inclusive school culture, and weaken communities by exacerbating the marginalization of some groups. In order to support the development of a more inclusive school culture, the school leader should engage parents as collaborative partners by communicating openly and often, displaying respect for their unique values, beliefs, and perspectives, and enlisting their involvement in shared decision-making (Leithwood et al., 2020).

In this case, the team meeting also reflected an absence of systematic, organized planning structures, which interfered with the provision of support and created conflict within the team. In order to overcome these challenges, the school leader should explore the implementation of Response to Intervention

(RTI) (Fuchs & Fuchs, 2006). Adopting a multitiered structure of service delivery like RTI would provide a process for timely assessment, evidence-based instruction, progress monitoring, and the use of data to inform instruction (National Centre of RTI, n.d.). The implementation of RTI also fosters collaboration as roles and responsibilities are clarified, and supports are organized so that teachers have greater awareness of the range of supports that are available and the strategies for implementation (Addison & Warger, 2011). One way to begin this process would be for the school leader to engage in professional learning about RTI along with the teachers, as a part of a Professional Learning Community (PLC) (Bender & Waller, 2011; Robinson et al., 2008). Leading these broad-based cultural and structural changes is challenging; however, the creation of a more equitable and inclusive school is worth the investment.

References:

Addison, P., & Warger, C.L. (2011). *Building your school's capacity to implement RTI.* ASCD.

Ainscow, M., & Sandill, A. (2010). Developing inclusive education systems: The role of organisational cultures and leadership, *International Journal of Inclusive Education,* 14(4), 401–416, doi: 10.1080/13603110802504903

Bender, W. N., & Waller, L. (2011). *RTI & differentiated reading in the K-8 Classroom.* Solution Tree Press.

Causton, J. & Theoharis, G. (2014). *The principal's handbook for leading inclusive schools.* Paul H. Brookes Publishing Co.

Fuchs, D., & Fuchs, L. S. (2006). Introduction to Response to Intervention: What, why, and how valid is it? *Reading Research Quarterly, 41*(1), 93–99. doi: 10.1598/RRQ.41.1.4

Katz, J. (2013). The three-block model of universal design for learning (UDL): Engaging students in inclusive education. *Canadian Journal of Education,* 36, 153–194.

Leithwood, K., Harris, A., & Hopkins, D. (2020). Seven strong claims about successful school leadership revisited. *School Leadership and Management,* 40(1), 5–22.

Morrison, B. E., & Vaandering, D. (2012). Restorative justice: Pedagogy, praxis, and discipline. *Journal of School Violence,* 11(2), 138–155, doi: 10.1080/15388220.2011.653322

Nation Center on Response to Intervention. (n.d.). *The essential components of rti.* Retrieved from http://www.rti4success.org/

Name: Nadine Bartlett
Position: Assistant Professor
Institutional Affiliation: University of Manitoba

Resources

Books

Boynton, M., & Boynton C. (2005). *The educator's guide to preventing and solving discipline problems.* Association for Supervision and Curriculum Development.

This book by Christine and Mark Boynton focuses on classroom management and school discipline. The book includes four sections and seventeen chapters, each section looks at the issue from a different perspective; the classroom perspective, the whole school perspective, the individual perspective and then concludes with a section dedicated to strategies. The section on the individual student would be especially useful to look at anger management, responding to disruptions, dealing with serious rule violations, and students with oppositional defiant disorder.

Videos

Jensen, S. (2019, October). *How can we support the emotional well-being of teachers?* [Video]. Ted Talk. https://www.ted.com/talks/sydney_jensen_how_can_we_support_the_emotional_well_being_of_teachers?language=en

This video presented by Sydeny Jensen is a Ted Talk calling for change in our education system for the better support for the mental health of our teachers and educators. Jensen talks about secondary trauma and how as educators we take home the burden of our students when we create relationships with them. She gives examples of how some schools are making small changes to support their educators' mental health.

PBS News Hour. (2014, January 8). *Are some U.S. school discipline policies too punitive?* [Video]. PBS News Hour. https://www.pbs.org/newshour/show/Are-some-U-S-school-discipline-policies-too-punitive

This video is an interview done by Hari Sreenivasan with Sherrilyn Ifill and Chester Finn, two stakeholders in education with opposing views on the matter. The interview tries to show two different views on suspension and disciplining students in the classroom. The school to prison pipeline is discussed as well as the guidelines released by the US government on school discipline.

Academic Articles

Puskar, K. R., Stark, K. H., Northcut, T., William, R., & Haley, T. (2010). Teach kids to cope with anger: Peer education. *Journal of Child Health Care,* 15(1), 5–13. doi: 10.1177/1367493510382932

This study by Kathryn Puskar, Kirsti Stark, Terri Northcut, Rick Williams and Tammy Haley examined the effects of an anger management program taught by peer educators to 4th to 8th grade students. The article examined the use of high school aged peer educators to implement the program and found that the younger students enjoyed having the high school students lead the activities and felt that they may want to lead it someday themselves. The use of peer educators was proven to be extremely successful in this study to communicate anger management and coping skills.

Professional Articles

Aguilar, E. (2017). *Helping teachers thrive.* Edutopia. https://www.edutopia.org/article/helping-teachers-thrive

Author Elena Aguilar wrote this article to help school leaders build and foster resilience in their teachers. The five tips Aguilar provides are for school leaders to implement themselves and watch as their teachers become more resilient to the challenges that may arise during the school year.

Department of Education and Training. *EFFECTIVE CONSULTATION: Improving outcomes for students with disability.* Canberra, Australia: Australian Government. Retrieved from https://docs.education.gov.au/system/files/doc/other/dse-fact-sheet-4-effective-consultation_1.pdf

This document presented by the Australian government shares how to have an effective consultation with all stakeholders to help students with disabilities. There is a list of five key principles to keep in mind and key issues to cover during the meeting. The document has a quick guide and tips for agreement on the last page where are both great reference tools when meeting with a school-based team.

Wheeler, R. (2017). *Suspensions don't teach.* Edutopia. https://www.edutopia.org/article/suspensions-dont-teach

Ryan Wheeler shares this article in order to educate teachers and school leaders about the alternative to suspensions, restorative justice. The article explains that by using restorative practices we will be teaching our students that their poor behavior affects those around them, and it tries to teach the students a good behavior, essentially replacing the bad behavior with a good one. The article concludes with five steps to implementing restorative justice in the classroom or school.

Websites

Alberta Education. (n.d.). *Medical/disability information for classroom teachers: Conduct disorder.* Learn Alberta. http://www.learnalberta.ca/content/inmdict/html/conduct_disorder.html

The Ministry of Education in Alberta maintains this site which contains a checklist of different implications that you should do as a classroom teacher for a student with conduct disorder. The site also includes a complete definition of conduct disorder and three sections; implications for planning and awareness, implications for instruction, and implications for social and emotional well-being. There are also a number of other disorders that the website provides implications on.

Education World. (2011). *Effective communication with parents.* https://www.educationworld.com/a_admin/effective-communication-with-parents.shtml

This article is based on the book *Communicate and motivate: The school leader's guide to effective communication* by Shelly Arneson. The article includes a question posed to administrators and three responses from different principals. The question looks at parent-teacher conferences and is an example of the information in the book by Arneson.

COMPLEX CASES

Chapter 24

"I Was on Autopilot"

CASE 1: COMPLEX CASES

Crosscutting Themes: Parents/Caregivers/Family.
Leadership Competencies: Collaboration, Problem-solving, Professional Learning, Communication.

"You're not going to guess who your 10 AM is," Fay, the school administrative assistant, said from her desk. Fay was one of those saving graces at a job like this—probably the only person I considered to be a friend in the building. Of course, I knew who she was referring to. Fay and I had both witnessed the relentless politics of the Bradleys, a couple who thought their little angel, Thomas, could do no evil. *Wrong.* Thomas *could* do evil and his teachers made sure to remind me of this every time I saw them. The past few weeks had been nonstop emails, phone calls, and meetings with the couple.

I was the principal at Vermont High School, a secondary school in a fairly prosperous part of our city. I'd been working there for five years at that point, and everything felt like it was about to explode. "Lucky me," I responded sarcastically to Fay as I stepped into my office. I closed the door behind me and sat down in my office chair.

That coffee was liquid gold after last night. My wife, Catherine, and I always left our discussions, which were usually very heated, till after 9:00 p.m. when our three kids were fast asleep. This particular discussion had gone on longer than expected. Catherine had thrown me for a loop when she talked about separating. "I think we need some time to ourselves," she had said. "It would be temporary." I told her that I would *never* consider separating. We had made vows to each other and we were not going to break those. After our discussion was over, I ended up falling asleep on the couch at 3:00 a.m.

Figure 24.1 Stressed Teacher. *Source*: https://www.istockphoto.com. Credit: Nicola Katie.

The first hour of work that morning involved what seemed to be an endless series of emails. Whenever I got to the end of the list, the email server would refresh to reveal another dozen waiting for my "immediate" response. One email in particular was important. A grade nine student named Jonathan had been displaying symptoms of depression and anxiety. His science teacher had noticed fresh cuts on his arm. Jonathan had been referred to the school councilor, Mr. Reece. Of course, his parents had been informed by the school, although everyone on Jonathan's crisis team knew that this did little to no good. Jonathan's parents were the polar opposite of Thomas'—inattentive, unconcerned, and neglectful.

I heard a knock on my door. I looked up from the blue light of the screen. It was Karen, a government ministry representative assigned to our district. She opened the door.

"Do you have a minute?"

"No, I don't."

"Sure. How can I help?"

"George, this isn't looking good, your literacy numbers and graduation rates aren't what we discussed a few months ago. Almost nothing has changed."

"Karen, I can assure you that everything in the last report has been looked after. Can we set up a meeting to go over your observations in detail? I need to know what you're seeing that I'm not seeing." Over her shoulder I can see the Bradleys enter the office—was it that time already?

"I'm more than happy to do that, George, but at this point I think we may need to get one of the superintendents involved."

At this point I'm just nodding, even though I think that getting a superintendent involved is a terrible idea. I need to get mentally prepared for this meeting with the Bradleys.

"I'll send you an email with my availability later this afternoon. But I need to go. I have a meeting in a few minutes with parents."

Karen nodded disapprovingly and exited. On cue I heard my office phone ringing; that would be Fay letting me know what I already knew. "Yes?"

"The Bradleys are here."

"Tell them I'll be with them in two minutes."

I'm opening the document I'd prepared for this meeting on my computer and hitting print. As I did this, I can feel my cellphone buzzing in my pocket. I reach into my pocket and pull it out absentmindedly. A single text appeared on the screen from my wife.

We need to talk again tonight. When will you be home?

I felt my throat get hard and my face numb slightly.

I walked to the door in a state of disbelief and opened it. I could see the annoyed faces of Mr. and Mrs. Bradley waiting in the office area. My own voice sounded distant, like it was coming from someone else.

"Hello, good to see you two again. Please come in."

The next fifteen minutes felt like I was watching myself from the ceiling. I was on autopilot, responding with nods and voicing empty, appeasing phrases as they vented. The truth is, the conversation didn't matter, the inevitable upcoming clash with the superintendent didn't matter; it was all so meaningless compared to that text.

My laptop computer, which has been put in sleep mode, suddenly sparked to life. An email. That's not supposed to happen unless the email is marked as urgent. From the corner of my eye I could see who the email was from. It was from Mr. Reece, the school counselor. I could only see the first few words of the email from the small notification box: The police just called.

Questions to Consider

1. Problems can snowball and compound very quickly, just as they did for George in this story. George kept trying to juggle all the problems himself. If you were to give advice to George, what might you suggest he do?
2. George has become cynical to many aspects of his work, including his superiors, elements of the bureaucratic process, and parents. Some of this

cynicism may even be justified. How does cynicism effect a job? Is it bad to be cynical?
3. George clearly has a lot on his plate. From his point of view, it seems like his family life and the troubled student in his school, Jonathan, should take priority. If you agree with George, what are ways in which he could make these a priority without neglecting his job responsibilities (if that's possible)?
4. What resources do you think George should pursue to help him with his problems? If those resources don't currently exist for principals to access, how would you suggest they be implemented?

Expert Opinion

> To let go of the desire to cure or rescue, to sit with the pain that compels us to reach for quick reforms, mindlessly write yet more grants that purport to offer, yet again, the solution to one or more horrible problems, to reframe standards in terms of our ability to remain open, to articulate and reflect on what we are feeling and experiencing, to face the terrors that gnaw at us, and to work through the fantasies that structure our thinking, to do these would be to begin to act ethically. (Taubman, 2000, p. 31)

This school principal's experience of a day on "autopilot" is all too familiar for school leaders. There were many days that I felt like I was on autopilot during my twenty-two years as a school administrator. I recall a parent saying to me one day that it must be so nice to be "the boss" and tell everyone what to do. I replied that their image of principalship was far from the truth. Our days are not our own; we are easily swept away by the multitude of requests and expectations that are placed in front of us. We are not in control; we are far more controlled by others and situations that arise. It seems that the more we seek to be responsive and available, the harder it is to be physically, emotionally, and intellectually present. On our most complex days we move to autopilot. We attempt to do what we can, hoping to respond competently while managing our feelings of incompetence, and most importantly do our best to interact with everyone in ethical and compassionate ways.

So we persevere through those challenging days. We take actions where we can, we reflect on our progress, we "recalibrate, take more actions, collect our stories, and calibrate again" (Bensen, 2014, p. ix). Understanding our own triggers, limits, and priorities for interaction can help us manage those seemingly impossible moments or days. In the craziness of autopilot we can find ourselves not reaching out to others, but rather withdrawing in an attempt to solve each new dilemma ourselves. In the most challenging times we need to step away from heroic (solo) decision-making (Furman, 2004) and instead, lean in to the support of our larger school community. Inviting others into our complex day promotes collaboration, community and inclusivity and helps school leaders manage the complexity of seemingly impossible days. Principalship is above all else a human enterprise and our central and most important focus is fundamentally the well-being of the students in our care (Shaprio & Stefkovich, 2010). Including others into our day can help us stay grounded in this important work.

Considerations to support my fellow colleagues to persevere (in the context of this case study):

Complex Parent Meetings

Require parents to articulate their purpose for the requested meeting. If their child is not in crisis, it is acceptable to say that you need time to gather information on their child's progress. Collaborating with others and setting up the meeting with a proactive purpose helps everyone to stay on track. With more adversarial parents, having clear expectations (code of conduct for your school and school jurisdiction) to address issues is critical to ensure a respectful and productive meeting. Bring others into the discussion with you, especially in times when you feel overwhelmed and vulnerable.

Prioritizing and Postponing Unexpected Requests

It is sometimes easy for education officials who are not in a school to forget about what life is like for a school principal. If these individuals happen to pop into your school unannounced, share a list of items you are dealing with at the moment. They need a reminder of what is happening in schools beyond standards and assessments. Validate that you are committed to school improvement and that you would be happy to have a focused and productive meeting with them, but it would need to be at a later date.

You, as principal, are also not the sole owner of school improvement. Bringing others on board offers future leaders and colleagues opportunities to take leadership roles and take ownership for school improvement.

Remember Students First

When the day seems to be at its craziest, step away and spend time with students in their classrooms. Find the places in your school where you know learning experiences are rich, authentic, and meaningful. Relish in those moments, support a student with their learning and share in their moments of success. This will ground you to your central purpose—students and their learning.

Establish a Student Support Team

Ensuring a strong collaborative school network to support vulnerable students is critical.

Ensuring that guidance counselors, classroom teachers, and resource teachers and support staff have processes to engage with complex learners and to support each other ensures that the principal is not the one having to be the expert or the one making all the critical moment to moment decisions. Surround yourself with capable staff who believe in the shared responsibility of all students.

Personal Challenges

The life of school leadership can be all encompassing, yet we must remember that we have personal lives that can also be very complex. Close your door and take time to make the call that will help you move forward for the day. You most likely can't resolve the issue, but seek to have a proactive plan that can help you manage the rest of your day in the best way possible.

Figure 24.2 Teachers Supporting Each Other. *Source*: https://www.istockphoto.com. Credit: monkeybusinessimages.

Final Thought

Remember to forgive yourself:

Principalship, like teaching and learning, is something that is never complete. Each day, each student, each situation teaches us about ourselves as leaders. Be kind and forgiving to yourself. Remember to breathe purposely and remember to be grateful to be able to do this important work: "By choosing integrity, I become more whole, but wholeness does not mean perfection. It means becoming more real by acknowledging the whole of who I am" (Palmer, 1998, p. 13).

References

Bensen, (2014). *Hanging in: Strategies for teaching the students who challenge us most.* ASCD.

Furman, G. (2004). The ethic of community. *Journal of Educational Administration,* 42(2), 215–235.

Palmer, P. (1998). *The courage to teach: Exploring the inner landscape of a teachers' life.* Jossey-Bass Publishers.

Shapiro, J. P. and Stefkovich, J. A. (2010). *Ethical leadership and decision making in education: Applying theoretical perspectives to complex dilemmas,* 3rd edition. Taylor & Francis Group, ProQuest Ebook Central, https://ebookcentral.proquest.com/lib/mtroyal-ebooks/detail.action?docID=547342

Taubman P. (2000). Teaching without hope: What is really at stake in the standards movement high stakes testing and the drive for "practical reforms". *Journal of Curriculum Theorizing* 16(3), 19–33.

Name: Joy Chadwick
Position: Assistant Professor
Institutional Affiliation: Mount Royal University

Resources

Book

Osborne, E.L., & Dowling, E. (2003). *The family and the school: A joint systems approach to problems with children.* 2nd ed. Routledge.

This book explores the relationship of family therapy and consultation to schools, discussing theoretical framework, implications, an interactional perspective, discussions of clinic in schools and the benefits for teachers, children and parents as well as the impact of joint intervention with teachers, children and parents in school settings. The book concludes that with an interactional approach, the two systems can overlap successfully with intentional practices such as counseling services and theoretical perspectives of child development.

Academic Articles

Pollock, K. & Hauseman, D. C. (2018). The use of e-Mail and principals' work: A double-edged sword. *Leadership and Policy in Schools*, 3, 382–393. doi: 10.1080/15700763.2017.1398338

This article by Katina Pollock and David Cameron Houseman focuses on the impact of emails, smartphones, and social networking for professionals. There is credit to technology making work easier or manageable but there are also emerging trends of principals' experience increased use of email without positive results such as lack of work-life balance when quick responses are expected, work intensification due to volume of emails, and extension of the typical workday. The journal discovers that email is the main contributor to work intensification and blurred home and work boundaries.

Taras, H. L., & Young, T. L. (2004). School-based mental health services. *Pediatrics*, 113(6), 1839+.

This journal article is a compilation of observations that school resources such as conflict resolution, enrichment and recreation, promotion of social and emotional development and programs combined with community resources such as youth development programs, and public health and safety both create a system for positive development and systems of prevention that work to engage all students and facilitate early intervention for those of high need. This article cites the importance of considering special education and mental health services, and school-based mental health services to provide positive, friendly, and open social environments for all students.

Professional Articles

Carny, P. & Parr, M. (2014). Resilient, active, and flourishing: Supporting positive mental health and well-being in school communities. *What Works Research into Practice*. http://www.edu.gov.on.ca/eng/literacynumeracy/inspire/research/WW_ResilientFlourish.Pdf

This article focuses on promoting well-being for both students and teachers to cope with adversity. Specifically noting aspects of well-being such as nourishment, activity and being physically and psychologically safe this article explains positive mental health, resiliency and then breaks down a continuum of support for all students and how to promote mental health in schools with student teacher and family strategies for well-being.

Websites

Children's Mental Health Ontario. (2020). *Teacher resources*. https://cmho.org/teacher-resources/

Children's Mental Health Ontario has compiled a set of resources (last updated 2020) for teachers. These resources are available to help encourage the conversation of mental wellness in the classroom, what the most likely mental health problems are present in today's classroom such as anxiety and mood disorders, ADHD, and behavioral disorders. The guide offers tips for early intervention and identification such as the ABCs of mental health, School training and provincial implementation of support as well as a guide to build classroom resources, and a reference guide for classrooms including important phone numbers.

Classroom Mental Health (2020). *A teachers toolkit for high school.* https://classroommentalhealth.org/

A resource from the University of Michigan for teachers to learn how to talk to students about mental health, community resources and how to use them, strategies on working with families, and signs of mood disorders. These resources have been compiled to support students while also reserving a section for self-care and for teachers to consider their own well-being as well.

EDUgains (n.d.). *Classroom educator mental health.* Edugains. https://www.edugains.ca/newsite/mentalHealth/index.html

This website is a variety of click button resources for teachers and education professionals. The site contains a list of videos on Mental health and the Ontario Curriculum, Supporting Learning Environments, and Continuing the Conversation. An educators guide to "Supporting Minds" is included containing early signs of mental health, and addiction problems along with strategies to support students in the classroom. The site also brings awareness and resources to the School Mental Health ASSIST program. Finally additional resources regarding Mental Health for parents are included.

Fleming, N. (2019, August 9). *Students can now miss school for a 'mental health day'.* Edutopia. https://www.edutopia.org/article/students-can-now-miss-school-mental-health-day

This web article explains how a new legislation in Oregon and Utah allows students five excusable mental health days in a three-month period. This was able to be legislated after research found that nearly a third of all high school students had experiences significant periods of sadness and hopelessness within the school year and 17% contemplated suicide. This represented a large need for mental health advocates, and awareness to help reduce the stigma around youth mental health and suicide.

Muir, T. (2018, October 24). *How to avoid principal burnout and love the job again.* We are Teachers. https://www.weareteachers.com/principal-burnout/

This web article written by Trevor Muir in 2018 focuses on principal burnout from frequent high-stress decision-making processes. The article speaks to inspire principals to remember why they started, that they believe in education, to focus on collaboration, and to incorporate parents into solution-oriented decision-making. This is a feel good article with strategies to re-engage in your work.

Ontario Principals Council. *Leading mentally healthy schools.* https://smh-assist.ca/wp-content/uploads/LMHS-Flipchart-EN-Web.pdf

The School Mental Health ASSIST (Ontario) program has created a flip chat by administrators for school administrators. This resource is expansive and includes many visuals explaining common language; the dual continuum model, which explains that one, can experience mental illness while maintaining well-being at the same time. The resource also breaks down tiers of intervention/prevention to gain practical skills for student and staff well-being.

Ontario Ministry of Education. (n.d.). *Exploring the "social" personal leadership resources: Perceiving emotions, managing emotions & acting in emotionally appropriate ways.* Ideas Into Action Bulletin 7. http://www.edu.gov.on.ca/eng/policyfunding/leadership/IdeasIntoActionBulletin7.pdf

This government document explores personal leadership resources. Specifically, with three resources, social, psychological and cognitive. The article breaks down each resource and communicates strategies to make them helpful for teachers and administration to put into practice. The article also specifically discusses the power of emotions and how they contribute to one's leadership and decision-making with strategies to improve one's ability to cope and instead create positive working environments through leadership.

Ontario Ministry of Education. (n.d.). *Quick facts for parents: Learning about mental health.* Edugains.http://www.edugains.ca/resourcesMH/ClassroomEducator/QuickFactsMentalHealth_eng%20D2.pdf

A PDF fact sheet provided by the Ministry of Education in Ontario provides resources and information for parents to understand mental health, and what students learn at school in regards to mental health at different ages. The fact sheet also provides tips on talking with children about mental health, and "more information" resources listed at the bottom for parents to continue their exploration.

Chapter 25

The Case of Bethany

CASE 2: COMPLEX CASES

Crosscutting Themes: Collaboration.
Leadership Competencies: Collaboration, Values Inclusion, Problem-solving, Communication, Policies and Procedures, Professional Learning.

Education is a right, not a privilege.

I had to read those words every day when I walked into the building. It was engraved above the front entranceway to the school. There is something decidedly intriguing about that statement. It sounded enlightened, progressive, and inclusive—and I want my school to be all of those things. But I was quickly learning that it was much harder to live out that statement than it was to say it.

I was the principal of a small middle school in a rural district. Bethany, a new student, had joined a grade seven class midway through the term. Bethany and her family had moved into town about two months ago. Bethany's parents hadn't mentioned an individual education plan (IEP) or any disabilities when she registered with the school—which now made sense.

I got plenty of feedback from the teachers on her first day. Bethany displayed many of the signs and symptoms of a behavioral exceptionality, including unexpected antisocial behavior, verbal outbursts, and trouble focusing on classroom activities.

When an awkward phone call was placed to Bethany's parents to inquire about their daughter, they acted as if what I was saying was no surprise. They weren't offended, they weren't alarmed, they were blasé and nonplussed.

They had argued that this was the way she had always been and her siblings were no different. I felt like they might have heard similar things in the past.

There was a Learning Support Teacher, Mrs. Kane, in the school, but she was limited in the support she could provide to Bethany due to her other heavy time commitments with other students. We had very little information from which to develop a plan. Fortunately, the team of teachers in my school were fantastic and were prepared to help to the greatest degree possible.

I ran on my condo building's treadmill every evening to try and reinvigorate myself.

I was exhausted even though I didn't like to admit it. I found that Bethany's case was on my mind more and more. Nevertheless, running helped with the stress. And you better believe I was stressed. I was starting to regularly receive emails from the teachers who taught Bethany about needing more classroom support, and I knew that wasn't possible. The funding wasn't there, especially for a child without a diagnosis. Sometimes during the lunch hour they would show up to my office, clearly agitated and concerned, and just talk about how out of control things were getting.

Bethany began having tantrums periodically and even sometimes went to the extent of throwing chairs, causing the classrooms to be evacuated. "Clearing the room" was protocol now, and it meant that every tantrum was interfering with every other child's education. Some of the classroom

Figure 25.1 Teacher Exercising to Cope with Stress. *Source*: https://www.istockphoto.com. Credit: Ljupco.

educational assistants were stepping in when they could to try and help, but it was abundantly clear that Bethany needed her own support worker.

I began getting the dreaded calls and emails from other parents at the school, inquiring and complaining about their own child's education. I understood where they were coming from. I would have had the same concerns if I was a parent or guardian of a child in the same class as Bethany.

Then it happened. Bethany's science teacher, Mr. Brown, unexpectedly applied for a stress leave. The minute I got the notice and saw that the union representative was CC'd on the email I knew we were entering new territory of stress on my staff. What's worse was that this meant I would be stepping in to find someone new to teach science. We were a small town, and finding a teacher who had expertise in science could take weeks.

It's terrible to say, but this kind of balancing act wouldn't have been necessary a few decades ago. Kids like Bethany wouldn't go to a typical school, they often would stay home or go to a special education school if the town or city had one. I often found myself wishing things worked the same way today but felt guilty whenever this thought crossed my mind. After all, I believed in inclusion of all students. What had happened to this deep-rooted belief?

Three weeks and many incidents, emails, and conversations later, I was at my breaking point. I had stopped running when I got home, I often went straight to bed. I was often lucky if I could get through an entire day without some kind of incident happening. My work with Bethany—and her teachers—took over more and more of my working hours. None of my other responsibilities or duties disappeared, they merely stacked up, waiting for me to attend to them.

My superintendent had been supportive but she had was also overwhelmed with a lot of complex cases. There was an upcoming Professional Development day, and she suggested we dedicate that day to finding ways to support the teacher in the school and to develop a plan for Bethany going forward. There was nothing ideal about the circumstances we were facing, so it was going to require creative thinking.

That day was tough, I still remember it now. We had to listen to a lot of heartbreak and stress from some of our friends and colleagues. We had to listen to frustrations we knew we didn't have the resources or tools to solve. And finally, we had to make compromises; I would have rather we didn't. In the end, we decided to reorganize one of the schedules of an educational assistant so that she could be available to support Bethany. This meant that the student who would normally be the focus of the assistant's time—Logan who had a significant cognitive and physical disability—would not have the assistant's full attention. As a result of the educational assistant's increased focus on Bethany, the number of incidents began to go down. But this new arrangement led to a new problem: I began getting calls from Logan's parents with concerns that his needs were not being met.

My job hasn't been the same since Bethany arrived at our school. She can be a sweet girl and I hope she prospers when she moves into high school in a few years. But we have to figure out a way to help us all be successful until that time arrives.

Questions To Consider:

1. This principal works in a rural district. This comes with its own set of funding, culture and resource challenges. How could the principal in this story have worked around these challenges?
2. The principal in this story runs every day to try and alleviate stress. What are coping mechanisms you might use to de-stress? How can you ensure these supporting habits don't fall by the wayside when things get tough?
3. The principal in this story had to make difficult choices and tradeoffs given the situation she faced. How would you have handled her situation? Was there something you disagreed with? Something you agreed with?

Expert Opinion:

Anyone can teach a child who is a good learner. But it makes us who we are as teachers when we bump into kids who struggle. That's when you have to work for it (Wendy Payne, Principal, Strawberry Vale School, Greater Victoria School District, British Columbia, Canada's Outstanding Principals Award winner, 2009).

The school is the heart of a rural community and newly arrived Bethany is a member of the community who belongs in this school [full stop]. Students such as Bethany, are unexpected; they puzzle and challenge us. They cause us to either close our classroom, and in many cases, our school doors, or alternatively, swing those doors open wide. The case of Bethany is a *shared* challenge, one for the entire school community, including parents, students, teaching and instructional support staff, the administrative and caretaking staff, even the school bus drivers. As Wendy Payne asserts, this is a school that needs to "work for it." A collaborative team approach, shared decision-making responsibility, and strong, clear lines of communication among *all* stakeholders is needed to understand and effectively teach and support Bethany throughout her school years. As Tschannen-Moran (2001) states, "When possible, solutions are evaluated in light of overarching goals and key values, it may result in a greater sharing of those values and goals" (p. 310). In this case, the entire school body needs to individually and collectively dig deep to consider and define what that slogan above their school entranceway really means for *their* school community. The school principal needs to initiate and lead this process by collectively "building a vision and setting direction, understanding and developing people, and redesigning the school to support teachers" and by extension, students (McLeskey & Waldron, 2015, p. 73). The resulting vision serves as a framework for developing and implementing school policies, procedures, and protocols that will guide daily problem-solving and decision-making. In this way, a proactive, rather than reactive approach to anticipating and being prepared to welcome all students with diverse learning needs will be in place. The process of developing a clear vision with articulated mission and goals will reveal strengths, and importantly, challenges and gaps in knowledge, skills, and resources to be addressed in order to enact their vision. The highlighted challenges and gaps will inform a range of professional development needs among the school's leadership and instructional staff. Professional development focused on the foundational principles and skills of collaboration, teamwork, and interpersonal communication are essential. Instructional frameworks, approaches, and strategies that address students' diverse learning needs such as, Universal Design for Learning and Differentiated Instruction (Tomlinson, 2017) are required in order to improve and optimize teaching and learning.

In essence, Bethany's presence in the school is an *opportunity* to advance principal leadership and teacher leadership that collectively will address all student needs, developing a truly inclusive school community in which every child and youth belongs.

References:

Award recipients, the learning partnership. (2020, May 15). Retrieved from https://www.thelearningpartnership.ca/programs/canadas-outstanding-principals/award-recipients

McLeskey, J., & Waldron, N. L. (2015, February). Effective leadership makes schools truly inclusive. *Kappan,* 96(5). 68–73.

Sider, S. (2019, April 1). Every child matters: What principals need to effectively lead inclusive schools. *The Conversation.* Retrieved from https://theconversation.com/every-child-matters-what-principals-need-to-effectively-lead-inclusive-schools-114249

Tomlinson, C. A. (2017). *How to differentiate instruction in academically diverse classrooms* (3rd ed.). Association for Supervision and Curriculum Development.

Tschannen-Moran, M. (2001). Collaboration and the need for trust. *Journal of Educational Administration,* 39(4), 308–331.

Name: Donna McGhie-Richmond
Position: Associate Professor
Institutional Affiliation: University of Victoria

Second Expert Opinion:

The case of Bethany addresses inclusion, school leadership, and special education in a manner in which the three aspects directly support and affect each other. As a school leader, while you can prioritize the different aspects, you cannot address them separately.

The aspect of school leadership should be a top priority. In order to be a strong school leader, you need to first take care of yourself. School leadership can be very stressful and often leads to feeling isolated. Every school leader should find a way to deal with the stresses of the job, which is a hobby, exercise, or spending time with family and friends. You also should set aside time to "unplug" from work. I would also encourage school leaders to find a network of peers who can provide you support and collaboration.

I would involve the special education department in a few ways. My district uses a process called Child Study Team (CST). When a teacher, parent, or administrator has concerns about a student, we start the CST process. All stakeholders can present information and possible solutions to help us set a goal for the student. The goal is evaluated and revisited in thirty days. I also provide information to the school psychologist and director of special education to seek their advice. If the team feels the student needs an evaluation for special education services, then you would want these individuals aware of the situation. Creating a team will help support not only the student but staff and family as well.

To help your school be a more inclusive environment, building leaders need to advocate and educate. To help students like Bethany be successful, we need to make sure resources are in place for them. This is where advocating comes into play. You need to continue to make stakeholders aware of the resources needed for students like Bethany. Along with advocacy comes education. Teaching different stakeholders through personal conversations can go a long way. Find those key individuals in your school community who have influence and get them in your corner.

Name: Jeffery Bell
Position: Principal
Institutional Affiliation: Bellaire Elementary School, Carlisle Area School District
Resources

Book

Mark Boynton & Christine Boynton. (2000). *Educator's guide to preventing and solving discipline problems.* Association for Supervision and Curriculum

Development. http://www.ascd.org/publications/books/105124/chapters/Dealing-with-Challenging-Students.aspx

This book written by Mark Boynton and Christine Boynton is an educator's guide to preventing and solving discipline problems in the classroom. It focuses on dealing with challenging students through a few specific strategies involving relationships and building a climate which promotes student interest, positive reinforcement and a focus on positive self and room talk. These strategies promote responsibility and leadership in the classroom which challenge students to turn negative self-concepts into a positive or helpful action. The key is to introduce these strategies gradually and monitor student comfort and success as you go, then scaffold these strategies. Positive self-talk is promoted in this chapter above academic strategies to ensure the emphasis on validating students' feelings, even if you don't agree with their actions shows that you value that student despite their behavior. The chapter finishes with academic strategies such as keeping a pace with the class, keeping it moving even when setbacks occur, setting high expectations as well as many positive disciplinary strategies to help teachers and principals create a culture of success and safety.

Video

Howcast, (2016, September 5). *How to connect with a challenging student: classroom management.* [Video]. YouTube. https://www.youtube.com/watch?v=DJwSB_cQ8Tc

This short three-minute video is part of a playlist focusing on classroom management. This video walks through the importance of positively connecting with a challenging student and the multiple ways to do this. In elementary schools, one-way to connect is to join them in a game they are playing at recess as a concerned friendly adult as this often helps to break down their feelings of resistance toward you. More solidified strategies such as the two by ten strategy which is for two minutes a day, ten days in a row, have a personal connection with particularly challenging students on anything they find interesting. Research shows that with this method behavior can improve up to 85% with this connection. The video discusses their theory behind student behavior and why this focuses time and positive interactions are important for students to feel connected and more accepted in the classroom.

Academic Articles

Chantrand, S. (2009). Funding issues and proactive responses in education. *Journal of Graduate Studies in Education.* 11(1), 17–21. https://files.eric.ed.gov/fulltext/EJ1230333.pdf

This journal focuses on the issues and possible responses for funding in special education. This author focuses on their experience in Manitoba such as issues of making necessary changes to align to policy, problems with different funding models and tiered funding models. Some suggestions are to re-distribute resources and to train educators to implement inclusive strategies effectively. This article explains the complexities of funding, the connection with policies and advocating for special education funding in the classroom. They claim reorganization is able to support inclusive education in a profitable way but there is a varying degree of implementation between boards, provinces, and countries. The article continues to suggest funding models similar to Finland and New Zealand as proactive responses to special education. There is also a notion to group students by tiers of necessary interventions to best allocate resources and thus funding, these suggestions help to include special educational needs in the general classroom and for educators and policymakers to examine funding models and necessary changes.

Hicks, J. M. (2004). It's an attitude. *Arts Education. 57(3).* 13–17. doi: 10.1080/00043125.2004.11653546

This article helps to argue for funding for education, for the topics that often get overlooked such as the arts and special education versus math, and science which usually is prioritized. The article encourages readers to re-define the way they look at funding schools by putting the arguments into context for investors with business language and comparisons. By using quotes from experienced teachers, they provide real perspectives to why a focus on curriculum and relating to student experience is the best way to invest in education, and activities which support these connections need to be prioritized such as the expression arts classes and more resources such as support teachers and educational assistants provide. This article specifically discusses the importance of the arts and how to promote art through multidimensional communications and how art connects to other subjects, as well as in a student's future career.

Kuravackel, G. M., Ruble, L. A., Reese, R. J., Ables, A. P., Rogers, A. D., & Toland, M. D. (2018). COMPASS for hope: Evaluating the effectiveness of a parent training and support program for children with ASD. *Journal of Autism and Developmental Disorders.* 48(2).

This article explained the intricacies of autism and the varying aspects at different stages of life. There are five major aspects of explanatory models of illness or chronic conditions which help to define coping strategies for individuals and families. Often these models include cultural and religious beliefs, social class, education and professional background as well as past experiences with illness and inconsistent and self-contradictory. Understanding the variety in descriptions or explanations will help individuals understand that autism is individual and there are different assessments and steps needed to best support individuals on a case-by-case basis.

Professional Articles

Minister of Education & Minister of Children and Youth Services. (2007). *Making a difference for student with autism spectrum disorders in Ontario schools. From evidence to action.* http://www.edugains.ca/resourcesSpecEd/SystemLeader/ASD/autismFeb07.pdf

This document focuses on the vision, foundation, how to make a difference and how to move forward when working with children with autism Broken down into three aspects, they explore student learning and assessment, research and knowledge mobilization, and partnerships and shared responsibility. Finally, suggestions and recommendations for moving forward and how to facilitate change, what our immediate priorities need to be as well as suggested short-term, and long-term priorities with an explanation on what will be different.

Minister of Learning Alberta. (2003). *Teaching students with autism spectrum disorder.* https://education.alberta.ca/media/385138/teaching-students-with-asd-2003.pdf

This professional article created by Alberta Learning Special Programs Branch was created for teachers and administrators to learn how to program for students with special needs and specifically students with autism This is one portion of a series of books which focuses on teaching for student differences, essential support skills for students, individualized program plans, teaching students who are deaf and hard of hearing, visual impairments and students with learning disabilities/gifted as well as emotional disorders or mental illness.

Ontario Ministry of Education. (2007). *Effective educational practices for students with autism spectrum disorder.* http://www.edu.gov.on.ca/eng/general/elemsec/speced/autismSpecDis.pdf

This resource from the Ontario Ministry of Education breaks down the foundation of autism with terminology as well as the importance of program planning while involving parents, individual learning profiles, assessments and IEPs all to support collaborative planning. Next the resource explores instructional strategies such as differentiated instruction and visual supports. These supports are important to consider the individual needs of each student and make a plan on how to foster their growth in literacy skills, mathematics, homework as well as environmentally by taking into consideration assistive technology, the structure of the learning environment as well as sensory considerations. Finally, this document discusses behavior management, social skills and communication strategies that are commonly used to support students with autism.

Websites

Greene, K. (n.d.). *Teaching students with autism spectrum disorder:10 ways to support.* Scholastic. https://www.scholastic.com/teachers/articles/teaching-content/teaching-students-autism-spectrum-disorder/

This website from Scholastic shares an article of a teacher sharing ten ways to support students with autism. This article would help to ground a teacher in their experience to ensure they are able to reflect on the student need first and then adapt the classroom to foster learning.

Horwood, M., Parker, P., & Riley, P. (2019, February 26). *Three principals are seriously stressed, Here's what we need to do about it.* The Conversation. http://theconversation.com/one-in-three-principals-are-seriously-stressed-heres-what-we-need-to-do-about-it-110774

This website article provides principal's accounts of where their stress stems from, and what supports they need to reduce stress and improve their quality of life both at work and at home by maintaining effective work-life balance. This article sources information from a 2018 Australian report on Principal Occupational Health, Safety and Well-being Survey. Principals identify being overburdened with red tape, under-resourced and mistreated. The website speaks to a global comparison of how to best support educators through a unified approach to education.

Ontario Teachers' Federation. (n.d.). *Autism spectrum disorder.* TeachSpecEd. https://www.teachspeced.ca/autism-spectrum-disorder-asd

This website sources strategies teachers would be able to implement from emotional regulation, gross motor skills, and self-esteem to name a few.

Shalaway, L. (n.d.). *25 sure-fire strategies for handling difficult students.* Scholastic. https://www.scholastic.com/teachers/articles/teaching-content/25-sure-fire-strategies-handling-difficult-students/

Scholastic created a list of teacher written articles to share their experiences and perspectives. This article focuses on handing difficult students and what to do when students act up and personalities clash. This article hones in on teacher discipline and the movement to use kind words, and encouragement over reprimands. Some of the twenty-five tips are to remain calm and set a positive tone, ensuring students understand that discipline is not blaming, and creating community through active listening and treating all students respectfully.

Keenan, B. (2017, February 2). *Challenging student behaviour: moving from the boot to the root.* Edutopia. https://www.edutopia.org/discussion/challenging-student-behavior-moving-boot-root

This website explores how children with challenging behaviors may be labeled as unmotivated and disrespectful, but it is the role of the teacher and administrator to understand that exclusionary discipline, even if the child is testing patience, creates isolation for that child without identifying the root cause of challenging behavior. This article promotes classroom-based, teacher-driven skill building in emotional learning to ensure student behavior can be assessed, and resolved. Much of this information comes from the assessment of lagging skills and unsolved problems (ALSUP) from Dr. Ross Greene's Collaborative & Proactive Solutions model. Using stories and breaking down the events, the website talks about the focus on the "why" and "when" of student behavior which helps to decide explicit instruction to build on skill development strategies to help the students.

Chapter 26

The Newspaper Article

CASE 3: COMPLEX CASE

Crosscutting Themes: Communication, Relationships/Trust.
Leadership Competencies: Communication, Differentiated Instruction, Fosters Relationships, Professional Learning.

Alejandro's Perspective

I've had a hearing impairment since I was born. I'm now sixteen years old and I still can't hear well. I have hearing aids and they help me a lot. When I was in elementary school, no one really knew what it meant if someone had hearing aids and there certainly wasn't any stigma around them. It's different now that I'm in high school. I'm in grade ten at Waterford Secondary School. I just moved to the school a couple of weeks ago because of a family move. I've found the teachers to be pretty good but one teacher, Mr. Logan, my math teacher, annoys me. He just started teaching here last week, so we're both new to the school. Every time I raise my hand and ask for clarification or to repeat the question because I didn't hear him, he gets upset. It's been starting to really bother me because I don't know what he expects me to do about it. And what makes it worse is that he's started to call on me to answer questions when I don't have my hand raised. It's so embarrassing to not know the answer because I can't hear the question.

Mr. Logan's Perspective

I barely slept last night. My partner and I were fighting again. It was a fight I was really hoping to avoid, mainly because it's the same issue each time:

She wasn't happy that we moved to this area to secure a teaching position. I'd been hoping she would come around to liking the area, but that hasn't happened thus far. I'm beginning to wonder if the move was worth it.

I started as the grade ten math teacher just last week. The students are great for the most part. You always have the one trouble maker or class clown, but they're pretty easy to deal with: Just don't give them attention and they eventually stop. But one of my students, Alejandro Gibson, is different. It's like he chooses not to listen to me and to not pay attention. He doesn't do the homework, and when I try and engage him in class and ask him questions, he looks annoyed at me and doesn't answer. I've tried my best to be patient, but it happens day after day. I'm new and still don't know who I should talk to about this. I've tried to connect with the principal, Linda Ramirez, but she always seems to be busy or away at meetings.

The school hasn't received Alejandro's Student Record from his previous school yet. Hopefully the document will provide some info on him.

Alejandro's Parents' Perspective

For the past few days, Alejandro has been coming home complaining about his math teacher, Mr. Logan. We've heard this teacher is new to the school. We are worried that Mr. Logan is going to deter Alejandro's confidence by

Figure 26.1 Teacher Searching for Answers. *Source*: https://www.istockphoto.com. Credit: damircudic.

always calling him out in class and not being patient with him. We are going to go speak with the principal about it.

Mr. Logan's Perspective

I was walking through the hall today on my way out to grab lunch when I ran into a couple, a man and woman in their mid-forties, peering into Principal Ramirez's dark office.

"Can I help you?" I asked the couple, as they were obviously confused.

"We're looking for Ms. Ramirez. Where is she?" the woman demanded.

"She is out of the office today," I said. "She will be back tomorrow. Can I help you in the meantime? I'm Carter Logan. I teach here." I extended my hand.

Their eyes narrowed. Neither of them shook my hand. "*You're* Mr. Logan, the same Mr. Logan who is making Alejandro fail math?" the man accused me.

I was startled. "Pa-Pardon? Alejandro isn't failing."

"Our son, Alejandro, is in your math class. He comes home from school every day saying how you have no patience with him and always call him out in class. He needs a good grade in math for his university application!" the man exclaimed.

Maybe it was the fact that my partner and I had yet another fight through text messaging just before this conversation or that I was on my fifth cup of coffee of the day, but I shot back: "Alejandro *never* listens to me in class. He's incredibly disrespectful. He never does the homework and when I try and engage him in class, he ignores me!"

I moved past the couple to head to the staff room. I couldn't deal with this. Not today.

"Excuse me?" Alejandro's mother said. I continued on my way out. Then I heard her mutter, "You would *think* teachers would have a little compassion for students with disabilities." I froze. "What?" I turned to face them.

"Alejandro has a hearing impairment. You know that right?" the woman said. "He has hearing aids, but they don't work very well. We're looking at getting him new ones."

"What? I had no idea! No one ever told me Alejandro had a hearing impairment." I was still trying to process the news.

Alejandro's father looked confused. "Didn't you take a look at Alejandro's Student Record? Wouldn't it say there that he has a hearing impairment? Didn't Ms. Ramirez or one of the staff have a conversation with you about Alejandro?"

I sighed. "I'm really sorry. We haven't received his Student Record yet. I promise you I had no idea. I'll try to work with Alejandro to come up with a solution."

The man and woman looked at each other. "No," Alejandro's mom finally said. "Alejandro needs a competent teacher. We're going to transfer him to a different math class. We'll speak to Ms. Ramirez when she returns." And with that, the couple walked through the front doors of the school and disappeared into the parking lot.

A Week Later

I was at home sipping my early morning coffee before heading to school when I grabbed the local newspaper and saw a piece by the newspaper's editor-in-chief, Dale Gibson. *Gibson.* That last name seemed familiar. *That's Alejandro's last name*, I thought, making the connection. *Maybe Dale is his dad?*

I skimmed the small article that Dale Gibson had written and immediately confirmed that Dale *was* Alejandro's dad. The article was a scathing opinion piece on public education. Dale suggested that some public educators are incompetent and encouraged readers to consider private schooling for their children. "From my own experience," Dale wrote, "There are some educators who don't care about our children. All they want to do is get your child through the system as fast as possible."

Figure 26.2 Teacher Reading Bad News Online. *Source*: https://www.istockphoto.com. Credit: FluxFactory.

I winced. The article was about *me*. Suddenly my phone buzzed, indicating that a new email had arrived in my inbox. I reached for my phone and saw the email was from Ms. Ramirez. It read:

> Come see me before class. We need to chat. If you haven't seen the paper yet, you probably should. I don't usually respond to articles—or even calls from reporters—but we need to respond to this article as soon as possible.

Questions To Consider:

1. Do you think Mr. Logan's claim that "it wasn't his fault" that he didn't know that Alejandro was hearing impaired is valid? Should he have taken more responsibility? Why or why not?
2. How would you have handled the situation if you ran into Alejandro's parents in the hallway?
3. What would be Principal Ramirez's role in this situation if she wasn't on vacation? How would her presence alter the situation and the outcome?

Expert Opinion:

Communication, relationships, and organization are at the center of inclusive schools. Without them extenuating circumstances such as those found in this case will unnecessarily lead to crises. There are lessons to be learned for school leaders, special educators and classroom teachers from this complex case.

Principal Ramirez, and her ability to attend to communication and relationship building, was hampered by both the busyness of her schedule and the short time frame within which to attend to the situation. Transformational leadership is fundamental to inclusive schools as it aids in the building of strong communication and relationships, but in many ways, it requires considerable time. Transformational principals empower teachers to go above and beyond and is integral in establishing healthy parental relationships. Without the time to engage in transformational leadership strategies, established organization, policies, and practices are fundamental.

Special educators can take on lead roles in student transitions, acting as communication links between parents, students, and teachers, and as resource persons for classroom strategies. Designating a special educator as mediator would avoid miscommunication, allowing for smooth transitions with the implementation of quality inclusive classroom strategies.

Communication is established and maintained through initial intake meetings centered around the needs of the student, and is communicated by special educators to all stakeholders.

Students with special needs often have a lower self-concept concerning their academics.

Extra vigilance is needed by classroom teachers, special educators and administrators to ensure that this is minimized by creating a climate of inclusion. Designating a resource person would aid in removing the barriers such as those experienced by Alejandro. In addition, using adaptive supports and good teaching practices to minimize stigma and providing a means by which classroom teachers avail of support in implementing classroom strategies, improves inclusivity.

There is no better substitute than good, honest, trusting relationships among principals, teachers and parents. However, on occasion there is simply not enough time to establish and maintain these relationships. This is where clear lines of communication, clarified roles and established procedures are of utmost importance in maintaining inclusive schools. Having a mentorship program for new teachers where they are paired with knowledgeable and seasoned staff members would help in their own transition to a new workplace and may help in avoiding the situation that Mr. Logan found himself in. Furthermore, a procedure for the intake of students into their new school would have facilitated Alejandro's transition. An initial transition meeting would bring together the parents, educators and school leadership to talk face-to-face regarding the needs of the student. Mentorship programs, transition meetings, and special educators as mediators would aid in avoiding misunderstandings.

Unfortunately for Principal Ramirez, these opportunities have passed and now there is a crisis. But at the heart of the crisis are frustrated parents, a hurting student and a confused teacher. Principal Ramirez will need to draw upon her transformational leadership skills, meeting with all stakeholders and listening with empathy to find a solution to this issue, and to see it as a learning experience to better inform the establishment of communication, relationship building and policy and procedures that are indispensable to inclusive schools.

Name: Jill Rose
Position: Instructional Resource Teacher
Institution Affiliation: Newfoundland and Labrador English School District

Resources

Academic Articles

Dawn, T. E. (2016). Communication behaviors of principals at high performing Title 1 elementary schools in Virginia: School leaders, communication, and transformative efforts. *Creighton Journal of Interdisciplinary Leadership.* 2(2), 2–16. https://eric.ed.gov/contentdelivery/servlet/ERICServlet?accno=EJ1152186

This academic article focuses on schools where most students live in poverty. This research focuses on a training program to improve and implement strategies learned from high-performing principals. They found five themes to leadership which were a student-centered approach to decision-making, transparency of decision-making, shared decision-making with principal and teachings, the role of faculty trust, and principal preparation. Principals were integral to motivating teachers toward these high-performing strategies with face-to-face and personal communications from principal to teachers. Additionally, school-division training in communication development was critical in the role of successful mentorship. In conclusion the research found that communication development was integral for trust in schools between principals and teachers which lead to effective instruction.

Professional Articles

Nakpodia, E. D. (2010). Influence of communication on administration of secondary schools in Delta Stateeria. *Academic Leadership,* 8(4).

This article focuses on communication systems in schools being vital to the smooth running of the organizations. This is important to ensure the communication is formalized as a social instruction to measure reciprocity among members. The transfer of information and connection with behavior is important to understand why organizations operate in different ways with different channels of communication as it links the people together within it.

Ferris State University. (n.s) Teaching strategies for hearing impaired students. *Disabilities Services, Retention and Student Success.* https://www.ferris.edu/htmls/colleges/university/disability/faculty-staff/classroom-issues/hearing/hearing-strategy.html

Ferris State University has created a set of resources in disabilities services to promote retention of students and student success. This specific page focuses on teaching strategies for hearing impaired students. The strategies include allowing the students to self-identify and to define how they would like to receive accommodations and/or communication from teachers as well as peers. The strategies also include: keep instructions brief, use clear requirements, present class information in a visual format and use more than one way to demonstrate the concept. They also consider the benefits of online content to refer back to, repeating questions and comments when participants speak to ensure all can hear and optimally provide a transcript or assisting the student in finding a note-taker.

Government of New Zealand. (2014). *A school's guide to dealing with the media.* Shaping Education. http://shapingeducation.govt.nz/wp-content/uploads/2014/02/Schools-Media-Check-Sheet.pdf

This article was published by the government of New Zealand to assist school leaders in dealing with the media. It is important to understand the obligations and how to prepare for the media and how to respond to news reporters in the school setting. Important steps are to first identify if your board has a media policy, who is authorized to speak to the media and under what circumstances, as well as what issues may arise if someone does not adhere to this.

Website

Hopkins, G. (2007). *Dealing with angry parents.* Education World. https://www.educationworld.com/a_admin/admin/admin474.shtml

This website focuses on a principal's perspective on how to tackle a variety of issues such as angry parents. There are a variety of links attached such as listening is key, put yourself in the parents shoes, a variety of calming techniques such as maintaining your own calm tone, how strong school communities often minimize angry visits, find a solution that works, the roles of administrative assistants and how they can assist as they are the first line of defense, a recommendation to quick responses as the most positive approach and finally, principal-suggested resources.

Impact Teachers. (2017, October 13). *4 teacher tips – Dealing with angry parents.* Impact Teachers. https://www.impactteachers.com/4-teacher-tips-dealing-with-angry-parents/teacher-tips

This website focuses on the experiences teachers have with parents and lists a few strategies to consider. They recognize that teachers will experience heightened emotions in these conversations but is important not to "fuel the fire" as parents are simply looking out for the best interest of their child. The tips are to listen and stay calm, empathize and categorize to ensure that you mitigate any misconceptions, be firm and take responsibility, apologize and come to a solution.

Pawlas, G. (2005). *Building relationships with the media.* Education World. https://www.educationworld.com/a_admin/columnists/pawlas/pawlas004.shtml

This website focuses on the important aspect of a principal's jobs to tell the school's story to the community. This article emphasizes the importance of using reporters as allies and ensuring your school and board have an overall communication plan. Some suggestions to build and maintain good relationships with the media are to return calls from reporters, help them meet deadlines, understand the job of the reporter, provide feedback, and avoid giving information that is difficult to interpret or understand. These tips along with being honest, using "no comment" when needed, and extending the same courtesy's you would any other visitor will help to provide a strong foundation to these relationships, and in turn positive media coverage for your school.

Weber, M. (2016, August 21). *10 challenges deaf students face in the classroom.* GettingSmart. https://www.gettingsmart.com/2016/08/10-challenges-deaf-students-face-in-the-classroom/

This news article provides the perspective of a student with hearing impairments. The website outlines ten challenges as well as strategies on how to mitigate them.

SUPPORTING NEW TEACHERS

Chapter 27

Figuring It Out On Your Own

CASE 1: SUPPORTING NEW TEACHERS

Crosscutting Themes: Advocacy, Collaboration.
Leadership Competencies: Differentiated Instruction, Values Inclusion, Professional Learning, Advocacy, Differentiated Leadership, Agency.

I've been the vice principal of Nith Valley Primary School for the past four years. I work along the principal, Alex Kendall who, admittedly, I don't always get along with. Two months ago, we hired a new teacher, Lisa Lester, as one of our grade one teachers. I was very impressed with Lisa in her interview. She had been a substitute teacher for a number of years and clearly had a passion for working with children. We hired her at the beginning of the school year for a full-time teaching role.

Shortly after the beginning of the school year, I checked in with Lisa to see how her first couple weeks had gone at the school.

She told me, "Well, it's been, it's been a difficult few weeks, honestly. It's been a bigger challenge than I was expecting."

I wasn't particularly surprised by this, as new teachers often find the transition to being in the classroom full-time challenging. But the more that Lisa spoke about her time at Nith Valley so far, the more I got the impression that she was incredibly overwhelmed. She talked for half an hour about how all of her students were so different from each other and how she didn't know how best to teach them.

"Sometimes I feel hopeless. Am I really teaching my students anything? I'm especially worried about the students with special education needs in my class. I feel so unprepared to authentically include them in the class. Like

Elsie. She's in a wheelchair. I often forget that she can't do some of the things that others are doing." Lisa sighed.

"Lisa, have you talked to your mentor teacher about this?" I asked. As a new teacher, Lisa had been assigned to be part of our school system's mentorship program which paired new teachers with more seasoned teachers.

"No, we have tried to connect but haven't found any time to actually do," she responded. "I think she has a really challenging class and is struggling with her own issues right now."

Lisa and I chatted for a few more minutes before I stepped out to finish some other work I had to get done. But I couldn't get Lisa's situation out of my head. That night I thought of multiple strategies that might help her.

The next day, I stepped into the principal's office to talk to Alex about the possibility of finding a different mentor at Nith Valley for Lisa.

> Lisa has been having a really hard time adjusting to being a teacher. Her assigned mentor is not available and we need to find someone else who can ease the transition for her. I can think of a couple of options of more experienced staff members or maybe we could even reach out to a retired staff member.

I couldn't contain my enthusiasm. I continued,

Figure 27.1 Teacher Mentoring Another Teacher. *Source*: https://www.istockphoto.com. Credit: fizkes.

I think Lisa needs particular help supporting her students with special education needs. Could we look into some additional board training to help her develop some strategies to work with students with special needs? Maybe we could get some additional training for the whole staff too?

Alex looked at me skeptically. "Well, there's nothing stopping you from identifying and assigning a new mentor," he responded. I could tell that he wasn't as enthusiastic about my idea as I was. He eyes darted to his computer screen, where I'm sure he had dozens of emails that he needed to respond to. I could tell that I didn't have his full attention.

I just don't know if any of the other teachers would be interested in participating. Everyone is so busy. But, I mean, you can see. As for the additional training, I can look into that. The board sometimes offers special education workshops.

That night, I was reflecting on my own teaching journey with my partner over dinner. He reminded me that I had a similar experience to Lisa when I started teaching. The most stressful years of my life were probably the years that I was in the substitute rotation, waiting for a full-time position to open up. Once I was offered one, I took it without hesitation. But after a month in, I was exhausted. I felt like I was on an island alone. I doubted that my education to become a teacher had prepared me adequately. I doubted the staff team I was on and if they were really there to support me. But most of all, I doubted my own teaching abilities and my ability to make a positive impact on my students.

During the next few weeks I waited to hear from Alex about whether or not the board was offering special education training. In the meantime, I offered to help Lisa myself by sitting in on some of her lessons. I observed her teaching habits and the relationships she had with her students and gave her feedback.

Alex didn't appreciate that I was doing this, as he thought it discouraged Lisa from growing on her own. Let's just say that we agreed to disagree on that one.

The following Friday, Alex came into my office as I was sending off some final emails before heading home for the weekend. I could tell by the look on his face that whatever he had to tell me wasn't what I wanted to hear. Alex sat down.

"The board isn't offering any additional special education training," he told me. "Budget cuts, you know." He sounded nonchalant and I was devastated by the news. "Listen, we can't do everything for Lisa. She just needs to push through. She will develop some perseverance through this. She is just going to have to figure things out on her own."

Figure 27.2 Teacher De-briefing with Another Teacher. *Source*: https://www.istockphoto.com. Credit: SDI Productions.

Questions To Consider:

1. What are strategies that you use to support new teachers, especially during the transition to full-time teaching?
2. What kinds of supports and training for supporting students with special education needs are particularly valuable to new teachers?
3. Many new teachers can over-extend themselves and become overwhelmed when they begin full-time teaching work. How can you ensure that these teachers maintain a healthy work-life balance?
4. What kinds of struggles might a new teacher experience especially in working with students with special education needs?

Expert Opinion:

Meeting the needs of diverse learners provides educators with incredible satisfaction when we are successful. Creating an inclusive environment with rich and meaningful programming, that encourages a student to thrive, allows educators to feel a sense of efficacy and moral purpose. But when educators, regardless of their role, struggle to find ways to support the success of exceptional learners, and when learners with special education needs have difficulty with self-regulation, achievement and engagement, educators feel ineffective and embarrassed that they are not fulfilling their professional duties. In order to ensure the success of diverse students, this case study highlights the need for three necessary and co-existing components. The first is the need to have a shared vision of inclusion and success for exceptional learners around which the whole staff rallies. The second is the need for a strategic professional learning plan for the whole staff, that is differentiated by experience, knowledge and individual classroom need. The third is the need for a comprehensive mentor program at both the system and school levels in order to support all educators as they transition into new roles.

This case study shows that the school has not collaboratively developed a shared vision of inclusion and success for all students. We know that not all principals come to the role with a deep understanding of special education, but a principal who sees him or herself as a co-learner and who has skills to build a shared vision around a moral imperative about students will create the conditions that allow students, regardless of ability, to thrive. Schools that put students with special education needs at the center of their planning empower teachers to create inclusive classrooms where all students belong and find success.

The case study also outlines the importance of providing rich data driven professional learning in the area of special education. There are many teachers who experience the same sense of being overwhelmed that Lisa demonstrates in this case. It isn't as much that she is a new teacher that is causing the stress, but rather her lack of relevant skills and knowledge in how to meet the wide diversity of needs in her class. This sense of being overwhelmed is also common within the experienced teacher community. Using a growth mindset model that focuses on practical, relevant, self-initiated and differentiated professional learning will support teacher growth.

The final piece that seems to be missing from this case is the need for strong mentorship programs, both at the system level for the principal and vice principal, as well as at the school level for Lisa. Alex needs a mentor that can help him become a better support for his vice principal. It appears that Alex is struggling to manage the workload, always being too busy for his VP. He needs to learn how to build in time each week to meet and discuss her learning needs and questions. Lisa, the new teacher, also requires better mentorship. Explicit time needs to be provided for Lisa and her mentor to meet regularly. The mentor seems to be struggling with similar issues regarding special education, and dedicated mentorship time can also be useful for co-learning.

Name: Carolyn Treadgold
Position: Professional Learning Specialist, Special Education Lead
Institutional Affiliation: Ontario Principals' Council

Resources

Books

Aniscow, M. (2004). *Special needs in the classroom: A teacher education guide.* Jessica Kingsley Publishers Ltd and UNESCO. https://www.eenet.org.uk/resources/docs/135116e.pdf

The guide shares strategies for responding to children's special needs in ordinary schools. It walks through school improvement through, and encourages teacher development, constructing a resource pack and supporting innovation. Theoretical and practical ideas for intentional collaboration are included.

Maich, K., & Hill, R. (2017). *Special education case studies.* Oxford University Press.

This book is a collection of case studies focused embedded in the Ontario special education model, intended to be utilized alongside resources that focus on special education policies, practices, and legislations. The cases cover primary, intermediate, junior, and senior stages of education, providing an accessible entry point for case-based discussion when direct observation is not possible or ethical.

Videos

Educational Impact (2013). *Mentoring & coaching: The journey of a first year teacher.* [Video]. YouTube. https://www.youtube.com/watch?v=5hrqMwEyfn0

A short video which explains the importance of mentor teachers in the first-year teacher guiding and motivating them through coaching. First year teachers find solace in having someone to ask questions to, with the absence of their associate/homeroom teacher from placements or previous classroom experience.

Academic Articles

Denton, D. W., & Heiney-Smith, J. (2020). Characteristics of an effective development program for mentors of preservice teachers. *Educational Studies, 46*(3), 337–351. doi: 10.1080/03055698.2019.1584854

This 2020 article by David W. Denton and Jill Heiney-Smith delves into the topic of effective development programs of mentors for preservice or new teachers. With increased likelihood for reliable student teaching being the end goal, this article explores how important strong mentor programs are for preservice teachers. Findings for this study suggest that subject areas for development include a focus on communication and relationships building. Furthermore, training which promotes reciprocity between mentors and teachers, along with an emphasis on mentor and teacher roles was found to be important. Finally, this study provides details about the mentors preferences for format, timing, frequency, and duration of development activities.

Professional Articles

Ontario Ministry of Education New Teacher Induction Program. (2010) A resource handbook for mentors. *NTIPMentor*. 1–53. http://www.edu.gov.on.ca/eng/teacher/NTIPMentor.pdf

A resource for mentor teachers created by the Ontario Ministry of Education for their New Teacher Induction Program. It provides time management suggestions, collaboration points and key ideas or highlights to showcase for your mentee with core development tools.

Websites

Morehouse, L. (2008, April 22). *Supporting teachers: Effective mentoring*. Edutopia. https://www.edutopia.org/mentor-teachers-effectiveness

This article provides narratives from teachers and staff on what were the most important aspects of having a mentor, or being a mentor to support first year teachers. Experiences, suggestions, and professional development celebrations were notes on how mentoring was most effective.

Ontario Teachers Federation. (n.d.). *Teaching Strategies for Students with Special Needs*. Teachspeced.https://www.teachspeced.ca/teaching-strategies-students-special-needs

Teaching strategies consolidated by the Ontario Teachers Federation for students with special needs with a variety of click buttons to identify needs (such as mobility needs). The individual pages then explore instructional, environmental, and assessment suggestions and strategies.

South Regional Education Board. (2018). *Mentoring new teachers: A fresh look*. SREB.org. https://www.sreb.org/sites/main/files/file-attachments/mentoring_new_teachers_2.pdf

A guide created in 2018 by South Regional Education Board for when working with new teachers, discussing continuum of support, action areas of exploring how good mentors are created through programming, addressing challenges that new teachers face, and explains the tiered process (low-level needs, mid-level needs, high-level needs) to respond to needs.

Tew, K. (2019, June 29). *The benefits of multiyear induction program*. Edutopia. https://www.edutopia.org/article/benefits-multiyear-induction-program

An article written by Kimberly Tew explaining the benefits of multiyear induction program (4 years) to support teachers in the difficult years. This was conducted after it was found 17% of new educators leave the profession in their first five years and where this attrition comes from. The factors the help reduce attrition can be accomplished even with one year of the induction program. The program is then explained and outlined; this would be helpful for schools beginning this partnership.

Chapter 28

The Case of Alexis

CASE 2: SUPPORTING NEW TEACHERS

Crosscutting Themes: Relationships/Trust, Communication.
Leadership Competencies: Communication, Differentiated Instruction, Professional Learning, Problem-solving, Lived Experience of Students, Embodies Professional Standards, Values Inclusion.

I was recently hired as the special education teacher at Fortuna Secondary School. My passion and drive to work with students with special education needs come from my eight-year-old nephew who has dyslexia. I've seen first-hand how difficult his education journey has been at times: some uncooperative teachers, classmates who don't understand, and one particular principal who didn't want my nephew to be *their* problem. Of course, this is not always the case. There have been some wonderful people in his life. But he has certainly been affected by some negative situations and people.

Much of my time in the university was focused on courses in special education, which is one of the reasons I was hired by Fortuna's principal this past February. I was quite surprised that I got a teaching position shortly after completing my teacher education program, but I was told that there was a need for special education teachers in the school. One of Fortuna's special education teachers had recently retired, so the school was looking for a permanent replacement.

This is my first full-time teaching position, and I really want to do a good job and make an impact on these kids. But, I'll admit, there is a lot I have to learn about being a teacher. In some situations, I just don't know what to do. For example, one of my grade twelve students, Alexis, is legally blind. Alexis takes a slightly reduced course load and moves between classes with the help of her guide dog, Maxwell. She completes one period a day in the resource room with me as an opportunity to provide her with extra support for the other classes she is taking.

I've never worked with a blind student before, so I'm still learning how to support her. I'm also just six years older than Alexis, so sometimes I think she doesn't consider me as a "real teacher."

One day Alexis came to me at the end of the school day. "Ms. Richmond? Can I talk to you?" she asked.

"Of course. What's going on?"

"Well, I don't really know how to say this." Alexis began. "But I, uh, I know you're a new teacher. So I know you don't have a *ton* of experience. But I wanted to talk to you about a few things that you're doing that aren't right."

I immediately felt self-conscious. What was this about? What was I doing wrong? What was Alexis going to say?

Alexis continued.

You don't explain what you're writing on the whiteboard, so I can never follow what you're doing in class. And nothing is ever in the same place in the classroom. Like the other day I was looking for the stapler and couldn't find it.

Figure 28.1 A Student Using Their Guide Dog. *Source*: https://www.istockphoto.com. Credit: Cylonphoto.

It seems to be moved to a different place every time I need it. The *old* resource teacher always made sure that everything was in the same spot in the class so I could easily find it. And the other day you gave us a handout that had instructions at the top, but I couldn't read what the instructions were. All of my other teachers give oral instructions to help me out. I'm applying for college soon and I need good grades to get in, so I'd really appreciate it if you helped me out a bit more.

I had no idea how to respond. I felt badly that I wasn't doing the best job of supporting Alexis and making it easy for her to follow my lessons. I finally said, "I'm so sorry about this." I thought I was going to break down and cry. "I will definitely explain what I write on the whiteboard and I'll give oral instructions from now on. I am *so* sorry."

"Did they teach you how to teach visually impaired students when you went to university?" Alexis asked in a slightly condescending tone. She crossed her arms.

"Ohhh, not really. You're the first blind student I've worked with," I admitted. I could feel my face turning bright red.

"Yeah, I can tell," Alexis said under her breath. And with that, she left the room with Maxwell beside her.

Feeling completely embarrassed, I immediately headed to the vice principal's office. Clarice Rosenberg has been my saving grace throughout my transition into full-time teaching. She has been teaching for over twenty-five years so she has been a great resource. She was always willing to chat, so I often told her about my stresses and struggles. Fortunately, Clarice was in her office so I knocked on the door. She looked up and said enthusiastically, "Hi! Come on in!"

Stepping into the office, I began to cry. "I need to talk to you," I said.

"Go ahead," Clarice invited and I sat down in the chair across from her. I told her all about the conversation with Alexis and how I wasn't doing a very good job supporting her. I explained that I didn't know how to work with blind students, but desperately wanted to help Alexis succeed so she could get into college.

"And to make matters worse, I'm only six years older than Alexis," I cried.

"It's so awkward teaching someone who isn't *that* much younger than me. I don't think she respects me very much because I'm so young. I don't know what to do. How can I help Alexis? Tell me what to do, Clarice."

Questions To Consider:

1. If you were Clarice, how would you respond to the situation? What would be your immediate steps and longer term actions?

2. What should Ms. Richmond do next? As a principal, what kinds of supports would you provide to her?
3. As a school leader, what do you do to support new teachers as they support students with special education needs?
4. In what ways can a principal support the unique needs of new teachers who may be very close in age to senior high school students? If a senior student has a special education need, does this proximity in age complicate the teacher-student relationship in any way?

Expert Opinion:

New teachers put undue pressure on themselves to be an "authority," both as a person in power and as an expert. I wonder if Ms. Richmond's insecurities around her own youth and her inexperience with blind students speak to this. I have observed that some new teachers attempt to establish a traditional hierarchical relationship with their students to live up to societal expectations for what a teacher should be. As well, I see these well-meaning, start-of-career teachers setting unrealistic expectations of themselves in their perceived need to be seen as an expert in all things related to their field. If I were Ms. Richmond's administrator, my first task would be to relieve her of these assumptions. I would reassure her that while wisdom does come with experience, the greatest lesson of age is not knowing more, but becoming comfortable, even a little delighted, about knowing very little. Far from showing weakness, being "wrong," or not doing something perfectly "right," opens a window for reflection and research. These questions or gaps are the exciting starting points into profession inquiry and self-discovery. One of the most powerful lessons we can model for our students, both typical and differently able, is how to adopt a growth mindset to face adversity. Like all our unique students, Alexa presents Ms. Richmond with an opportunity to connect, learn, and grow as an inclusive educator.

Empathy is at the foundation of strong relationships and universally designed inclusive education; working to see the school and learning through the lens of each student is critical for building effective teacher-student relationships. As an inclusion teacher, I would nudge Ms. Richmond to become well-versed and proficient at Universal Design for Learning (UDL), a user-centric and empathetic approach to co-creating accessible learning plans. The first step in UDL is to get to know and understand the user or student, in this case Alexa. Having a candid conversation with Alexa, asking her what has and hasn't worked for her, is the starting point in this collaborative approach to learning. Giving Alexa a voice in her program helps her to develop a sense of agency and independence, which is important for all students, but especially senior secondary students on the verge of adulthood.

Moving forward, Ms. Richmond's role can then evolve into co-designer, co-learner, and ally; to maintain that relationship, I would advise her to

Figure 28.2 Student Using Assistive Technology. *Source*: https://www.istockphoto.com. Credit: Zuraisham Salleh.

regularly elicit Alexa's feedback around her program design and delivery to continually edit and improve it. This is the heart of empathetic, inclusive design.

Over the course of her teaching career, Ms. Richmond will likely have the pleasure of meeting a myriad of differently abled students, all of whom will enrich her practice. Each of these students, like Alexa, will present a diverse collection of strengths and stretches, lessons for Ms. Richmond to learn and wisdom for her to gain. Co-designing and co-learning with these unique students will enable their autonomy while at the same time providing a needed boost to Ms. Richmond's confidence as an inclusive educator.

Name: Grania Bridal
Position: Vice Principal
Institutional Affiliation: Sooke School District #62, British Columbia.

Resources:

Books

Ontario Ministry of Education. (2017). *Special education in Ontario: Kindergarten to grade 12*. Ontario Ministry of Education. http://www.edu.gov.on.ca/eng/document/policy/os/onschools_2017e.pdf

This policy and resource guide, created by the Ontario Ministry of Education in 2017, focuses on special education within Ontario specifically for students in kindergarten through to grade 12. This document outlines that transcribers or interveners may play an important role for students who are blind or have low vision. The qualifications for teaching special education and teaching students who are blind or have low vision are also outlined in this document. Information regarding additional qualifications for working with blind or low vision students is also included in this resource guide. Furthermore, there is information about Provincial Schools which are schools operated by the Ministry of Education for students who are Deaf or hard of hearing, are blind or have low vision, or are deafblind.

Wang, J., Odell, S. J., & Clift, R. T. (2010). *Past, present, and future research on teacher induction.* Rowman & Littlefield Education,

This book addresses the importance and impact of mentored learning on professional development of new teachers. Using research-based examples, Wang, Odell and Clift explain the effects that mentoring has on teacher performance and student achievement. Using both theory and practical applications, this book provides insight into developing effective teacher induction programs for teacher educators, teachers, policymakers and any other stakeholders in the education realm. This book includes the components of the induction programs theory: policies, research, responsibilities of universities and school districts, impact of technology, ethnicity, equity, and studies of teacher retention.

Videos

CSDB Channel. (2017, January 25). *Behaviour: Strategies and supports for blind low vision students* [Video]. YouTube. https://www.youtube.com/watch?v=A_yjEXeEPJE

This video discusses the basics, developing positive behaviors, challenges, consequences, setting limits, common struggles and tactile tools, when it comes to supporting behavior issues with students who are blind or have low vision. Tactile tools used as support can be great positive reinforcement for students who are blind or have low vision. Tactile reinforcement includes some form of token system where a student may physically touch and feel how many tokens they have earned, and thus, know how many more they need before they receive some form of delayed gratification. Similarly, tokens may be taken away as a form of delayed consequence.

Academic Articles

Saenz-Armstrong, P. (2020, July 9). Supporting teachers through mentoring and collaboration. *National Council on Teacher Quality.* https://www.nctq.org/blog/Supporting-teachers-through-mentoring-and-collaboration

Saenz-Armstrong makes a case for the constant need for new teachers that are effective regardless of their setting. Administrators look for ways to minimize the cost of turnover that an unprepared or overwhelmed teacher workforce can cause on a school board or district. The author of this article analyzes current length of teacher orientations and the differing mentoring programs in 124 large school districts in the United States. Recommendations made following this study include: increasing orientation time for new teachers, structuring mentoring programs for novice teachers and addressing their needs through this for two years, prioritize collaborative planning time between teachers, and commit to professional development.

Professional Articles

The Conversation. (2019, January 2). *Six ways to support new teachers to stay in the profession.* The Conversation. https://theconversation.com/six-ways-to-support-new-teachers-to-stay-in-the-profession-106934

This article details six ways to support new teachers to stay in the profession. One such method is the partnership between schools and universities; their collaboration can provide informed professional learning opportunities to build the capacity for mentor teachers to better support new teachers. This article also mentions the benefits of a planned orientation for introducing new teachers into their new workplace. Allocation of an effective mentor teacher is another way in which new teachers are more likely to remain in the profession. Creating a school community of mentors and incorporating ongoing strategic induction programs are strong courses of action as well. Finally, the article explains that constant evaluation of the induction and mentoring program is important for continued improvement and growth.

Richards, L. (2017, December 5). *10 tips for teaching blind or visually impaired students.* We Are Teachers. https://www.weareteachers.com/teaching-blind-students-visually-impaired/

This piece provides tips for teachers with students who are blind or visually impaired. Richards writes about practical tips and things to keep in mind that can be utilized by educators in their classrooms. Some points she makes include; always using student names when addressing them, do not avoid words like "see" or "look," verbalize rather than gesture, and avoid asking a student if they can see something. Richards also mentions finding the optimal seating for low vision students, depending on what their unique vision case is crucial. This article also provides information regarding how you can be a confident sighted guide for students who require it when moving from classroom to classroom.

Mulvahill, E. (2019, August 2). *Give your first-year teachers everything they need to succeed.* We Are Teachers. https://www.weareteachers.com/supporting-first-year-teachers/

Elizabeth Mulvahill touches on key points such as creating a stable and positive school environment, giving new teachers scaffolded assistance, being transparent and proactive about offering school operational information, and how to set up novice teachers for success. A big takeaway from this article is the importance of pairing up new teachers with a mentor. Mentor teachers are to provide support to new teachers by helping them manage their time, get meaningful feedback, and be especially supportive when it comes to disciplining students and dealing with parent issues.

Websites

National Council on Teacher Quality. (n.d.). *Monthly suggestions for supporting new teachers*. National Council on Teacher Quality. https://www.nctq.org/dmsView/Monthly_Suggestions_for_Supporting_New_Teachers

The National Council on Teacher Quality have released this website in a portable document format for easy downloading. This document provides a month to month timeline for supporting new teachers during the school year, and it runs from summer months to the end of the school year come May. In the beginning of the academic year, there is a focus on orientation, setting up classrooms, and student management plans. Throughout the school year, incorporating new teachers into the larger school community is a focus, along with professional development and the opportunity for new teachers to observe more seasoned teachers. The end of the document entails reflection or self-assessment and celebration of accomplishments.

Ontario Teachers Federation. (n.d.). *Blind/vision impaired*. Teachspeced. https://www.teachspeced.ca/blindvision-impaired

This webpage, titled "Blind/Vision Impaired," is available on the Ontario Teachers' Federation Teachspeced website, and focuses solely on the instructional, environmental, and assessment strategies for working with students who are blind/vision impaired. Specific instructional strategies include utilizing assistive technology, media sources, describing in detail, reading writing on the board aloud, and much more. Environmental supports include reducing auditory noise in the classroom, keeping items in predetermined places, and using preferential seating. Some assessment strategies are to provide extra time, oral tests, and scribing. At the bottom of this webpage, a list of useful resources including assistive technology, braille information, and numerous links are available.

Chapter 29

Overinvested?

CASE 3: SUPPORTING NEW TEACHERS

Crosscutting Themes: Relationships/Trust, Agency/Efficacy.
Leadership Competencies: Advocacy, Collaboration, Policies and Procedures, Legal Requirements, Lived Experience of Students, Values Inclusion, Professional Learning.

Amir Wasem's Perspective

I was hired as a new History and Social Studies teacher at Redwood Secondary School last month. It's my first real teaching job. I graduated with a Bachelor of Education degree three years ago and have been in supply teaching since. I applied for this position without much hope of being successful, but when I was offered the job, I was ecstatic! It's difficult to land a teaching job in the area I live. I was excited to start teaching.

Many of Redwood's students have special education needs—from extreme behavior issues to significant learning challenges. To help support these students, the school has four resource teachers who provide individualized support to students and also to their teachers. I took a special education class in the university, but don't have too much experience working with students with special education needs, so I am particularly appreciative of the help the resource teachers can provide.

This past Monday I was getting ready to head home for the day when I heard a knock on my door. I was surprised to see Garrett, one of the students in my grade ten history class. Garrett has attention deficit hyperactivity disorder (ADHD).

"Hi Mr. Wasem," Garrett started quietly.

"Garrett, hi," I said. "What are you still doing here? It's 3:45. School ended over an hour ago."

"I don't want to go home," Garrett sighed.

"Why not?" I asked him. For the next hour, Garrett opened up to me about how he is in foster care.

He told me how difficult it is to focus on his schoolwork when he's with his foster family because there are seven other kids who live there. He complained that the other kids always run around the house and yell making it difficult for Garrett to get any homework done. He admitted that it usually takes him a long time to concentrate on homework because he has ADHD and if he is able to concentrate, the other kids in the house interrupt him.

"My other teachers get mad at me when I fall asleep in class—especially Mrs. Callaghan. I really try not to, but I can't help it because I try to do my work at night when it's quiet in the house."

I didn't know what to say. My six years of the university certainly didn't prepare me for a situation like this.

Over the next couple of days, I couldn't get Garrett off of my mind. I felt sorry for him and wanted to help. His visits to my office became more frequent, and I began letting him use my classroom as a study space when he wanted. At the end of the week, I stopped by the principal's office to see if she knew about Garrett's home life.

Figure 29.1 Student and Teacher Having a Serious Conversation. *Source*: https://www.istockphoto.com. FatCamera.

"Yes, I'm aware of Garrett's situation at home," Kathleen Nichols, the principal, told me. "He was taken from his mom when he was two years old and has been in foster care ever since."

"It's so sad," I commented.

> He is really struggling with completing his homework. And, as you know, he has ADHD, which I think has just intensified his struggles at home and at school. We *have* to do something. I was thinking of calling his case worker and requesting that he be moved to a quieter, calmer home.

Kathleen stopped me.

"Amir, I understand that you care for Garrett. But the reality of it is, we can't do anything. Technically, we're not responsible for what happens outside of the school. He's not being mistreated with his foster family."

I was shocked by Kathleen's lack of concern. How could she say that?

The next few days were difficult for me because I had become personally invested in helping Garrett. Thinking about Garrett's situation consumed my days and my nights. I had shared Garrett's situation with my partner, Siba, who is a social worker. The two of us would often talk about ways to support Garrett. I was losing hours of sleep and began showing up late for work.

Two weeks after my initial conversation with Kathleen, she called me into her office to talk again. "You look terrible," she said frankly. I was too tired to care. She continued, "You should take a personal day to stay at home and get a bit of a break."

"What?" I cried. "No! I'm only losing sleep because I'm so worried about Garrett."

Kathleen sighed. "I know. But we've already been over this. We really can't get involved unless something serious occurs that threatens Garrett's safety or well-being."

I turned to walk away. "I'll take tomorrow off. But I'll have to do some thinking. If I'm not able to help my students, I shouldn't be teaching here."

Kathleen Nichols' Perspective

I hired Amir at the beginning of the school year because of how impressive he was in the interview. He seemed to have excellent interpersonal skills, patience, and passion for teaching. I hired him right away because I've found that committed and enthusiastic teachers who want to be in the classroom and make a real difference in students' lives are key to effective schools. I've been trying to support him as best I can, and I do understand his concern with Garrett's situation. But I think Amir has become overinvested.

When I first started teaching, it took me a long time to learn the boundaries between professional life and personal life. I think it's good for him to

Figure 29.2 Burnt Out Teacher. *Source*: https://www.istockphoto.com. Fizkes.

learn this now rather than further down the road. I admire his commitment to helping Garrett, but part of the reason that I've encouraged him to step back from the situation is because he is going to burn out if he takes every child's difficult situation on as his own personal mission. Yes, we need to support students with all of their complexities, whether those be special education needs or family situations or otherwise. But I can tell that he doesn't appreciate the lesson that I'm trying to help him understand. What else can I do to help him?

Questions To Consider

1. What are some strategies that Kathleen can use to support Amir?
2. Students with complex, intersecting needs including special education needs and familial needs, provide challenging cases for new teachers, experienced teachers, and principals alike. Given Amir's new role as a teacher in the school, what supports could be provided to best support him when confronted with complex student needs.
3. Do you agree with how Kathleen handled the situation? What would you have done differently or the same?
4. In what ways could the learning resource teachers have been involved in supporting Garrett and Amir? What supports or resources could they provide?

Expert Opinion

Administrators work with all stakeholders to establish a framework that creates an equitable and inclusive school culture. According to the book *The Principal as Leader of the Equitable School* (2012), the goal is to create a caring, productive, and collaborative environment that enhances the learning experiences of students with special education needs and allows them to realize their full potential. For student achievement, an inclusive school includes criteria such as having high expectations for each and every student, believing that all students can learn, and a commitment to reducing the achievement gap. And for their well-being, schools should develop a holistic approach to support their students. Kathleen should reflect on her school's philosophy toward equity and inclusion, and ensure that her intent, behavior, and actions reflect these values.

Another goal as administrators is to build trusting relationships among all stakeholders. Kathleen can continue building a strong, trusting relationship with Amir by actively listening to him. She can create a "brave space" encouraging open and honest conversation, giving him a voice.

She also needs to value different perspectives and understand that people speak from different sets of experiences. This pluralistic approach allows for a diversity of views and approaches that can inform processes, policies, and strategies to address gaps and challenges.

In fostering collective responsibility for student achievement and well-being, Kathleen should work collaboratively with all stakeholders to find a student-centered solution. She should recognize that Garrett is self-advocating and that we want this from all our students. From here, she should develop Amir's capacity, competency, and confidence in responding to complex student needs by explaining the processes in place to support these students. She could encourage Amir to seek advice or support from the special education resource teachers. This could be followed up by bringing the student to school-based team (SBT). Collaboratively, SBT could explore alternative programming, strategies, and work through next steps on how to support Garrett. Parent engagement would be the next step. A meeting with Garrett and his foster parents to discuss these strategies would ensure success at home and at school.

This case also presents an opportunity to build Amir's professional capacities, as the challenges that teachers encounter early in their careers are an opportunity to learn. Kathleen could pair Amir with a mentor, encourage him to develop goals for professional growth and provide opportunities for his professional development with a focus on supporting students with special needs.

As administrators, we need to be self-aware of our potential biases and assumptions that may impact our ability to support teachers and those students with special needs. We need to constructively respond to the emotions of our staff, as their well-being has a significant impact on their performance.

In a review of evidence about teacher emotions and their consequences for classroom practice and student learning, Leithwood and Beatty (2008) recommend leaders attend to the feelings or effects of staff members, both individually and collectively. This, they argue, is because teachers' perceptions and motivations can have significant effects on the quality of instruction, student learning, job satisfaction, morale, stress, and more. When Kathleen sees that he is struggling, as evidenced by his distressed appearance and lateness, she is quick to judge and makes suggestions that further his distress. Rather than asking him to take a personal day which dismisses his emotions she could, as an example, refer him to the school board's Employee Assistance Program.

References

Leithwood, K., & Beatty, B. (2008). *Leading with teacher emotions in mind.* Thousand Oaks, CA: Corwin Press.

Ontario Principals' Council. (2012). *The principal as leader of the equitable school.* Corwin Press.

Name: Shemira Sheriff
Position: Vice Principal
Institutional Affiliation: Waterloo Region District School Board

Resources

Books

Boogren, T. H. (2015). *Supporting beginning teachers: The classroom strategies series.* Marzano Resources.

In this book, Tina Boogren delves into key concepts such as giving new teachers time and professional guidance to develop into expert teachers. Using research, the author details four types of support new teachers require to grow and develop within their first year of teaching: physical, emotional, instructional and institutional. Furthermore, this book provides essential strategies in developing an effective mentoring program schoolwide, for kindergarten to grade 12 mentors, coaches and school leaders.

Videos

TEDx Talks (2018, July 16). *Learn to shine bright- the importance of self care for teachers.| Kelly Hopkinson | TEDxNorwichED* [Video]. YouTube. https://www.youtube.com/watch?v=5O5QIqlDxjg

This TEDx Talk is about the importance of self-care for teachers to avoid burnout and other negative outcomes. Kelly Hopkinson, the speaker in the video, speaks about how many teachers may neglect their self-care. In a recent study, 1 in 83 teachers took long term leave from their work due to pressures of work, stress and anxiety.

Hopkinson suggests placing as great of an interest in staff well-being as we do in student mental health, as she speaks to her struggles to cope as a teacher herself.

PBS NewsHour. (2013, July 4). *Mentorship for new educators helps combat teacher burnout* [Video]. YouTube. https://www.youtube.com/watch?v=7P5uSQ9E-NU

This YouTube video can be found on the PBS NewsHour channel. Mentorship is explored as a route to combat teacher burnout, in particular for new teachers entering the workforce. The advantages of having a mentor teacher with many years of experience under their belt to assist new teachers are discussed. Mentor teachers may help new teachers with professional development, leadership training, and support with classroom management. Teachers who feel supported, appreciated and valued have been shown to stay in the profession.

Academic Articles

Skaalvik, E. M., & Skaalvik, S. (2007). Dimensions of teacher self-efficacy and relations with strain factors, perceived collective teacher efficacy, and teacher burnout. *Journal of Educational Psychology,* 99(3), 611–625. doi: 10.1037/0022-0663.99.3.611

The authors examined 224 elementary and middle school teachers, after developing and analyzing the Norwegian Teacher Self-Efficacy Scale. Strong supports were found for the following components of teacher efficacy: Instruction, Adapting Education to Individual Students' Needs, Motivating Students, Keeping Discipline, Cooperating With Colleagues and Parents, and Coping With Changes and Challenges. Collective teacher efficacy and teacher burnout were also strongly related to teacher self-efficacy.

Professional Articles

Iteach (2019, May 29). *Setting healthy boundaries: As a teacher and in your personal life.* Iteach. https://www.iteach.net/blog/setting-healthy-boundaries/

This professional article emphasizes the importance of setting healthy boundaries both in your professional and personal life. Boundaries are defined as guidelines, rules or limitations that are set by someone, meant to create safe and permissible ways for others to behave toward them. This article focuses on three main topics titled: setting boundaries as a teacher, communication boundaries as a teacher, and teachers need to set emotional boundaries. The last section explains that teachers need to maintain a professional role and avoid acting in a peer or parental role with their students, offering strategies and alternative approaches for teachers to practice.

Ontario College of Teachers (n.d.). *A self-reflective professional learning tool.* Ontario College of Teachers. https://www.oct.ca/-/media/PDF/A%20Self%20Reflective%20Professional%20Learning%20Tool/EN/SPE%20Self-Reflection%20Brochure%20EN%20ACCESSIBLE%20WEB.pdf

This document, created by the Ontario College of Teachers, provides resources for educators looking to develop their professional self-reflective skills. Keeping the Ontario *Ethical Standards for the Teaching Profession* and *Standards of Practice for the Teaching Profession* in mind, this document is designed to assist teachers in thinking about their professional practice. Through numerous writing prompts and sentence starters, readers are guided to thinking critically about their professional practice, as it pertains to Ontario ethical standards and standards of practice.

Gill, S. (2015, September 30). *Effective support for teaching staff who are struggling.* SecEd. https://www.sec-ed.co.uk/best-practice/effective-support-for-teaching-staff-who-are-struggling/

This article was written by Sonia Gill to shed light on what effective support looks like for teaching staff who are struggling. Gill offers recommendations for principals and mentor teachers for how they can best support teachers. She suggests that honest and specific feedback be given to teachers often, both of you should be in agreement with what said teacher should focus on, and work together to create your picture of success. Gill also mentions that celebrating successes and making time for reflection together are key points for future progression.

Websites

Tapp, F. (n.d.). *Teacher burnout: Causes, symptoms, and prevention.* Hey Teach!. https://www.wgu.edu/heyteach/article/teacher-burnout-causes-symptoms-and-prevention1711.html

This informational article, written by Fiona Tapp, explains the causes, symptoms, and prevention techniques for teacher burnout. Teacher burnout has been defined as "a state of chronic stress that leads to physical and emotional exhaustion, cynicism, detachment, and feelings of ineffectiveness and lack of accomplishment." Burnout can be caused by educators who become perfectionists and do not take time for self-care. Symptoms mentioned in the article include: fatigue, sleep issues, periods of forgetfulness, trouble concentrating, appetite and weight issues, depression and anxiety. Finally, strategies and resources for avoiding or preventing burnout are mentioned at the end of this article.

The Graide Network (2019, February 26). *Teacher burnout solutions & prevention - How to retain talented educators.* The Graide Network. https://www.thegraidenetwork.com/blog-all/teacher-burnout-solutions-prevention

This article outlines three coping mechanisms educators develop when dealing with burnout over time: exhaustion, cynicism toward aspects of their job, feelings of inefficacy or incompetence. The Graide Network defines educators who experience burnout to be in one of three categories: frenetic, underchallenged or worn out. Prevention strategies mentioned include: giving teachers more control over their daily lives, helping teachers modify their reactions, publicizing and looking for early detection of warning signs, offering mental and physical health amenities, and creating a clear path for addressing symptoms.

References

ABC10. (2019, May 17). *Teens talk about the transition from middle school to high school* [Video]. YouTube. https://www.youtube.com/watch?v=rojP6Tj2OF4&feature=youtu.be

Aguilar, E. (2011). *20 tips for developing positive relationships with parents.* Edutopia. https://www.edutopia.org/blog/20-tips-developing-positive-relationships-parents-elena-aguilar

Aguilar, E. (2017). *Helping teachers thrive.* Edutopia. https://www.edutopia.org/article/helping-teachers-thrive

Alber, S. R., & Heward, W. L. (1996). "GOTCHA!" Twenty-five behavior traps guaranteed to extend your student's academic and social skills. *Intervention in School and Clinic. 31*(5), 285–289. doi: 10.1177/105345129603100505

Alberta Education. (n.d.). *Medical/disability information for classroom teachers: Conduct disorder.* Learn Alberta. http://www.learnalberta.ca/content/inmdict/html/conduct_disorder.html

American Federation of Teachers. (2007). *Building parent-teacher relationships.* Reading Rockets. https://www.readingrockets.org/article/building-parent-teacher-relationships

Angelle, P., & Bilton, L. N. (2009). Confronting the unknown: Principal preparation training in issues related to special education. *Journal of Scholarship & Practice, 5.* 5–9.

Aniscow, M. (2004). *Special needs in the classroom: A teacher education guide.* Jessica Kingsley Publishers Ltd UNESCO. http://www.eenet.org.uk/resources/docs/135116e.pdf

Anxiety Canada. (n.d.). *Social anxiety disorder.* https://www.anxietycanada.com/articles/social-anxiety-disorder/

Arneson, S. (2017). *Communicate and motivate: The school leader's guide to effective communication.* Routledge.

ASCD Guest Blogger. (2018, June 6). *Inclusive classrooms: Looking at special education today.* ASCD in Service. http://inservice.ascd.org/inclusive-classrooms-looking-at-special-education-today/

Asperger's Society of Ontario. (n.d.). *Asperger's society of Ontario.* Asperger's Society of Ontario. http://www.aspergers.ca/

Australian Government Department of Social Services. (2017). *Disability advocacy.* Department of Social Services. https://www.dss.gov.au/disability-advocacy-fact-sheet

Autism Advocate. (2009). *School transitions in the elementary grades.* Autism Advocate, https://www.autism-society.org/wp-content/uploads/2014/04/school-transitions-in-the-elementary-grades.pdf

Autism Canada. (n.d.). *Autism explained.* Autism Canada. https://autismcanada.org/autism-explained/

Autism Society. (2020). *About the Autism society.* https://www.autism-society.org/about-the-autism-society/

Autism Society Newfoundland and Labrador. (2003). *Strategies for classroom management.* https://www.autism.nf.net/service-provider/resources-for-educators/strategies-for-classroom-management/

Autism Speaks Canada. (n.d.). *Asperger syndrome.* Autism Speaks Canada. https://www.autismspeaks.ca/about-autism/what-is-autism/asperger-syndrome/

Autism Support Network. (2017). *Advocacy roadmap.* Autism Support BC. https://autismsupportbc.ca/advocacy-roadmap/

Autism, Life skills, Social Skills. (n.d.). *Necessary life skills for teens with autism.* Learning For a Purpose. https://learningforapurpose.com/2018/01/11/necessary-life-skills-for-teens-with-autism/

Autism360. (2016, February 4). *ADHD and autism in the classroom.* https://www.autismag.org/adhd-and-autism-in-the-classroom/

Baker, L., Diggs, L., & Royal, M. (2019, February). *The evolving relationship: Principals and their supervisors.* National Association Secondary School Principals. https://www.nassp.org/2019/02/01/the-evolving-relationship-principals-and-their-supervisors/

Barrett, D. (2019). Determination and partnerships: Keys to successful inclusion for secondary students. *Inclusive Education.* https://inclusiveeducation.ca/wp-content/uploads/sites/3/2019/02/Determination-and-Partnerships-Keys-to-successful-inclusion-for-secondary-students.pdf

Barrett, D. (n.d.). Determination and partnerships: Keys to successful inclusion for secondary students. *Inclusive Education.* https://www.edweek.org/ew/articles/2018/10/17/the-important-role-principals-play-in-special.html

Barrett, D. (n.d.). *Determination and partnerships: Keys to successful inclusion for secondary students.* Inclusive Education. https://www.edweek.org/ew/articles/2018/10/17/the-important-role-principals-play-in-special.html

Bateman, D., Gervais, A., Wysocki, T. A., & Cline, J. L. (2017). Special education competencies for principals. *Journal of Special Education Leadership, 30*(1), 48–56.

Benner, A. D., Boyle, A. E., Bakhtiari, F., Buchmann, M., Malti, T., & Steinhoff, A. (2017). Understanding students' transitions to high school: Demographic variation and the role of supportive relationships. *Journal of Youth and Adolescence, .46*(10), 2129–2142.

Bennett, S. (2009). *What works? Research into practice: Including students with exceptionalities*. ETFO-OTS. http://etfo-ots.ca/wp-content/uploads/2013/08/Including-Students-with-Exceptionalities.pdf

Bethel School District. (2013). *Field trip checklist teacher's responsibility*. http://media.bethelsd.org/home/services/operations/documents/risk_management/forms/field_trip/Teacher_Checklist_Nov_2013.pdf

Beveridge, S. (2005). *Children, families and schools: developing partnerships for inclusive education*. Routledge.

Billingsley, B. S., McLeskey, J., & Crockett, J. B. (2014). *Moving toward inclusive and high-achieving schools for students with disabilities*. https://ceedar.education.ufl.edu/wp-content/uploads/2017/12/Principal-Leadership-IC-2017-Revision.pdf

Boogren, T. H. (2015). *Supporting beginning teachers: The classroom strategies series*. Marzano Resources.

Boyle, B., While, D., & Boyle, T. (2004). A longitudinal study of teacher change: what makes professional development effective? *The Curriculum Journal, 15*(1), 45–68. doi: 10.1080/0958517042000189470

Boyle, C., Topping, K., Jindal-Snape, D., & Norwich, B. (2012). The importance of peer-support for teaching staff when including children with special educational needs. *School Psychology International, 33*(2), 167–184. doi:10.1177/0143034311415783

Boynton, M., & Boynton, C. (2000). *Educator's guide to preventing and solving discipline problems*. Chapter 13. http://www.ascd.org/publications/books/105124/chapters/Dealing-with-Challenging-Students.aspx

Boynton, M., & Moynton C. (2005). *The educator's guide to preventing and solving discipline problems*. Association for Supervision and Curriculum Development.

BP Children. (2011). *Webinar series 1* [Video]. Vimeo. https://vimeo.com/22245908#embed

BP Children. (n.d.). *Teachers*. BP Children. https://www.bpchildren.com/teachers

Bright Hub Education. (2010, March 29). *Teaching strategies for hearing impaired students*. https://www.brighthubeducation.com/special-ed-hearing-impairments/67528-tips-and-strategies-for-teaching-hearing-impaired-students/

Brown, B. (2017, April 7). *Daring classrooms*. [Video]. YouTube. https://www.youtube.com/watch?v=DVD8YRgA-ck

Buckmann, M. S., & Pratt, C. (1999). Supporting students with Asperger's syndrome who present behavioral challenges. *Indiana Institute on Disability and Community*. https://www.iidc.indiana.edu/irca/articles/supporting-students-with-aspergers-syndrome-who-present-behavioral-challenges.html

Burke, M., Meadan-Kaplansky, H., Patton, K., Pearson, J., Cummings, K., & Lee, C. (2018). Advocacy for children with social-communication needs: perspectives from parents and school professionals. *The Journal of Special Education, 51*(4), 191–200. doi: 10.1177/0022466917716898

Burriss, K. (2002). What general educators have to say about successfully including students with down syndrome in their classes. *Journal of Research in Childhood Education, 16*(1), 28–38.

Cameron, D. L. (2016). Too much or not enough? An examination of special education provision and school district leaders' perceptions of current needs and common approaches. *British Journal of Special Education, 43*(1), 22–38.

Campbell T. A., Brownlee A., & Renton C. A. (2016). *What works? Research into practice: Pedagogical documentation: Opening windows onto learning.* Ontario Ministry of Education.

Canadian Council on Learning. (2009). Does placement matter? Comparing the academic performance of students with special needs in inclusive and separate settings. *Lessons in Learning.* http://www.cclcca.ca/pdfs/LessonsInLearning/03_18_09E.pdf

Canadian Down Syndrome Society. (n.d.). *Down syndrome resources for teachers & schools.* CDSS.ca. https://cdss.ca/teachers-schools/

Canadian Human Rights Commission. (n.d.). *Left out: Challenges faced by persons with disabilities in Canada's schools.* Canadian Human Rights Commission—Commission Canadienne des Droits de la Personne. https://www.chrc-ccdp.gc.ca/eng/content/left-out-challenges-faced-persons-disabilities-canadas-schools

Canadian Mental Health Association. (n.d.). *Bipolar disorder.* Canadian Mental Health Association. https://cmha.bc.ca/documents/bipolar-disorder/

Canadian Teachers' Federation. (2021, May 3). *Mental health.* https://www.ctf-fce.ca/?s=mental+health&x=0&y=0.

Carny, P. & Parr, M. (2014). Resilient, active, and flourishing: supporting positive mental health and well-being in school communities. *What Works Research into Practice.* http://www.edu.gov.on.ca/eng/literacynumeracy/inspire/research/WW_ResilientFlourish.Pdf

Carrier, C. (n.d.). *Teacher support for refugee children in Canada.* British Columbia Teachers' Federation. https://bctf.ca/uploadedFiles/Public/SocialJustice/Programs/GlobalEd/Teacher%20Guide%20PDF.pdf

CBC. (2019, February 17). *'I felt helpless': Teachers call for support amid 'escalating crisis' of classroom violence.* CBC Radio. https://www.cbc.ca/radio/thesundayedition/the-sunday-edition-for-february-17-2019-1.5017616/i-felt-helpless-teachers-call-for-support-amid-escalating-crisis-of-classroom-violence-1.5017623

CBC News: The National. (2016, May 30). *Struggling to adapt: One Syrian refugee family's story.* [Video]. YouTube. https://www.youtube.com/watch?v=6CFYoJQKM7A

Centre for global Education. (2018). Teaching for global competence in a rapidly changing world. *Asia Society.* doi: 10.1787/9789264289024-en.

Chandler K. (2015, September 9). *Support services for children with special needs.* KidSpot. https://www.kidspot.com.au/school/primary/learning-and-behaviour/support-services-for-children-with-special-needs/news-story/911e36a9cb6680a16fe168fe9e0971d3

Chantrand, S. (2009).Funding issues and proactive responses in education. *Journal of Graduate Studies in Education. 11*(1), 17–21.

Child & Adolescent Bipolar Foundation. (2007). *Educating the child with bipolar disorder.* Child & Adolescent Bipolar Foundation. https://www.dbsalliance.org/pdfs/BMPN/edbrochure.pdf

Childminding, Monitoring, Advisory and Support Canada. (2015). *Caring for Syrian refugee children: A program guide for welcoming young children and their families*. Childminding, Monitoring, Advisory and Support Canada. https://cmascanada.ca/wp-content/uploads/2015/12/Supporting_Refugees/Caring%20for%20Syrian%20Refugee%20Children-final.pdf

Children's Mental Health Ontario. (2020). *Teacher resources* https://cmho.org/teacher-resources/

Clark-Howard, K. (2019). Inclusive education: How do New Zealand secondary teachers understand inclusion and how does this understanding influence their practice? *Kairaranga, 20*(1) 46–57.

Classroom Mental Health. (2020). *A teachers toolkit for high school*. https://classroommentalhealth.org/

Cobb, C. (2015). Principals play many parts: A review of the research on school principals as special education leaders 2001–2011. *International Journal of Inclusive Education, 19*(3), 213–234. doi: 10.1080/13603116.2014.916354

Cohen, E. (2015). Principal leadership styles and teacher and principal attitudes: Concerns and competencies regarding inclusion. *Procedia-Social and Behavioral Sciences, 186*, 758–764.

Community Living New Brunswick. (n.d.). *Other strategies for achieving social inclusion through recreation.* New Brunswick Association for Community Living. https://nbacl.nb.ca/module-pages/other-strategies-for-achieving-social-inclusion-through-recreation/

Connections for Students Phase II Regional Advisory Group. (n.d.). *Connections for students: Meeting minutes templates*. Edugains. http://www.edugains.ca/resourcesSpecEd/ASD/BoardDevelopedResources/CapacityBuilding/ConnectionsForStudents_Meeting_Minutes_Template-3.pdf

Conners, H. (2016, December 2). *'Inclusion' is the classroom challenge teachers are too afraid to talk about, educator says*. CBC News. https://www.cbc.ca/news/canada/nova-scotia/nova-scotia-teachers-classrooms-inclusion-work-to-rule-1.3879240

Conners, H. (2016, December 2). *'Inclusion' is the classroom challenges teachers are too afraid to talk about, educator says*. CBC. https://www.cbc.ca/news/canada/nova-scotia/nova-scotia-teachers-classrooms-inclusion-work-to-rule-1.3879240

Cook, C. R., Coco, S., Zhang, Y., Fiat, A. E., Duong, M. T., Renshaw, T. L., Long, A. C., & Frank, S. (2018). Cultivating positive teacher-student relationships: Preliminary evaluation of the establish-maintain-restore (EMR) method. *School Psychology Review, 47*(3), 226–243. doi: 10.17105/SPR-2017-0025.V47-3

Cooper, V. (2005). *Support staff in schools promoting the emotional and social development of children and young people*. National Children's Bureau.

Council of Ministers of Education, Canada. (2008). *Report two: Inclusive education in Canada: The way of the future*. http://www.cmec.ca/Publications/Lists/Publications/Attachments/122/ICE2008-reports-canada.en.pdf

Council of Ontario Directors of Education. (2014). *What parents can do to help their children develop healthy relationships*. Parent toolkit. http://www.ontariodirectors.ca/Parent_Engagement/2014_PE_Docs/40714_Code_ParentToolKit_E.pdf

Council of Ontario Directors of Education. (n.d.). *Building partnerships for the future: Engaging parents of students with special needs.* Ontario Directors. http://www.ontariodirectors.ca/CODE_Webinars/files/CODE_Parents_EN.pdf

Coyle, S., & Malecki, C. (2018). The association between social anxiety and perceived frequency and value of classmate and close friend social support. *School Psychology Review, 47*(3), 209–225. doi: 10.17105/SPR-2017-0067.V47-3

CSDB Channel. (2017, January 25). *Behaviour: Strategies and supports for blind low vision students* [Video]. YouTube. https://www.youtube.com/watch?v=A_yjEXeEPJE

Cunningham, T. (2020). *How do I choose between the different types of assistive technology to make sure my students have the tools they need to succeed?* LD@school. https://www.ldatschool.ca/choose-assistive-technology/

Cusson, M. (2010). *Empirically based components related to students with disabilities in tier I* [Unpublished doctoral dissertation] The University of Texas at Austin.

Dabbs, L. (2012, March 26). *A school principal must be a support to teachers.* Kids discover. https://www.kidsdiscover.com/teacherresources/school-principal-support-teachers/

Davies, L. (2006). *Oppositional defiant disorder in children.* Kelly Bear. http://www.kellybear.com/TeacherArticles/TeacherTip68.html

Davies, N. (2016, January 7). *Oppositional defiant disorder in the classroom.* Headteacher-Update. http://www.headteacher-update.com/best-practice-article/oppositional-defiant-disorder-in-the-classroom/112142/

Davis, M. (2013, May 16). *Transition resources for parents, teachers, and administrators.* Edutopia. https://www.edutopia.org/blog/transition-resources-teachers-matt-davis

Dawn, T. E. (2016). Communication behaviors of principals at high performing title 1 elementary schools is Virginia: School leaders, communication, and transformative efforts. *Creighton Journal of Interdisciplinary Leadership, 2*(2), 2–16.

De Luca, C. (2013). Toward an interdisciplinary framework for educational inclusivity. *Canadian Journal of Education, 36*(1), 305–348.

De Matthews, D. E., Serafini, A., & Watson, T. N. (2021). Leading inclusive schools: Principal perceptions, practices, and challenges to meaningful change. *Educational Administration Quarterly, 57*(1), 3–48. doi: 10.1177/0013161X20913897

Dempster, K., & Robbins, J. (2017). *How to build communication success in your school: A guide for school leaders.* Routledge

Denton, D. W., & Heiney-Smith, J. (2020). Characteristics of an effective development program for mentors of preservice teachers. *Educational Studies, 46*(3), 337–351. doi: 10.1080/03055698.2019.1584854

Denver Academy. (2012, October 16). *How are you smart? What students with learning disabilities are teaching us* [Video]. YouTube. https://www.youtube.com/watch?v=OdqaUcq7YVQ

Department of Education and Early Childhood Development. (2013). *Policy 322.* http://www2.gnb.ca/content/dam/gnb/Departments/ed/pdf/K12/policies-politiques/e/322A.pdf

Department of Education and Training. *EFFECTIVE CONSULTATION: Improving outcomes for students with disability*. Canberra, Australia: Australian Government. Retrieved from https://docs.education.gov.au/system/files/doc/other/dse-fact-sheet-4-effective-consultation_1.pdf

Department of Health & Human Services. (n.d.). *Down syndrome and learning*. Better Health Channel. https://www.betterhealth.vic.gov.au/health/HealthyLiving/down-syndrome-and-learning

Dickenson, P. (2017). What do we know and where can we grow? Teachers preparation for the inclusive classroom. In P. Dickenson, P. Keough, & J. Courduff (Eds.). *Preparing Pre-service Teachers for the Inclusive Classroom* (pp. 1–22). IGI GLobal.

Dollarhide, C., Smith, A., & Lemberger, M. (2007). Critical incidents in the development of supportive principals: Facilitating school counselor–principal relationships. *Professional School Counseling, 10*(4), 360–369.

Down Syndrome Association of Greater St. Louis. (n.d.). *What students with down syndrome want teachers to know: Information for para professionals*. DSAGSL.org. https://dsagsl.org/wp-content/uploads/2019/02/Paraprofessional-Powerpoint-20141.pdf

Down Syndrome Education. (n.d.). *Resources*. Down-Syndrome.org. https://www.down-syndrome.org/en-us/resources/

Dubec, R. (2018). *Foster inclusion in the classroom*. Teaching Commons Lakehead University. https://teachingcommons.lakeheadu.ca/foster-inclusion-classroom

Dusenbury, L. (2012). *Creating a safe classroom environment*. Education World. https://www.educationworld.com/a_curr/creating-safe-classroom-environment-climate.shtml

Edmunds, A. L., & Macmillan, R. B. (eds.). (2010). *Leadership for inclusion: A practical guide*. Sense Publishers.

Education Corner. (n.d.). *Teaching students with Asperger's syndrome*. Education Corner: Education That Matters. https://www.educationcorner.com/teaching-students-with-aspergers-syndrome.html

Education World. (2011). *Effective communication with parents*. https://www.educationworld.com/a_admin/effective-communication-with-parents.shtml

Education World. (2015, March 30). *Stress relief for teachers and students*. https://www.educationworld.com/a_curr/strategy/strategy063.shtml

Educational Impact. (2013). *Mentoring & coaching: The journey of a first year teacher* [Video]. YouTube. https://www.youtube.com/watch?v=5hrqMwEyfn0

EduGains. (n.d.). *Classroom educator mental health*. Edugains. https://www.edugains.ca/newsite/mentalHealth/index.html

EduGains. (n.d.). *Educator support guide for transition planning*. The Ontario Ministry of Education. http://www.edugains.ca/resourcesSpecEd/IEP&Transitions/BoardDevelopedResources/TransitionPlanning/SupportGuides/EducatorSupportGuideforTransitionPlanning.pdf.

EduGains. (n.d.). *Special education advisory committee*. Ontario Ministry of Education. http://www.edugains.ca/newsite/SpecialEducation/prolearnfac/seac.html

Edutopia. (2015, April 7). *Sharing data to create stronger parent partnerships* [Video]. YouTube. https://www.youtube.com/watch?v=kL5lO8gMrR0

Edutopia. (2019, January 14). *The power of relationships in schools* [Video]. YouTube. https://www.youtube.com/watch?v=kzvm1m8zq5g

Edutopia. (2017, May 3). *The sensory room: Helping students with autism focus and learn* [Video]. Edutopia. https://www.edutopia.org/video/sensory-room-helping-students-autism-focus-and-learn

Egale Canada Human Rights Trust. (n.d.). *Preparing students for the transition of a transgender or gender diverse peer.* Government of Newfoundland and Labrador. https://www.gov.nl.ca/eecd/files/k12_safeandcaring_pdf_preping_students_diverse_peer.pdf

Elksnin, K. L., & Elksnin, N. (1989). Collaborative consultation: Improving parent-teacher communication. *Academic Therapy, 24*(3) 261–269. doi: 10.1177/105345128902400302

Ellerbrock, C. (2012). *Help students transition to high school smoothly.* AMLE. https://www.amle.org/BrowsebyTopic/WhatsNew/WNDet/TabId/270/ArtMID/888/ArticleID/117/Help-Students-Transition-to-High-School-Smoothly.aspx

Ennab, F. (2017). Being involved in uninvolved contexts: Refugee parent involvement in children's education. *Canadian Centre for Policy Alternatives Manitoba.* https://www.policyalternatives.ca/sites/default/files/uploads/publications/Manitoba%20Office/2017/04/Refugee_parent_involvement.pdf

Equity and Inclusive Education Strategy, Ontario. (2009). *Quick Facts.* http://www.edu.gov.on.ca/eng/policyfunding/equity_quick_facts.html

Ferris State University. (n.s) Teaching strategies for hearing impaired students. *Disabilities Services, Retention and Student Success.* https://www.ferris.edu/htmls/colleges/university/disability/faculty-staff/classroom-issues/hearing/hearing-strategy.html

Finley, T. (2017, March 13). *Mastering classroom transitions.* Edutopia. https://www.edutopia.org/article/mastering-transitions-todd-finley

Fischer, M. W. (2005, November). *Handling parent complaints—The good, the bad, and the ugly.* Education World. https://www.educationworld.com/a_curr/voice/voice082.shtml

Fleming, N. (2019, August 9). *Students can now miss school for a 'mental health day'.* Edutopia. https://www.edutopia.org/article/students-can-now-miss-school-mental-health-day

Foundation for People with Learning Disabilities. (2013). *Moving on... Tips for pupils moving to secondary school.* https://www.mentalhealth.org.uk/sites/default/files/moving-on-top-tips-for-pupils.pdf

Friend, M. P., & Cook, L. (2017). *Interactions: Collaboration skills for school professionals* (2nd ed.). Pearson.

Fullan, M. (2011). *Change leader: Learning to do what matters most.* Jossey-Bass.

Gelfer, J. I. (1991). Teacher-parent partnerships: Enhancing communications. *Childhood Education, 67*(3), 164–167, doi: 10.1080/00094056.1991.10521602

Gill, S. (2015, September 30). *Effective support for teaching staff who are struggling.* SecEd. https://www.sec-ed.co.uk/best-practice/effective-support-for-teaching-staff-who-are-struggling/

GLSEN. (2017, November 13). *How to support transgender students* [Video]. YouTube. https://www.youtube.com/watch?v=kq19QdOfH1Y

Government of New Brunswick. (2016). *New Brunswick receives international award for inclusive education.* http://www2.gnb.ca/content/gnb/en/news/news_release.2016.02.0085.html

Government of New Zealand. (2014). *A school's guide to dealing with the media.* Shaping Education. http://shapingeducation.govt.nz/wp-content/uploads/2014/02/Schools-Media-Check-Sheet.pdf

Grade 8 to 9 Transition Planning. Pathways & Student Success. (2021). Retrieved 3 May 2021, from https://studentsuccess.hcdsb.org/sample-page/transition-planning/.

Grant, L. M. (2013). *How does a principal use intention and strategy in the enactment of advocacy leadership?* ProQuest Dissertations Publishing.

Greene, K. (n.d.). *Teaching students with autism spectrum disorder: 10 ways to support.* Scholastic. https://www.scholastic.com/teachers/articles/teaching-content/teaching-students-autism-spectrum-disorder/

Griffin, D., & Galassi, J. (2010). Parent perceptions of barriers to academic success in a rural middle school. *Professional School Counseling, 14*(1), 87–100. doi: 10.1177/2156759X1001400109

Guetzloe, E. (2006, March). *Practical strategies for working with students who display aggression and violence.* Child and Youth Care-Online. https://www.cyc-net.org/cyc-online/cycol-0306-guetzloe.html

Guralnick, M., Connor, R., & Johnson, L. (2011). The peer social networks of young children with down syndrome in classroom programmes. *Journal of Applied Research in Intellectual Disabilities, 24*(4), 310–321. doi: 10.1111/j.1468-3148.2010.00619.x

Halton Catholic District School Board. *Helping your teen transition to a Halton Catholic Secondary School.* Burlington, Ontario. Retrieved from https://studentsuccess.hcdsb.org/wp-content/uploads/2014/08/Engaged-Parents-Successful-Students.pdf

Hanhimäki, E., & Tirri, K. (2009). Education for ethically sensitive teaching in critical incidents at school. *Journal of Education for Teaching, 35*(2), 107–121.

Hasan, S. (2018, August). *Social phobia factsheet for schools.* Kids Health. https://kidshealth.org/en/parents/social-phobia-factsheet.html

HealthLink BC. (n.d.). *Bipolar disorder in children: School issues.* HealthLink. https://www.healthlinkbc.ca/health-topics/ty6942

Hicks, J. M. (2004). It's an attitude. *Arts Education. 57*(3), 13–17. doi: 10.1080/00043125.2004.11653546

Hoerr, T. (2017, March). *Principal connection. connecting with students' parents.* ASCD Educational Leadership. http://www.ascd.org/publications/educationalleadership/mar17/vol74/num06/Connecting-with-Students'-Parents.aspx

Hopkins, G. (2007). *Dealing with angry parents.* Education World. https://www.educationworld.com/a_admin/admin/admin474.shtml

Horne, V. (2015). *Five useful ways teacher can help pupils transition to secondary school*. The Guardian. https://www.theguardian.com/teacher-network/2015/jul/01/five-useful-ways-teachers-pupils-transition-secondary-school

Horwood, M., Parker, P., & Riley, P. (2019, February 26). *Three principals are seriously stressed, here's what we need to do about it*. The Conversation. http://theconversation.com/one-in-three-principals-are-seriously-stressed-heres-what-we-need-to-do-about-it-110774

Howcast. (2016, September 5). *How to connect with a challenging student: Classroom management* [Video]. YouTube. https://www.youtube.com/watch?v=DJwSB_cQ8Tc

Howell, G. L. (2016). *The relationship between school leaders' behaviors and teachers' perceptions of their value in promoting a culture of inclusive education* (Paper 3822) [Doctoral dissertation]. Electronic Thesis and Dissertation Repository: http://ir.lib.uwo.ca/etd/3822

Hughes, J., & Lackenby, N. (2015). *Achieving successful transitions for young people with disabilities: a practical guide*. Jessica Kingsley Publishers.

Hume, K., Sreckovic, M., Snyder, K., & Carnahan, C. (2014). Smooth transitions: helping students with autism spectrum disorder navigate the school day. *TEACHING Exceptional Children, 47*(1), 35–45. doi: 10.1177/0040059914542794

Hurley, K., (2018, September 26). *Classroom accommodations to help the anxious child at school*. Psycom. https://www.psycom.net/classroom-help-anxious-child-at-school/

Hurlington, K. (2010, February). Bolstering resilience in students: Teachers as protective factors. *What Works? Research into Practice*. http://www.edu.gov.on.ca/eng/literacynumeracy/inspire/research/WW_bolstering_students.pdf

Impact Teachers. (2017, October 13). *4 teacher tips—Dealing with angry parents*. Impact Teachers. https://www.impactteachers.com/4-teacher-tips-dealing-with-angry-parents/teacher-tips

Inclusive Education Canada. (2013). *School principals leading the way to inclusive schools: Implementation steps for moving forward*. Inclusive Education Canada. https://inclusiveeducation.ca/wp-content/uploads/sites/3/2013/07/School-Principals-Leading-the-Way-to-Inclusive-Education.pdf

Inclusive Schools. (2015, August 20). *The principal's responsibilities in supporting quality instruction*. https://inclusiveschools.org/the-principals-responsibilities-in-supporting-quality-instruction/

Iowa Student Learning Institute. (2016, February 26). *It makes us feel stupid: School from a special education student perspective* [Video]. YouTube. https://www.youtube.com/watch?v=WQ1BjgI55YE

Iteach. (2019, May 29). *Setting healthy boundaries: As a teacher and in your personal life*. Iteach. https://www.iteach.net/blog/setting-healthy-boundaries/

Jacobs, D. S. (2019). *Safety and consent for kids and teens with autism or special needs: A parents' guide*. Jessica Kingsley Publishers.

Jahnukainen, M. (2015). Inclusion, integration, or what? A comparative study of the school principals' perceptions of inclusive and special education in Finland and in Alberta, Canada. *Disability & Society, 30*(1), 59–72.

Jensen, S. (2019, Oct). *How can we support the emotional well-being of teachers?* [Video]. Ted Talk. https://www.ted.com/talks/sydney_jensen_how_can_we_support_the_emotional_well_being_of_teachers?language=en

John Adams Elementary School. (n.d.). *Drop-off and pick-up procedures.* ACPS.k12. https://www.acps.k12.va.us/Page/1561

Jones, P., Whitehurst, T., & Egerton, J. (2012). *Creating meaningful inquiry in inclusive classrooms: Practitioners' stories of research.* Routledge Ltd.

Kalambouka, A., Farrell, P., Dyson, A. & Kaplan, I. (2007). The impact of placing pupils with special educational needs in mainstream schools on the achievement of their peers. *Educational Research 49*, 365–382.

Katherine Hampsten. (2016, February). *How miscommunication happens (and how to avoid it)* [Video]. TED-ed. https://www.ted.com/talks/katherine_hampsten_how_miscommunication_happens_and_how_to_avoid_it?language=en

Keenan, B. (2017, February 2). *Challenging student behaviour: moving from the boot to the root.* Edutopia. https://www.edutopia.org/discussion/challenging-student-behavior-moving-boot-root

Kelley, K. (2017, August 10). *50 tips and tricks to facilitating a more inclusive classroom.* We Are Teachers. https://www.weareteachers.com/tips-tricks-inclusive-classroom/

KGW News. (2019, February 4). *Classrooms in crisis: Outbursts plaguing Oregon classrooms* [Video]. YouTube. https://www.youtube.com/watch?v=Om7yVbuap9k

Killoran, I., Zaretsky, H., Jordan, A., Smith, D., Allard, C., & Moloney, J. (2013). Supporting teachers to work with children with exceptionalities. *Canadian Journal of Education, 36*(1), 240–270.

Kipps-Vaughan, D., Ponsart, D., & Gilligan, T. (2012). Teacher wellness: Too stressed for stress management? *Communique, 41*(1), 1, 26–28.

Knox County Schools TV. (2018, June 6). *Calming corners* [Video]. YouTube. https://www.youtube.com/watch?v=U2HdaOyh09Q

Kokina, A. (2012). *Social story interventions: An examination of effectiveness in addressing transition difficulties of students with autism spectrum disorders.* [Doctoral Dissertation, Lehigh University] *ProQuest Dissertations.*

Kuravackel, G. M., Ruble, L. A., Reese, R. J., Ables, A. P., Rogers, A. D., & Toland, M. D. (2018). COMPASS for hope: Evaluating the effectiveness of a parent training and support program for children with ASD. *Journal of Autism and Developmental Disorders, 48*(2), 404–416.

Ladau, E. (2014, May 2). *Communication is the key to inclusive field trips.* Think Inclusive. https://www.thinkinclusive.us/communication-is-the-key-to-inclusive-field-trips/

Lakhani, K. (2016, June 21). *How to support a child with autism in the classroom.* Autism Speaks. https://www.autismspeaks.org/blog/five-ways-teachers-can-support-students-autism

Lambert, M., & Bouchamma, Y. (2019). Leadership requirements for school principals: Similarities and differences between four competency standards. *Canadian Journal of Educational Administration and Policy, 188*, 53–68.

LD @ School. (n.d.). *Resources.* https://www.ldatschool.ca/resources/

References

Leithwood, K., Day, C., Sammons, P., Harris, A., & Hopkins, D. (2006). *Seven strong claims about successful school leadership*. National College for School Leadership. http://dera.ioe.ac.uk/6967/1/download%3Fid=17387&filename=seven-claims-about-successful-school-leadership.pdf

Leithwood, K., Day, C., Sammons, P., Harris, A., & Hopkins, D. (2006). *Successful school leadership: What it is and how it influences student learning*. Research Report 800. Department for Education.

Leithwood, K., Patten, S., & Jantzi, D. (2010). Testing a conception of how school leadership influences student learning. *Educational Administration Quarterly, 46*(5), 671–706.

Litvinov, A. (2017, July 16). *School funding facts, Pt. 3: How to advocate for public school resources*. Education Votes National Education Association. https://educationvotes.nea.org/2017/07/16/school-funding-facts-pt-3-advocate-public-school-resources/

Logsdon, A. (2020, May 17). *Using person-first language when describing people with disabilities*. Very Well Family. https://www.verywellfamily.com/focus-on-the-person-first-is-good-etiquette-2161897

London, R. A. (2016). Family engagement practices in california schools. *Public Policy Institute of California*. https://www.ppic.org/content/pubs/report/R_616RLR.pdf

MacCormack, J., Sider, S., Maich, K., & Specht, J. (2021). Self-determination and inclusion: The role of Canadian principals in catalysing inclusive-positive practices. *International Journal of Education Policy and Leadership, 17*(2). https://journals.sfu.ca/ijepl/index.php/ijepl/article/view/969/289

Madden, M. (2019, September 9). *For Syrian refugee children, back to school brings major challenges*. Concern Worldwide. https://www.concernusa.org/story/syrian-refugee-children-back-to-school/

Maich, K., & Hall, C. (2016). *Autism spectrum disorder in the Ontario context*. Toronto: Canadian Scholars Manitoba Education and Training. (2017). *Supporting transgender and gender diverse student in Manitoba schools*. Manitoba Education and Training. https://www.edu.gov.mb.ca/k12/docs/support/transgender/full_doc.pdf

Manitoba Education. (2004). *Working together: A handbook for parents of children with special needs in school*. Manitoba Education. https://www.edu.gov.mb.ca/k12/specedu/parent/pdf/workingtogether.pdf

Mason, V. (2013). *Challenges to instructional leadership practices: Superintendent and principals' experiences*. Library and Archives Canada.

Mastros, S. (2014, October 31). *Field trip management for special needs students*. BusBoss. https://www.busboss.com/Blog/bid/202049/Field-Trip-Management-for-Special-Needs-Students

McHatton, P. A., Boyer, N. R., Shaunesy, E., & Terry, P. M. (2010). Principals' perceptions of preparation and practice in gifted and special education content: Are we doing enough? *Journal of Research on Leadership Education, 5*(1), 1–22. doi: 10.1177/194277511000500101

Meador, D. (2019, February 21). *How teachers can build a trusting relationship with their principal.* ThoughtCo. https://www.thoughtco.com/build-a-trusting-relationship-with-their-principal-3194349

Meador, D. (2019, January 29). *How principals can provide teacher support.* Thought Co. https://www.thoughtco.com/suggestions-for-principals-to-provide-teacher-support-3194528

Minister of Education & Minister of Children and Youth Services. (2007). *Making a difference for student with autism spectrum disorders in Ontario schools.* From Evidence to Action. http://www.edugains.ca/resourcesSpecEd/SystemLeader/ASD/autismFeb07.pdf

Minister of Learning Alberta. (2003). *Teaching students with autism spectrum disorder.* https://education.alberta.ca/media/385138/teaching-students-with-asd-2003.pdf

Ministry of Education. (2002). *Transition planning: A resource guide.* OAFCCD. http://www.oafccd.com/documents/transitionguide.pdf

Ministry of Education. (2013). *Engaging parents in their children's learning.* Edu.gov.ca http://www.edu.gov.on.ca/eng/policyfunding/leadership/pdfs/issue20.pdf

Ministry of Education. (2019). *Supporting students with autism spectrum disorder.* Edu.gov.ca. http://www.edu.gov.on.ca/eng/general/elemsec/speced/autism.html

Ministry of Labour, Training and Skills Development. (2019, October 21). *Student safety plan.* Ontario.ca. https://www.ontario.ca/document/workplace-violence-school-boards-guidelaw/student-safety-plan

Moghtader, L., & Shamloo, M. (2019). The correlation of perceived social support and emotional schemes with students' social anxiety. *Journal of Holistic Nursing and Midwifery, 29*(2), 106–112. doi: 10.32598/JHNM.29.2.106

Montgomery County Public Schools TV. (2018, June 15). *FYI... Parent engagement and MCCPTA advocacy* [Video]. YouTube. https://www.youtube.com/watch?v=e6gFQiuByDY

Moran, K. (2020, March 12). *9 of the biggest parent communication mistakes (plus how to fix them).* We Are Teachers. https://www.weareteachers.com/parent-communication-mistakes/

Morehouse, L. (2008, April 22). *Supporting teachers: Effective mentoring.* Edutopia. https://www.edutopia.org/mentor-teachers-effectiveness

Moshman, R. (n.d.). *Supporting kids with oppositional defiant disorder in the classroom: What teachers need to know.* Classroom Management. https://www.boredteachers.com/classroom-management/teachers-need-to-know- oppositional-defiant-disorder-odd

Muir, T. (2018, October 24). *How to avoid principal burnout and love the job again.* We are Teachers. https://www.weareteachers.com/principal-burnout/

Mulvahill, E. (2019, August 2). *Give your first-year teachers everything they need to succeed.* We Are Teachers. https://www.weareteachers.com/supporting-first-year-teachers/

Murry, F. (2005). Effective advocacy for students with emotional/behavioral disorders: how high the cost? *Education & Treatment of Children, 28*(4), 414–429.

Myles, J. M. (2019). *Developing intercultural competence: A shift in thinking.* Education Canada. https://www.edcan.ca/articles/developing-intercultural-competence/

Nakpodia, E.,D. (2010). The influence of communication on administration of secondary schools in Delta State, Nigeria. *International NGO Journal, 5*(8), 194–198.

National Academies of Sciences, Engineering, and Medicine. (2016). *Parenting matters: Supporting parents of children ages 0-8.* Washington, DC: The National Academies Press. https://www.nap.edu/read/21868/chapter/7

National Council on Teacher Quality. (n.d.). *Monthly suggestions for supporting new teachers.* National Council on Teacher Quality. https://www.nctq.org/dmsView/Monthly_Suggestions_for_Supporting_New_Teachers

National Deaf Children's Society. (2016, March 22). *Tips for teaching deaf children with a mild hearing loss* [Video]. YouTube. https://www.youtube.com/watch?v=jylb7TDn2Tk&t=2s

National Institute of Mental Health. (n.d.). *Bipolar disorder in children and teens.* National Institute of Mental Health. https://www.nimh.nih.gov/health/publications/bipolar-disorder-in-children-and-teens/index.shtml

National Policy Board for Educational Administration. (2015). *Professional standards for educational leaders 2015.* http://www.wallacefoundation.org/knowledge-center/Documents/Professional-Standards-for-Educational-Leaders-2015.pdf

Niblett, B. (2017). *What works? Research into practice,* Facilitating Activist Education. http://www.edu.gov.on.ca/eng/literacynumeracy/inspire/research/tips_activist_educators.html

Obiakor, F., Harris, M., Mutua, K., Rotatori, A., & Algozzine, B. (2012). Making inclusion work in general education classrooms. *Education & Treatment of Children, 35*(3), 477–490. doi: 10.1353/etc.2012.0020

Ontario College of Teachers. (n.d.). *A self-reflective professional learning tool.* Ontario College of Teachers. https://www.oct.ca/-/media/PDF/A%20Self%20Reflective%20Professional%20Learning%20Tool/EN/SPE%20Self-Reflection%20Brochure%20EN%20ACCESSIBLE%20WEB.pdf

Ontario College of Teachers. (2018, November 8). *Professional advisory: Supporting students' mental health.* Ontario College of Teachers. https://www.oct.ca/Home/Resources/Advisories/Mental%20Health

Ontario Equity and Inclusive Education Strategy Quick Facts. (n.d.). http://www.edu.gov.on.ca/eng/policyfunding/EquityQuickFacts.pdf.

Ontario Human Rights Commission. (n.d.). *Appropriate accommodation.* Ontario Human Rights Commission. http://www.ohrc.on.ca/en/guidelines-accessible-education/appropriate-accommodation

Ontario Ministry of Education New Teacher Induction Program. (2010). *A resource handbook for mentors.* NTIP Mentor. http://www.edu.gov.on.ca/eng/teacher/NTIPMentor.pdf

Ontario Ministry of Education. (2007). *Effective educational practices for students with autism spectrum disorder.* http://www.edu.gov.on.ca/eng/general/elemsec/speced/autismSpecDis.pdf

Ontario Ministry of Education. (2007). *Shared solutions: A guide to preventing and resolving conflicts regarding programs and services for students with special education needs.* Edu.gov.on.ca. http://www.edu.gov.on.ca/eng/general/elemsec/speced/shared.pdf

Ontario Ministry of Education. (2012, October). *Parent engagement.* Capacity Building Series K-12. EduGains. http://www.edugains.ca/resourcesLIT/Professionalearning/CBS/CBS_ParentEngage.p

Ontario Ministry of Education. (2017). *Special education in Ontario: Kindergarten to grade 12.* Ontario Ministry of Education. http://www.edu.gov.on.ca/eng/document/policy/os/onschools_2017e.pdf

Ontario Ministry of Education. (2020, May 7). *Special needs support.* Children. http://www.children.gov.on.ca/htdocs/english/specialneeds/index.as

Ontario Ministry of Education. (n.d.). *Quick facts for parents: Learning about mental health.* Edugains. http://www.edugains.ca/resourcesMH/ClassroomEducator/QuickFactsMentalHealth_eng%20D2.pdf

Ontario Ministry of Education. (n.d.). *Exploring the "social" personal leadership resources: Perceiving emotions, managing emotions & acting in emotionally appropriate ways.* Ideas into Action Bulletin 7. http://www.edu.gov.on.ca/eng/policyfunding/leadership/IdeasIntoActionBulletin7.pdf

Ontario Principals Council. *Leading mentally healthy schools.* https://smh-assist.ca/wp-content/uploads/LMHS-Flipchart-EN-Web.pdf

Ontario Teachers Federation. (n.d.). *Mentoring—Survive & thrive.* Surivethirve. https://survivethrive.on.ca/article-category/mentoring/?topic=34&level=Elementary&article_category=17

Ontario Teachers Federation. (n.d.). *Teaching strategies for students with special needs.* Teachspeced.https://www.teachspeced.ca/teaching-strategies-students-special-needs

Ontario Teachers' Federation. (2015). Parent engagement. *Ontario Teachers Federation.* https://www.parentengagement.ca/

Ontario Teachers' Federation. (2020). *Modeling effective communication.* Ontario Teachers Federation. https://www.parentengagement.ca/modules/modeling-effective-communication/context-background/

Ontario Teachers' Federation. (n.d.). *Autism spectrum disorder.* TeachSpecEd. https://www.teachspeced.ca/autism-spectrum-disorder-asd

Ontario Teachers' Federation. (n.d.). *Learning disabilities.* TeachSpecEd. http://www.teachspeced.ca/?q=node/695

Ontario Teachers' Federation. (n.d.). *Self-advocacy skills.* TeachSpecEd. http://www.teachspeced.ca/?q=node/720

Ontario Teachers' Federation. (n.d.). *Transition skills.* Teach Spec Ed. https://www.teachspeced.ca/transition-plans?q=node/728

Osborne, E. L., & Dowling, E. (2003). *The family and the school: A joint systems approach to problems with children: Vol.* (2nd ed.). Routledge.

Passman, B. (2008). Case in point: knowledge, skills, and dispositions. *Journal of Special Education Leadership, 21*(1), 46–47.

Pathways & Student Success. (2021). Retrieved 3 May 2021, from https://studentsuccess.hcdsb.org/sample-page/transition-planning/.

Pawlas, G. (2013). *The administrator's guide to school-community relations.* Routledge.

Pawlas, G. (2005). *Building Relationships with the Media.* Education World. https://www.educationworld.com/a_admin/columnists/pawlas/pawlas004.shtml

PBS NewsHour. (2013, July 4). *Mentorship for new educators helps combat teacher burnout* [Video]. YouTube. https://www.youtube.com/watch?v=7P5uSQ9E-NU

PBS NewsHour. (2014, January 8). *Are some U.S. school discipline policies too punitive?* [Video]. PBS News Hour. https://www.pbs.org/newshour/show/Are-some-U-S-school-discipline-policies-too-punitive

Peel District School Board. (n.d.). *Special education programs and services.* Peel Schools. https://peelschools.org/parents/specialed/Pages/default.aspx

Pelletier, J., Laska, M., Nanney, M., & Pratt, R. (2018). Cross-sector collaboration on Safe Routes to School policy advocacy and implementation: A mixed methods evaluation from Minnesota. *Journal of Transport & Health, 9*, 132–140. doi: 10.1016/j.jth.2018.04.004

Perras, C. (2015). *Learning disabilities and mental health.* LD@schools. https://www.ldatschool.ca/learning-disabilities-and-mental-health/

Perras, C. (2016). *Elementary to secondary: transition planning for students with LDs.* LD@School. https://www.ldatschool.ca/transitionelementarysecondary/

Phillips, M. (2012, November 27). *Parents and teachers: Turning conflicts into partnerships.* Edutopia. https://www.edutopia.org/blog/parent-teacher-conflicts-into-partnerships-mark-phillips

Polluck, K. & Hauseman, D. C. (2018). The use of e-mail and principals' work: A double-edged sword. *Leadership and Policy in Schools, 3*, 382–393. doi: 10.1080/15700763.2017.1398338

Pont, B. (2013). Learning standards, teaching standards and standards for school principals: A comparative study. *Centre of Study for Policies and Practices in Education (CEPPE).* http://www.oecd.org/officialdocuments/publicdisplaydocumentpdf/?cote=EDU/WKP(2013)14&docLanguage=En

Porter, G. & Towell, D. (2017). *Advancing inclusive education: Keys to transformational change in public education systems.* http://inclusiveeducation.ca/2017/04/21/advancing-inclusive-education/

Puskar, K. R., Stark, K. H., Northcut, T., William, R., & Haley, T. (2010). Teach kids to cope with anger: Peer education. *Journal of Child Health Care, 15*(1), 5–13. doi: 10.1177/1367493510382932

Rauhala, J. (2018, September 20). *Building relationships with teachers.* Edutopia. https://www.edutopia.org/article/building-relationships-teachers

Richards, L. (2017, December 5). *10 tips for teaching blind or visually impaired students.* We Are Teachers. https://www.weareteachers.com/teaching-blind-students-visually-impaired/

Rigler, M., Rutherford, A., & Quinn, E. (2015). *Independence, social, and study strategies for young adults with autism spectrum disorder.* Jessica Kingsley Publishers.

Riva, N. (2016, September 6). *'A lot of kids' needs are not being met': Lots of labels, lack of resources for students with special needs.* CBC. https://www.cbc.ca/news/canada/special-ed-iep-support-1.3751522

Roberts, J. (2016). *Let's behave as a team.(cooperation of schools and parents in addressing students' behavioural problems)(Parents' View).* Times Educational Supplement, 5218.

Robinson, K. (2018). Four secondary teachers' perspectives on enhancing the inclusion of exceptional students. *Exceptionality Education International, 28* (1), 1–21.

Robson, D. (2018, April 16). *How to help kids who struggle with daily transitions.* CBC. https://www.cbc.ca/parents/learning/view/how-to-help-kids-who-struggle-with-transitions

Rogozinsky, D. (2018). *What to do when parents don't understand boundaries.* Study.com. https://study.com/blog/what-to-do-when-parents-don-t-understand-boundaries.html

Rosenberg, D. (2020). Finding time for new teachers to thrive. *Educational Leadership, 77,* 61–65. http://www.ascd.org/publications/educational-leadership/jun20/vol77/num09/Finding-Time-for-New-Teachers-to-Thrive.aspx

Rosenberg, D., & Miles, K, H. (2018). *Growing great teachers: How school system leaders can use existing resources to better develop, support, and retain new teachers and improve student outcomes.* ERStrategies. https://files.eric.ed.gov/fulltext/ED593368.pdf

Ross, D. J., & Cozzens, J. A. (2016). The principalship: essential core competencies for instructional leadership and its impact on school climate. *Journal of Education and Training Studies, 4*(9), 162–176.

Ross, J. A., & Gray, P. (2006). Transformational leadership and teacher commitment to organizational values: The mediating effects of collective teacher efficacy. *School Effectiveness and School Improvement, 17*(2), 179–199.

Royal Botanic Gardens. (2019, March). *Health and safety risk assessment.* KEW. https://www.kew.org/sites/default/files/2019-03/Risk%20assessment%20for%20visiting%20schools%20Kew%202019.pdf

Rubin, A. (2018, April 9). *4 professional boundaries principals need to consider.* We Are Teachers. https://www.weareteachers.com/principal-professional-boundaries/

Ruef, Michael B., Higgins, Cindy, Glaeser. Barbara C. J., & Patnode, Marianne. (1998). Positive behavioral support: Strategies for teachers. *Intervention in School and Clinic. 34*(1), 21–31.

Saenz-Armstrong, P. (2020, July 9). Supporting teachers through mentoring and collaboration. *National Council on Teacher Quality.* https://www.nctq.org/blog/Supporting-teachers-through-mentoring-and-collaboration

Samules, A, C. (2018). The important role principals play in special education. *Education Week. 38*(9), 26–28. https://www.edweek.org/ew/articles/2018/10/17/the-important-role-principals-play-in-special.html

San Bernardino Unified School District. (2017, October 4). *Relationship building: Parent/teacher communication* [Video]. YouTube. https://www.youtube.com/watch?v=LTKOhxE4LNc

San Bernardino Unified School District. (2018, February 16). *Differentiation within the inclusion classroom model.* YouTube. https://www.youtube.com/watch?v=7G_PuCIpaaM

Scholastic. (n.d.). *Understanding Asperger's in the classroom.* Scholastic. https://www.scholastic.com/teachers/articles/teaching-content/understanding-aspergers/

Schultz, T., Schmidt, C., & Stichter, J. (2011). A review of parent education programs for parents of children with autism spectrum disorders. *Focus on Autism and Other Developmental Disabilities, 26*(2), 96–104. doi: 10.1177/1088357610397346

Scott, A. E. (2004). Counselor development through critical incidents: A qualitative study of intern experiences during the predoctoral internship. *Dissertation Abstracts International, 65,* 1681A.

Severance, C., Tierney, J., & Johnson, D. (2019, February 1). *Classrooms in crisis: Verbal, physical, sometimes violent outbursts plaguing Oregon classrooms.* KGW8. https://www.kgw.com/article/news/classrooms-in-crisis-verbal-physical-sometimes-violent-outbursts-plaguing-oregon-classrooms/283-490a6255-23d0-4bab-af74-895102734e78

Shalaway, L. (n.d.). *25 sure-fire strategies for handing difficult students.* Scholastic. https://www.scholastic.com/teachers/articles/teaching-content/25-sure-fire-strategies-handling-difficult-students/

Shields, C. M. (2010). Transformative leadership: Working for equity in diverse contexts. *Educational Administration Quarterly, 46*(4), 558–589.

Shin, S. H., & Slater, C. L. (2010). Principal leadership and mathematics achievement: An international comparative study. *School Leadership and Management, 30*(4), 317–334.

Shmoop. (2020). *Understanding your students' home lives.* https://www.shmoop.com/teachers/beyond-teaching/personal-care/students-home-lives.html

Shultz, T. R., Able, H., Sreckovic, M. A., & White, T. (2016). Education and training in autism and developmental disabilities. *Parent-teacher collaboration: Teacher Perceptions of What Is Needed to Support Students with ASD in the Inclusive Classroom, 51*(4), 344–354.

Sider, S. (2012, Dec 12). *Working as a team.* [Video] Vimeo. https://vimeo.com/55498214

Sider, S. (2020). School principals and students with special education needs in a pandemic: Emerging insights from Ontario, Canada. *International Studies in Educational Administration, 48*(2), 78–84. http://cceam.net/wp-content/uploads/2020/08/ISEA-2020-48-2.pdf#page=84

Sider, S., Maich, K., & Morvan, J. (2017). School principals and students with special education needs: Leading inclusive schools. *Canadian Journal of Education, 40*(2), 1–31.

Sider, S., Maich, K., Morvan, J., Villella, M., Ling, P., & Repp, C. (2021). Inclusive school leadership: Examining the experiences of school principals in supporting students with special education needs. *Journal of Research in Special Educational Needs 21*(2), 233–241. https://doi.org/10.1111/1471-3802.12515

Simplican, S. C., Leader, G., Kosciulek, J., & Leahy, M. (2015). Defining social inclusion of people with intellectual and developmental disabilities: An ecological model of social networks and community participation. *Research in Developmental Disabilities, 38,* 18–29.

Skaalvik, E. M., & Skaalvik, S. (2007). Dimensions of teacher self-efficacy and relations with strain factors, perceived collective teacher efficacy, and teacher burnout. *Journal of Educational Psychology, 99*(3), 611–625. doi: 10.1037/0022-0663.99.3.611

Social Sciences and Humanities Research Council of Canada. (2017, October). *Supporting Refugee Students in Canadian Classrooms.* Cities of Migration. http://citiesofmigration.ca/wp-content/uploads/2018/04/What-Works-Monograph_Supporting-Refugee-Students-in-Canadian-Classrooms_Oct.-2017.pdf

Solomon, M. (2018, August 7). *How to help young adults with autism transition to adulthood.* Spectrum News. https://www.spectrumnews.org/opinion/viewpoint/help-young-adults-autism-transition-adulthood/

South Regional Education Board. (2018). *Mentoring new teachers a fresh look.* SREB.org. https://www.sreb.org/sites/main/files/file-attachments/mentoring_new_teachers_2.pdf

Specht, J. A., & Metsala, J. L. (2018). Predictors of teacher efficacy for inclusive practice in pre-service teachers. *Exceptionality Education International, 28,* 67–82.

Specht, J., McGhie-Richmond, D., Loreman, T., Mirenda, P., Bennett, S., Gallagher, T., Young, G., Metsala, J., Aylward, L., Katz, J., Lyons, W., Thompson, S., & Coulter, S. (2016). Teaching in inclusive classrooms: Efficacy and beliefs of Canadian preservice teachers. *International Journal of Inclusive Education, 20*(1), 1–15.

Special Education Services. (2016). *A manual of policies, procedures and guidelines.* https://www2.gov.bc.ca/assets/gov/education/administration/kindergarten-to-grade-12/inclusive/special_ed_policy_manual.pdf

Stevenson-Jacobson, R., Jacobson, J., & Hilton, A. (2006). Principals' perceptions of critical skills needed for administration of special education. *Journal of Special Education Leadership, 19*(2), 39–47.

Storey, K., & Hunter, D. (2014). *The road ahead: transition to adult life for persons with disabilities.* IOS Press.

Szidon, K., Ruppar, A., & Smith, L. (2015). Five steps for developing effective transition plans for high school students with autism spectrum disorder. *Teaching Exceptional Children, 47*(3), 147–152. doi: 10.1177/0040059914559780

Szumski, G., Smogorzewska, J. & Karwowski, M. (2017). Academic achievement of students without special educational needs in inclusive classrooms: A meta-analysis. *Educational Research Review, 21,* 33–54. doi: 10.1016/j.edurev.2017.02.004.

Tapp, F. (n.d.). *Teacher burnout: Causes, symptoms, and prevention.* Hey Teach!. https://www.wgu.edu/heyteach/article/teacher-burnout-causes-symptoms-and-prevention1711.html

Taras L. Howard & Young, L.Thomas. (2004). School-based mental health services. *Pediatrics, 113*(6), 1839.

Tavanger, H. (2017, November 8). *Creating an inclusive classroom.* Edutopia https://www.edutopia.org/article/creating-inclusive-classroom

Teaching Students with Emotional & Behavioral Disorders. (2009). *Oppositional defiant disorder in the classroom—Strategies & advice.* Bright hub education. https://www.brighthubeducation.com/special-ed-behavioral-disorders/26631-strategies-for-teaching-children-with-oppositional-defiant-disorder/

Teachnology. (n.d.). *Inclusion in the classroom.* Teachnology. http://www.teach-nology.com/teachers/special_ed/inclusion/

TEDx Talks. (2018, July 16). *Learn to shine bright- the importance of self care for teachers.| Kelly Hopkinson | TEDxNorwichED* [Video]. YouTube. https://www.youtube.com/watch?v=5O5QIqlDxjg

TEDx Talks. (2013, November 7). *Building relationships between parents and teachers: Megan Olivia Hall at TEDxBurnsvilleEd* [Video]. YouTube. https://www.youtube.com/watch?v=kin2OdchKMQ

Teutsch, F., & Gugglberger, L. (2019). Analysis of whole-school policy changes in Austrian schools. *Health Promotion International, 35*(2), 331–339. doi./10.1093/heapro/daz006

Tew, K. (2019, June 29). *The benefits of multiyear induction program.* Edutopia. https://www.edutopia.org/article/benefits-multiyear-induction-program

The Canadian Safe School Network. (n.d.). *Welcoming refugee children to the classroom.* The Canadian Safe School Network. https://cssn.me/welcoming-refugee-children-to-the-classroom

The Conversation. (2019, January 2). *Six ways to support new teachers to stay in the profession.* The Conversation. https://theconversation.com/six-ways-to-support-new-teachers-to-stay-in-the-profession-106934

The Institute for Education Leadership. (2013). *Ontario leadership framework.* https://www.education-leadership-ontario.ca/en/resources/ontario-leadership-framework-olf

The Institution for Education Leadership. (2013, September) *The Ontario leadership framework.* Edugains. http://www.edugains.ca/resources21CL/SchoolLeader/SettingDirections/OLF_User_Guide.pdf

The State of Victoria. (2009). *Addressing parents' concerns and complaints effectively policy and guides.* Education Victoria Government. https://www.education.vic.gov.au/Documents/school/principals/management/parentsconcerns.pdf

The Understood Team. (n.d.). *4 benefits of inclusive classrooms.* [Video] Understood.org. https://www.understood.org/en/learning-attention-issues/treatments-approaches/educational-strategies/5-benefits-of-inclusion-classrooms

The Understood Team. (n.d.). *Assistive technology for learning: What you need to know..* https://www.understood.org/en/school-learning/assistive-technology/assistive-technologies-basics/assistive-technology-what-it-is-and-how-it-works

The Graide Network. (2019, February 26). *Teacher burnout solutions & prevention - How to retain talented educators.* https://www.thegraidenetwork.com/blog-all/teacher-burnout-solutions-prevention

Thomas, R. L. (2016). The right to quality education for refugee children through social inclusion. *Journal of Human Rights and Social Work, 1*(4), 193–201. doi: 10.1007/s41134-016-0022-z

Thompson, P. A. (2017). Effective leadership competencies of school-based special education administrators. *Journal of Special Education Leadership, 30*(1), 31–47.

Today. (2017, March 2). *How one high school is welcoming refugee students | TODAY.* [Video]. YouTube.https://www.youtube.com/watch?v=rMGVJu_M-dc

Tompkins, A. (2018, June 25). *Principal hotline: I'm buried in parent requests. What do I do?*. WeAreTeachers. https://www.weareteachers.com/buried-in-parent-requests/

Toulouse, R. P. (2013). Fostering literacy success for first nations, Métis and Inuit students. *What Works? Research into Practice.* http://www.edu.gov.on.ca/eng/literacynumeracy/inspire/research/WW_Fostering_Literacy.pdf

Trainor, A. A. (2010). Diverse approaches to parent advocacy during special education home-school interactions. *Remedial and Special Education, 31*(1), 34–47. doi: 10.1177/0741932508324401

Transequality: National Centre for Transgender Equality. (n.d.). *What are my rights at school?* https://transequality.org/know-your-rights/schools

Tranter, D. & Kerr, D. (2016). *Understanding self-regulation: Why stressed students struggle to learn.* Edu.Gov.on.Ca. http://www.edu.gov.on.ca/eng/literacynumeracy/inspire/research/ww_struggle.html

Vyas, B. (2020). *Perspectives of the superintendent and principal: Leadership for technology integration.* ProQuest Dissertations Publishing.

Wang, J., Odell, S. J., & Clift, R. T. (2010). *Past, present, and future research on teacher induction.* Rowman & Littlefield Education

WeAreTeachers. (2019, April 2). *What teachers need to know about students with ODD (oppositional defiant disorder).* https://www.weareteachers.com/students-with-odd/

Weber, M. (2016, August 21). *10 challenges deaf students face in the classroom.* GettingSmart. https://www.gettingsmart.com/2016/08/10-challenges-deaf-students-face-in-the-classroom/

Westerberg, D., Newland, R., & Mendez, J. L. (2020). Beyond the classroom: The protective role of student–teacher relationships on parenting stress. *Early Childhood Education Journal, 48*(5), 633–642. doi: 10.1007/s10643-020-01024-w.

Weymouth, B. B., & Buehler, C. (2018). Early adolescents' relationships with parents, teachers, and peers and increases in social anxiety symptoms. *Journal of Family Psychology, 32* (4), 496–506. doi: 10/1037/fam0000396

Wheeler, R. (2017). *Suspensions don't teach.* Edutopia. https://www.edutopia.org/article/suspensions-dont-teach

Winton, S. (2011). Managing conduct: a comparative policy analysis of safe schools' policies in Toronto, Canada and Buffalo, USA. *Comparative Education, 47*(2), 247–263. doi: 10.1080/03050068.2011.554088

Winzer, M. (2017). Canadian teachers' associations and the inclusive movement for students with special needs. *Canadian Journal of Educational Administration and Policy*, (116). https://journalhosting.ucalgary.ca/index.php/cjeap/article/view/42813

Woods, A. D., Morrison, F. J., & Palincsar, A. S. (2018). Perceptions of communication practices among stakeholders in special education. *Journal of Emotional and Behavioural Disorders, 25*(4), 209–224. doi: 10.1177/106346617733716

Yamamoto, J. K., Gardiner, M. E., & Tenuto, P. L. (2014). Emotion in leadership: Secondary school administrators' perceptions of critical incidents. *Educational Management Administration & Leadership, 42*(2), 165–183.

Yin, R. K. (2013). *Case study research: Design and methods* (5th ed.). Sage.

Zaretsky, L., Moreau, L., & Faircloth, S. (2008). Voices from the field: School leadership in special education. *Alberta Journal of Educational Research, 54*(2), 161–177.

About the Contributors

The expert commentaries in this book are provided by inclusive education and school leadership scholars as well as school principals and other school leaders. Thirty-one contributors from Canada, the United States, and Australia provided commentaries and offered suggestions to strengthen the cases as well as resources.

The contributors are:

Jacqueline Specht
Mélissa Villella
Emma Hosey
Erin Keith
Tricia van Rhijn
Sheila Bennett
Monique Somma
Gabrielle Young
Jeffrey MacCormack
Gillian Parekh
Umesh Sharma
Lisa Devall-Martin
Lise-Anne St-Vincent
Nadia Rousseau
Carolyn Salonen
Carolyn FitzGerald

Jhonel Morvan
Lillian Scibetta
Douglas Matear
Scott Miller
Jordan Shurr
Anders Lunde
Ardavan Eizadirad
Nadine Bartlett
Joy Chadwick
Donna McGhie-Richmond
Jeffery Bell
Jill Rose
Carolyn Treadgold
Grania Bridal
Shemira Sheriff

About the Authors

Dr. Steve R. Sider is a former school administrator and current university faculty member who researches inclusive education and school leadership. He directs the Centre for Leading Research in Education and has held six national research grants exploring how school principals' leadership competencies are nurtured.

Dr. Kimberly Maich is a current university professor, psychologist, and behaviour analyst, as well as a former autism consultant to schools, vice principal, resource teacher, and guidance counsellor in charge of special services.